MW01222019

Andrew Ryder
The Challenge to Academic Freedom in Hungary

De Gruyter Contemporary Social Sciences

Volume 6

Andrew Ryder

The Challenge to Academic Freedom in Hungary

A Case Study in Authoritarianism, Culture War and Resistance

DE GRUYTER

ISBN 978-3-11-074958-8
e-ISBN (PDF) 978-3-11-074981-6
e-ISBN (EPUB) 978-3-11-074993-9
ISSN 2747-5689
e-ISSN 2747-5697

Library of Congress Control Number: 2021952145

Bibliographic information published by the Deutsche Nationalbibliothek
The Deutsche Nationalbibliothek lists this publication in the Deutsche Nationalbibliografie;
detailed bibliographic data are available on the Internet at http://dnb.dnb.de.

© 2022 Walter de Gruyter GmbH, Berlin/Boston
Cover image: © Oláh Gergely Máté
Printing and binding: CPI books GmbH, Leck

www.degruyter.com

Acknowledgements

Our solidarity must be affirmed by a shared belief in a spirit of intellectual openness that celebrates diversity, welcomes dissent, and rejoices in collective dedication to truth (bell hooks, 2014, 33).

I wish to thank Michaela Göbels and Anthony Mason of De Gruyter Press for their support and assistance. I also need to thank Linda Bell, Sarah Cemlyn, Andrew Chandler, Brian Foster, Miklos Hadas, András Pap, Lynne Tammi and Toby Whitty for reviewing sections of the book.

I dedicate the book to my partner Henrietta Réz and son Arthur and to the memory of the late Tom Sweeney, the inspirational campaigner for education and Travellers' rights.

About the Author

Andrew Ryder is an associate professor in the Institute of Political and International Studies at Eötvös Loránd University in Budapest, Hungary. Prior to this he held academic positions at the Corvinus University Budapest and the universities of Bristol and Birmingham. Ryder has a longstanding history of social justice activism and campaigning. He is a fellow of the Royal Society for Arts.

Contents

List of Abbreviations

AFI   Academic Freedom Index
BLM   Black Lives Matter
CEU   Central European University
CoE   Council of Europe
CUS   Critical University Studies
ELKH   Eötvös Loránd Research Network
ELTE   Eötvös Loránd University
EU   European Union
HAS   Hungarian Academy of Sciences
LGBTQ   lesbian, gay, bisexual, transgender and queer
NGO   Non-Governmental Organisation
OSF   Open Society Foundation
REF   Roma Education Fund
RREN   Roma Research and Empowerment Network
SZFE   University of Theatre and Film Arts
UNESCO   United Nations Educational, Scientific and Cultural Organization
USSR   Union of Soviet Socialist Republics

https://doi.org/10.1515/9783110749816-001

Preface

There is little consensus as to what academic freedom means. The concept is not well defined in legal terms either: it is a concept that relies greatly on custom, convention, or even tradition. An important attempt to define and enshrine academic freedom occurred in 1988 when the Magna Charta Universitatum was endorsed by 388 rectors from Europe and beyond and which has since been ratified by 776 universities in 81 countries. The Magna Charta defines academic autonomy and freedom as a fundamental principle. The charter declares that in order to meet the needs of the world around it, research and teaching must be morally and intellectually independent of all political authority and economic power. In the charter, academic freedom includes the freedom of teachers and students to teach, study, and pursue knowledge and research without unreasonable interference or restriction from the law, institutional regulations, or public pressure (Magna Charta, 2020). Academic freedom is said to entail fair and transparent funding regimes for research, facilitate the pursuit of knowledge, and encourage openness and flexibility. For others, it can entail a responsibility to peers and the general community (European Review of History editorial committee, 2020). Under all of these definitions, there is cause for concern in Hungary. The extent of this concern is evidenced by the fact the European Parliament initiated an Article 7 procedure against Hungary, designed to deal with concerns about member states and their respect for the rule of law. Concerns related to academic freedom were part of the grounds for this action.

This book seeks to give an overview of the extensive higher education reforms of the Hungarian Government under Prime Minister Viktor Orbán, it places them in the historical, political, and social context of a country that could be described as the first non-democratic member state of the EU. Freedom House, an NGO that tracks the health of democracy and human rights across the world, now describes Hungary as a hybrid regime that is partly free, in the same category are Hong Kong, India, and Indonesia (Freedom House, 2020). Whatever the validity of this claim, serious concerns are being raised about Orbán's vision of his self-proclaimed "illiberal democracy". The fate of Hungary's universities and academic freedom is an important indicator as to the legitimacy of concerns expressed about Hungary's political direction.

Why is an Englishman concerning himself with Hungarian higher education? Personally, I was concerned enough about the fate of a university I worked at for the last decade in Hungary to resign because of concerns about its institutional autonomy in the wake of its privatisation. I have to say there have been times I wanted to leave the country and considered returning to my native Brit-

https://doi.org/10.1515/9783110749816-002

ain. I decided to stay though. My child was born in Hungary, my partner is Hungarian, I have lived here for many years, to be candid Brexit Britain does not seem a good place to return to given the huge insecurities that now hang over my country of birth, now outside the EU. These were concerns I considered deeply in my book on Brexit (Ryder, 2020), concerns which led to me drawing parallels between the trajectories of both Britain and Hungary, two countries that seemed to be in the thrall of authoritarian populism and nationalist exceptionalism. I stayed because Hungary feels like home, in that sense even though I am British and my grasp of the Hungarian language remains shamefully poor, there are things in this country I care about deeply. It seemed like a time to take a stand. Here, with a touch of irony, let me quote Orbán (2018 state of nation address) "A good soldier does not fight because he hates that which stands in opposition to him, but because he loves that which stands behind him because he loves Hungary and the Hungarian people." In writing this book I am trying to be a "good soldier".

The book provides an overview of Orbán's higher education reforms but also the political, philosophical, and historical context of those changes. The book will probe the reasons for ideological conflict between the academy and state through concepts like 'culture war' and authoritarian populism. The book will explore how the Orbán administration has introduced a series of reforms leading to limitations being placed on the Hungarian Academy of Sciences, Gender Studies no longer being recognised by the State and the relocation to Vienna of the majority of teaching operations of the Central European University because of government pressure. The book also explores new reforms that ostensibly appear to give universities autonomy, but critics assert these reforms are in fact changes that will lead to cronyism and pro-government interference in academic freedom. More broadly, the book will assess to what degree commodification tames academia, reducing the scope for intellectual dissent and counter-hegemonic narratives. The book can be seen as reflecting the ideals of Critical University Studies in exposing and offering a critique of marginality, exploitation, and oppression in the higher education sector.

Critical University Studies (CUS), is a lens of analysis that believes neoliberal policies and practices primarily position higher education in relation to the market and such forces dictate the operations of the modern-day university. CUS scholars seek to expose and critique forms of institutional oppression shaped by market forces and or hegemonic ideologies and doctrines. CUS scholars often have a predilection for activism and solutions grounded in social change and movements that are transformative (Rangel, 2020). As a CUS scholar, it is my contention that Hungary can be viewed as an outlier for what can happen when a fusion of neoliberalism and authoritarian nationalism emerges. Hungary presents an important case study for what can happen to academic freedom but also the scope and nature of resistance. It is my hope that the stories and narrative presented in this volume can provide valuable lessons but also inspire.

Much of the book is filled with personal testimony. I interviewed around 40 people, mostly academics and students. Some of the interviews just provided general contextual information, but in each chapter, the direct testimony of some of the contributors is presented. In some cases, this testimony is anonymised and, in some cases contextual information has been changed to protect the identity of those who gave testimony (where only a first name of those giving testimony is mentioned these are invented names for those who wished to be anonymised). Alas, such is the level of fear it was necessary to take such precautions. The book is also reflexive, I narrate my personal story during various stages of the text. I, together with those who provided testimony, describe the dissonance and personal dilemmas we experienced in the face of government higher education reforms but also reasons for and approaches to dissent.

The book seeks to develop links between micro and macro analysis. Weiss and Fine (2012) call for 'critical bifocality', which is a contrast to the prevailing normative practice of studying groups and communities as if they were bounded and in a silo. In contrast, they appeal for research "to make visible the linkages, leakages, tensions, and solidarities within and among groups across time and space". Hence, the book relies heavily on semi-structured interviews with actors involved and affected by the changes outlined above, and weaves personal testimony with societal and political developments as well as providing historical and cultural context. Discussions and interviews encouraged reflexivity. Reflexivity encourages researchers and subjects to understand the lifeworld in which they have entered or are located and how they and their values, identity, and history interact with that lifeworld (Wray-Bliss, 2005). Reflexivity enables a 'self-concept' to become apparent, the set of values, purposes, and conceptions that an individual acquires through a variety of social structures, that continues to evolve through life. Hence, some of the interviews and discussions were in-depth and probed interviewees' life stories and encouraged them to reflect upon and consider how their self-concept shaped their actions and interpretations of the events this book recounts.

In this sense, the book seeks to determine why some choose to 'cross a line' and speak up and speak out. Differing strategies from a range of actors are profiled in the book which also discusses why those tactics were employed but also the personal motivations for such actions and the consequences. As will become evident, Hungary has had a difficult and traumatic history marked by crisis and dissent, often steered by competing forms of national identity. In these struggles, intellectuals have been prominent in defending or attacking these profound political and cultural shifts. How do the new generation of dissident thinkers compare to those who came before them in Hungarian intellectual circles? The book will seek to answer this question through interviews and conversations with leading contemporary Hungarian thinkers. These conversations, often involving exploration of personal as well as institutional selves lay the foundation of the book.

In many respects, this book is a collaborative effort in the sense that contributors were invited to comment upon and reflect on the draft versions of the book and their comments and suggestions helped shape the final output. Such collaboration encouraged something of a dialogic approach in devising the book, I wanted to create a conversation in which I and other actors involved in Hungarian higher education could try and make some sense of the institutional, political and cultural changes in Hungary that were impacting upon academic life. At the centre of this dialogic approach has been the question how we should respond and act in the face of a process of state capture motivated in part by perceptions of the Hungarian radical right that Hungarian academia is gripped by left-wing bias and the tyranny of political correctness. For some of these radical right idealogues, academia is a cultural threat to tradition and national identity. This is the crux of what has been styled 'culture war', a concept that will be discussed in more depth later.

The pandemic unsurprisingly added to a general sense of anxiety in Hungary and perhaps added to the desire in this book to identify new directions, especially as in the case of this book, new directions in the intellectual life of my adopted home. Living in a state of constant fear, as many of us did for ourselves and our families over the lifespan of the pandemic, perhaps added to my resolve to challenge, while I had the chance, aspects of Hungarian society that I found oppressive and intimidating. The threat and fear of illness made me value and savour more than ever before the chance to think, write and resist. During the pandemic, we were forced to change the way we lived and we managed to adapt. We could do so again! Ongoing political, economic, and environmental dislocation and instability suggests the time is ripe for paradigm shift, deep and fundamental change. My commitment to critical thinking and transformative change seems to have been strengthened by my experiences of the pandemic.

The case of the renowned academic and philosopher Ágnes Heller is one that seems to offer some insights into Orbán's culture war where tradition and conservatism are revered, and dissent and divergence are discouraged and even punished. At the start of Orbán's second period of government (prior to 2010 he was prime minister between 1998 and 2002), Ágnes Heller found herself facing serious reputational charges from the Hungarian government. Ágnes Heller (1929 – 2019) was a Hungarian philosopher and academic, she held a number of academic posts including the Hannah Arendt Professor of Philosophy at the New School, New York, in her later years she returned to Hungary and was professor emeritus at Eotvos Lorand University in Budapest. Heller was active within what became known as the 'Budapest School', a philosophical forum influenced by the eminent thinker György Lukács. This intellectual circle, like Lukács, challenged conventional Marxist orthodoxy appealing for notions of Marxism that were more humanistic and favourable to agency and personal freedom (Dorahy, 2020). Such sentiments were in conflict with the prevailing centralism of the Stalin and Brezhnev eras. Such thinking brought Heller into conflict with the authorities. Partly because of her support for the 1956 uprising she was sacked from her university post, expelled from the Hungarian Communist Party, and banned from conducting any research until the early 1960s. After having resumed her career, Heller again found herself targeted by the authorities in the 1970s and again expelled from the Communist Party, leading to her spending part of her life as a dissident living and teaching in exile in Australia and the USA.

At the time of the latest allegations made against Heller she was 82-years-old and a prominent critic of Orbán, frequently accusing him of being a tyrant. Heller was accused alongside other philosophers of embezzling state research funds. The German news outlet Deutsche Welle had the following to say "Though the accusations quickly went up in smoke, state-loyal media carried out a smear campaign against the 'leftist philosophers' and 'opinion distorters,' declaring them guilty" (Verseck, 2012). These accusations caused something of a scandal in liberal circles with the leading German philosopher, Jürgen Habermas, expressing profound concerns in a letter of support at what he described as trumped-up charges that represented a form of political persecution (Habermas and Nida-Rümelin, 2011). The charges were dropped because of a lack of evidence. Commenting on the matter in an interview with a journalist, Heller said "They make these kinds of accusations, spread them all over their loyal media outlets, and thus blacken the names of their opponents. By targeting liberals, they blacken the name of liberalism itself. 'Liberal' here is a dirtier word than 'Nazi' or 'communist'" (FT, 2013). András Máté, a Hungarian philosopher and activist in the Hungarian Academic Network, commented on the case of Heller in one of the interviews I conducted:

> The horror of this was the lack of respect for such an important Hungarian cultural figure, this incident was the prelude for the story that has unfolded in the last decade with reference to the contempt the Orbán government seem to have for academics. If this could be done to Heller it could be done to anyone (interview with Máté).

The action against Heller was interpreted by some observers as the regime's first attempt to control the critical intelligentsia in Hungary. For many critics of the Orbán government, this is the fear we have, that bullying, autocracy, and challenges to academic freedom will become endemic in Hungarian society. There is a legitimate fear that the forces that imperilled and buffeted the life of Heller and so many others in the darkest pages of Hungarian history could be set to return. Towards the end of her life Heller and several other Jewish faculty members at Eotvos Lorand University in Budapest were subject to an antisemitic act when their office doors were plastered with bumper stickers that read: "Jews, the university is ours, not yours!" As a Holocaust survivor whose own father died in the concentration camps, the decline of Hungary must have been profoundly disturbing for Heller.

Such is the rise in antisemitism that Orbán and members of the Fidesz circle have not shied away from what some consider to be antisemitic rhetoric despite Orbán in the past condemning antisemitism. In 2013 Orbán told the World Jewish Congress in Budapest that his country would not tolerate antisemitism (Mendonça, 2013). However, some observers argue that Orbán's vendetta with George Soros has antisemitic undertones, this is discussed in the book.

In my interpretation of the events outlined in this book, I can be described as a critical scholar, someone who seeks to challenge hegemony and oppressive practices and see the norms and values that govern our world rewritten to reflect the principles of social justice. I am though a critical thinker in the Habermasian sense, hence I promote deliberation and the search for a radical consensus at the core of which would be new and open forms of learning where freedom of thought and expression is sacrosanct. The book can also be viewed as an attempt to speak 'truth to power', standing up to authority and speaking out for what is right. Speaking truth to power, is a term that will recur in this text and can be viewed as a concept similar to satyagraha (truth-force) as pioneered by Mahatma Gandhi. For Gandhi truth had a moral force that could by standing up for what is right transform but do so through persuasion and dignity in struggle.

Ultimately though, I believe such transformative change can only come about when we return to the trajectory of what became known as the 'Glorious Thirty' – an age of economic growth and welfare expansion that spanned the post-war period. The Glorious Thirty could with time have overcome its imperfections, such as bureaucratic statism and the snail's pace of such gradualism, and become a force for meaningful and incremental steps towards achieving social justice. This trajectory though was broken with the advent of neoliberalism that has become increasingly entwined and complicit in the rise of radical nationalism and authoritarianism. Such viewpoints provide a frame for the analysis in the book and contend that neoliberalism and authoritarianism both present a profound threat and challenge to academic freedom.

With reference to neoliberalism and its impact on higher education, universities have become like corporations with formulae, incentives, and targets guided by the principles of 'new managerialism' (Miller, 2010). Academia can in fact be viewed as a field of power dominated by commercial principles and notions, reliant upon an audit culture that exalts and promotes competitive academic activity (Sparkes, 2007). In this marketplace, academic work is susceptible to market pressures, and the search for truth and accountability is less apparent.

Authoritarianism is an insular worldview that has little tolerance for alternative views and its disregard for fact has led some observers to classify the present times as one characterised by a 'post-truth' politics, where emotion trumps fact. The public sphere is increasingly slanted and distorted through Orwellian manipulation, stoking irrationality and blind loyalties that present a threat to academic freedom and the ideals of an open society (Economist, 2016).

To return to Heller, she said of the Orbán regime "Tyrannies always collapse, but whether Hungarians will escape with their sanity and sufficient clarity for a new start remains to be seen" (cited in the New York Times, 2019). Universities rightly or wrongly have been perceived as important centres of dissent and alternative visions of society. I hope to determine in this book what the intellectual counter-narrative to Orbán is. The dissident movement of the communist period that reached its zenith in the 1980s was like a civil society in embryo, it contained the germ of what became known as transition society in the 1990s. It is evident today that this vision was flawed with a naive adulation of western democracy that allowed largely unfettered neoliberalism to undermine social support mechanisms. The increase in poverty, the emergence of oligarchy, and the rise in xenophobia with a civil society that in some cases became hierarchical, elitist, and donor-driven were factors that contributed to illiberalism in Hungary. This book seeks to assess whether in the words of Heller the dissidents of today might enable their nation to escape with its sanity or whether they will repeat the mistakes of dissident movements of the past in Central Eastern Europe. Can Hungary be saved? Can it be transformed?

Chapter One
Setting the Context: Academic Freedom and Hungarian Society

This chapter gives a detailed interpretation of academic freedom and places it in a historic framework. It also provides insights into the relationship between the state and academia and the impact of neoliberalism on higher education. It reviews authoritarianism in Hungary, detailing its rise, and nature and its implications for academic freedom through a discussion of 'the culture war'. The chapter also provides a historical overview of the development of higher education in Hungary. The chapter thus provides contextual background to a series of case studies and testimonies presented in the main body of the book.

Defining Academic Freedom

Academic freedom can be perceived in many ways. It can be seen as an individual right, including freedom of opinion and expression and freedom of association. It is a fundamental freedom for academics within the law to question and test conventional wisdom and develop new ideas without undue harassment or interference. It is a freedom that does not constrain research questions or the freedom to teach the truth as we see it (Russell, 1993).

Another dimension of academic freedom is the institutional right of autonomy for academic institutions. Correspondingly, public authorities are expected to respect academic freedom and to protect it. Academic freedom is not codified as a stand-alone, autonomous right under international law. However, *the Charter of Fundamental Rights of the European Union* is an exception that explicitly guarantees academic freedom and is a binding obligation, while other bodies like the Council of Europe and United Nations also seek to uphold academic freedom (Vrielinka et al, 2011). UNESCO (1997) in a 'soft law' instrument endorsed a statement affirming that 'the right to education, teaching, and research can only be fully enjoyed in an atmosphere of academic freedom'. However, it would appear that alignment to these ideals may be lower in EU states than might be expected, a problem compounded by trying to get countries to conform to 'soft law' like the UNESCO recommendation and the limited and/or convoluted powers of intervention afforded by other protections for academic freedom. This, coupled with the rapid speed of change in the function and management of universities and increased political turbulence and extremes, has arguably led to an increasing di-

https://doi.org/10.1515/9783110749816-003

lution of academic freedom. As a consequence, the protection of the academic freedom of the majority of the individual academic staff in Europe's universities has probably diminished over recent years (Karran, 2009, Pap, 2021). Universities have often been the centre of political and intellectual dissent, and thus authoritarian regimes in the past and present have been fearful of academia and have sought to curb its autonomy and freedom (Kori, 2016). A key task for this book is to determine the relevance of these issues to Hungary.

In September 2018 the European Parliament voted in favour of launching Article 7 (Treaty on the EU) proceedings against the Hungarian government, based on a European Parliament Report prepared by MEP Judit Sargentini. The Sargentini Report adopted by the European Parliament in September 2018 called on the Council of the EU to use Article 7 (this procedure has the potential to suspend Hungary from certain rights in the EU for infringing the rule of law). The report mentioned the expulsion of the CEU, the Government ban on Gender Studies, and the discrimination against Roma students in primary and secondary schools. More could have been said in this report on the deeper structural changes introduced in education, as are outlined in this chapter (Zeigler, 2019). Nevertheless, it was a landmark moment, being the first time article 7 was activated by the European Parliament.

It should also be noted that in 2018 the Academic Freedom Index (AFI) placed Hungary in category B alongside countries like Columbia and Haiti, other EU member states are in category A. The index is formed through expert assessments based on indicators that measure academic freedom and autonomy and shows a serious deterioration in academic freedom in Hungary since 2010 (Kinzelbach et al, 2020). An updated version of the AFI in 2021 placed Hungary in category C, together with Burma, Brazil, and India. All other EU member states, apart from Hungary, are included in category A (Kinzelbach et al, 2021).

Universities have long been an ideological battleground. *Modernisation theory* suggests a link between university education and mass protest and the university is often celebrated as a site of critique and dissent. In contrast though, in autocratic states, universities have been compliant in the legitimation of dictators and the indoctrination of students, and the use of *knowledge outputs* to bolster such regimes (Dahlum and Wig, 2021). Some warn that constraints on academic freedom will lead to a deterioration in the quality of public debate and the maintenance of pluralist democracy. The central aim of this book is to assess the level of threat to academic freedom in Hungary, a nation-state that Prime Minister Viktor Orbán has described as an "*illiberal* democracy".

The Historic Development of Academic Freedom

Academic freedom, the right and freedom to investigate and debate issues without intimidation, fear and censorship is a concept that some would argue has ancient origins (Nelson, 2010). The Socratic tradition of learning and investigation as developed by the ancient Greek philosopher Socrates, encouraged the presentation of a hypothesis but then encouraged refutation to test, temper, and develop the argument presented. Socrates was put on trial by the Athenian state, charged with and convicted of corrupting the Athenian youth and not worshipping the gods of the city-state. For Socrates, seeking the truth and asking challenging questions was at the centre of his work, but this challenged and threatened the interests of powerful élites who conspired to remove Socrates through prosecution. Socrates was punished by being ordered to drink hemlock, a poison. The actions against him can be viewed as an early assault on intellectual freedom (Cabtree, 2003). However, as democracy in ancient Greece gave way to tyrants and given that the Roman Empire rested on the supreme and dictatorial powers of the Emperor, any fledgling notion of free intellectual inquiry was stifled. Intellectual freedom was further stunted with the rise of Christianity which marked the late Roman Empire and middle ages as a period where the nature of enquiry was hemmed in by superstition and irrationality. It was an age where church leaders were seen as the arbiters of what was legitimate thought. The inquisition and other waves of church-led persecution are testaments to the intellectual and religious tyranny of those times.

Universities were established in Europe from the eleventh century, but these were not the first, since such institutions had been established in the Middle East, Africa, and Asia before the establishment of the first European university in Bologna in 1088. The medieval universities in Europe developed as supra-national institutions under the jurisdiction of Papal power and combined practical learning for the 'higher' vocations or professions with a search for universal truths. The latter goal was sometimes impeded by religious dogma but the secularization of higher education or transference of control to the state helped limit such tension (Berdahl, 1990). With the advent of the Renaissance, notions of intellectual freedom were rekindled. Tensions and notions of intellectual and religious freedom of enquiry were evident in the sixteenth century with the clash between Martin Luther, a theologian, and professor in Wittenberg, Germany, and church authorities wedded to the Catholic faith. Luther was profoundly disturbed by what he perceived as the corruption, decadence, and lack of spirituality of the Catholic Church. Luther challenged the supremacy of the pope and the clerical élite and was excommunicated by the Pope in 1521 for his views. This rupture over what can be described as an issue of freedom of thought and faith led to the Reformation and religious and social revolt across Europe that laid the foundations for the Enlightenment. As Durkheim noted, the advent of Protestantism unleashed new intellectual freedoms and represented a paradigm shift that brought about huge philosophical, cultural, and scientific changes in a Europe that was no longer so tightly constrained by superstition and the rigid dogma of the Catholic Church (Jones, 1986). As a consequence, enlightenment ideals emphasised the importance of *democracy* and *liberty* and placed limits on the secular power of the church, concepts that spawned the industrial revolution and the rise of the modern nation-state.

The nation-state gave rise to the modern-day university as one of the core institutions in society that shaped and moulded national character and intellectual leadership. In this sense, the university entered more directly into the realm of politics, not just through the state's funding of universities. Questions and tensions arose about the autonomy of academic institutions and the role they should play not only in terms of national identity formation but also in their challenges to the status quo. Consequently, the concept of academic freedom became more defined and codified. For example, Wilhelm von Humboldt's educational reforms and the establishment of the University of Berlin (now Humboldt University) emphasised the importance of *Lehrfreiheit* (freedom to teach) and *Lernfreiheit* (freedom to learn), both of which were encapsulated in *Akademische Freiheit* (academic freedom), providing something of a prototype for other universities (Anderson, 2004). In Britain Cardinal Henry Newman, a key intellectual pioneer in the nineteenth century believed that universities should operate without religious dogma. Newman felt critical scholarship and universal knowledge, where knowledge pursued for its own ends and not for instrumental purposes, should shape the learning environment (Matthews et al, 2021). Despite the great influence of these liberal principles and the pioneering work conducted by Humboldt, Germany though was also to become the scene of one of the greatest challenges to academic freedom in the modern age. During the Third Reich, academic freedom and institutional autonomy were eradicated under the Nazis. Academics who were critical of the regime were dismissed and replaced by intellectually subservient Nazi academics (Beveridge, 1959). Elsewhere totalitarianism challenged academic freedom, particularly in the USSR.

From the 1930s, The Hungarian thinker and polymath Michael Polányi[1] considered both the purpose of scientific enquiry and the challenges presented by totalitarianism. This was a concern that deepened following his visit to the Soviet

---

[1] Michael Polányi was the brother of Karl author of the landmark book 'The Great Transformation' (1944).

Union in 1935 where he met the lead communist politician Nikolai Bukharin, a strong advocate of a centralised command economy. Bukharin argued that distinctions between the pure and applied sciences in the capitalist West deprived scientists of the consciousness of their social functions, creating an illusion of pure science. Bukharin felt the freedom of scientists must be subservient to the comprehensive planning of the Soviet economy and the five-year economic programmes (Polányi, 1939). During the 1930s, a growing body of researchers and academics became aligned to the view that planning and the state could play an important role in scientific development, most importantly the betterment of society. A leading proponent of such a view in the 1930s was the scientist John Bernal (1975), who believed that if scientists were left to their own devices they would be less likely to develop innovations and discoveries that could be applied to the needs of society. Bernal asserted that capitalism, with its reliance on competition and profits, pushed science into searching for the means to maximise profit rather than the social improvement that would benefit all.

In contrast to this shift to Soviet-style socialism and a vogue for centralisation in Science, Polányi advocated a society where free intellectuals search for truth for its own sake. A prerequisite for such a state of affairs was for science to be free from political, ideological, and economical influences. Polányi (1936, 117) felt that if scientists were too closely aligned with power then they "forfeited their right to restrain governments in the name of truth" and that "unless intellectuals make a new departure, inspired by unflinching veracity, the truth will remain powerless against propaganda." Polányi, therefore, felt that totalitarianism impeded academic freedom and he rejected the classical, liberal conception of liberty. In his view, such individualism and its failure to recognise and nurture transcendent moral values had, in crisis, mutated societies into forms of totalitarianism. In other words, denying the reality of transcendent moral ideas opens a door to totalitarianism. Polányi argued that there was a strong interconnection between independent science and political liberty (Polányi 1937, Hartl, 2011).

Polányi reasoned that knowledge production could operate in a manner somewhat akin to the free market where the actions of consumers can determine the demand and hence to a degree the value of an intellectual product (Beddeleem, 2020). Likewise, Polányi (1962) argued that scientists in a 'republic of science' should be free to engage in open debate and pursue truth as an end in itself rather than be shackled to power and authority. It could be argued that Polányi was trying to promote a form of academic dissensus where debate and an exchange of views in open discussion could help determine the value of scientific outputs and arguments. Such an approach could provide an antidote to the scourge of totalitarianism (Polányi 1998).

Polányi was not alone in his criticism of Marxist notions of Science. John Bernal's book (1939) '*The Social Function of Science*' made the case Bukharin had made to Polányi for closely harnessing Science to the cultural and material needs of society. In a review of Bernal's book John Randal Baker (1939, 175) attacked this viewpoint:

> The doctrine of those who profess that the only proper objects of scientific research are to feed people and to protect them from the elements, that research workers should be organised in gangs and told what to discover, and that the pursuit of knowledge for its own sake has the same value as the solution of crossword puzzles.

Baker and Polányi were to be instrumental figures in establishing the Society for Freedom in Science (1940–1963), a network of thinkers that sought to promote and defend open and free intellectual thought. Interestingly, another active member was the Austrian economist Frederick von Hayek, like Polányi an émigré of Central Europe who had, since 1931, been Professor of Economics at the London School of Economics. Hayek had allied himself with Polányi because his disposition to more laissez-faire approaches to the needs of society made him recoil from the socialism and planning espoused by groups like the 'Social Relations of Science' movement (Beddeleem, 2017). Hayek was to become a leading luminary of what we now term neoliberalism. Some would argue that this philosophical viewpoint has had a more profound influence in the last forty years on science and enquiry than the views propounded by Polányi in this sphere, leading to market principles increasingly being applied to academic institutions.

Liberalism, Commodification and Audit Culture

The post-war period, in countries like Britain, witnessed the ascendancy of Keynesian economics and central planning and development of a welfare state, what the French economist Jean Fourastié (1979) called the 'Les Trente Glorieuses' the *glorious thirty*, a 'gilded age' in which, from 1945 to 1975, living standards rose dramatically (see the preface for earlier discussion). However, western society avoided the authoritarian excesses of soviet power in the USSR by maintaining liberal democracies and promoting and developing human rights frameworks that emphasised the value and importance of liberty and freedom of speech. These socioeconomic and political initiatives were a response to totalitarianism, namely a desire to prevent the re-emergence of totalitarianism in Europe which was perceived to have been spawned by the economic crisis, poverty, and weak checks and balances within the political system. Another motive for such efforts was to stem the tide of the Soviet advance in what became known as *the Cold War.*

The Cold War was to be played out in several spheres including the intellectual. The U.S government and its Central Intelligence Agency pumped resources into cultural propaganda, including the *Congress for Cultural Freedom* established in 1950, whose mission was to minimise western academics' alignment with Marxist thinking. Congress issued a 'Freedom Manifesto', committed to the protection of freedom of expression, and denounced the restrictions on such freedoms imposed by totalitarian states (Saunders, 2000). A key facet of such propaganda was the claim that unlike in the USSR, where independent thinkers were purged and ostracised, western academics had real and meaningful academic freedom.

Interestingly, the Society for Freedom in Science (see the previous discussion) was drawn into the orbit of the Congress for Cultural Freedom, causing some tensions regarding autonomy and independence which was one factor in the decline of the Society for Freedom in Science (Reinisch, 2000). Discord within the Society also materialised because of a dispute between two of its founding members; Polányi and Baker. Polányi supported a proposed strike by academic staff at Göttingen University on account of a former Nazi, Leonhard Schlüter, being appointed as Minister for Education in Lower Saxony. Baker disapproved, as in his mind strike action was incompatible with a liberal democracy where reasoned argument and elections should be sovereign (Reinisch, 2000). The incident can be viewed as one of the first indicators of a rift and tension between liberal-minded progressives and more libertarian thinkers on the role of the academy and how it should be managed, a tension that presaged later disputes around the role of academic institutions and academic freedom in the 1980s onwards, a period that the discussion will return to shortly.

A product of the Cold War was the imposition of restrictions on the political activities and loyalties of both students and academics in the USA that sought to constrain and even prohibit the influence of communism. An important incident occurred at the University of California when its leadership in 1949 stipulated that all faculty must sign an oath declaring that they were not members of the Communist Party as a condition of employment. Some members of the faculty refused to sign the oath and lost their positions. By the late 1960s, the influence of such codes and the hysteria of the Cold War were on the wane. Universities in North America and Western Europe became the centres of the counterculture of the time, with faculty members and students being vociferous in challenging the prevailing cultural and political norms by for example opposing the war in Vietnam and encouraging radical politics and thinking (Hensby, 2019). The Free Speech Movement at Berkeley and activism at other college campuses led to growing calls for freedom of speech/academic freedom in universities and challenges to bans on political activities on campus in response to attempts by university leaders to punish and reprimand those involved in supporting and promoting the work of the burgeoning civil rights movement (Cohen, 2010).

The theories of Bourdieu (1986, 1988) are useful in helping us to comprehend the academic environment during the 1960s/70s. Bourdieu characterised the academy as being structured hierarchically. Those at the pinnacle of the pyramid had achieved and attained their position through the possession of forms of capital (economic, cultural, social, and symbolic) and were likely to share similar dispositions which incorporated common viewpoints and stratagems that maintained and upheld their supremacy but also served to marginalise and devalue those located in subordinate positions in the academic field. Bourdieu described such disputes as being positioned between *the conservatives* (orthodoxy) and those with a more subversive disposition (heretics). The field of academic discipline is in fact in permanent conflict, since academics frequently engage in strategies of 'position taking' directed towards the maximising of symbolic gain (Bourdieu, 1993). During these decades those who might be labelled as 'heretics' sought to challenge and expand the boundaries of what was considered to constitute the role of the academy and its ability to initiate transformative change, a debate that had implications for the developing notions of academic and intellectual freedom.

According to Bourdieu the power of those at the pinnacle of the university hierarchy was also attributable to the *secularisation* of that power through titles and notions that formalised and recognised forms of knowledge (cultural capital) legitimised and made pre-eminent the outputs of those located in the academic institution(s). Bourdieu's depiction of those at the pinnacle of academic power structures also provides insights into how the modern academic was becoming more like a manager and entrepreneur reliant on connections with power and hence contracts and funding. The modern academic also seems to rely upon marketing, patronage, and clientelism and not solely the value and impact of their academic outputs and intellectual prowess. Bourdieu was aware of how commercialism was transforming the basis of academic capital (recognition and achievement in research and scholarship) and was being supplanted through appeals to market principles (Collyer, 2015). The *conservatives* or *traditionalists* in academic circles can also be charged with what Freire (1972) called banking education, where the teacher deposits information into their students as they might deposit money into a bank. Didactic forms of teaching minimise the capacity for learning through critical thought and challenge.

The ascendancy of neoliberalism was bolstered through the disintegration of the communist system of the Soviet Union and a sense of triumphalism, as expressed in Frances Fukuyama's (1992) 'end of history' assertion, which contended that liberal democracy was the apotheosis of our socio-cultural evolution. In other words, there had been a triumph of capitalist liberal democracy and no capitalist democracies should ever see any need to revert to autocracy. Such comments now seem naïve and fanciful, especially since capitalism in some countries has bolstered and supported forms of autocracy. This sense of triumphalism led to what Joseph Stiglitz (2009) termed as market fundamentalism an unquestioning faith in neoliberalism and principles of the market, which found shape in the policies of the World Bank and International Monetary Fund. This new economic order forced and coerced weaker and more vulnerable economies, especially in the third world to fall into line with the neoliberalism of the west (the Washington Consensus) but also permeated all forms of life through an audit culture and marketisation of institutions (Brown, 2015).

Consequently, neoliberalism has meant the application of free-market principles to the academy has become more pronounced (Ivancheva, 2011). This process of change has been particularly marked in the UK and US where the impact of neoliberal ideas as articulated through Thatcherism, Reaganism and the Third Way of Blair had a profound influence on institutions like universities. Critics assert contrary to the views of Hayek, discussed earlier, that the free market has in effect constrained intellectual and academic freedom. The *marketisation* of society rooted in government economic discourses of competition is visible within higher education performance indicators and targets. Marketisation is also evident in the increasing role of non-academic managers, the adoption of line-management authority hierarchies, coupled with strategic planning, quality assurance, annual appraisals, and audits that now function as a regular part of university governance. Academics in the neoliberal university can be said to have become 'unprofessionalised', in that their expertise in the classical sense is no longer so strongly valued, their collegial power through bodies like senates being diluted through *audit culture*. They have therefore become 'atomised'.

Market forces in higher education have also weakened tenure with teaching becoming more precarious through casual employment practices. The effects of this neoliberalism in academia have significant impacts on the emotional wellbeing of staff, on job satisfaction, on morale, on personal stress, and on the ability for staff to cope with ever-increasing workloads the unrealistic expectations placed upon them. For those who do not make the grade, the consequences can be extreme, with long and productive careers ending in redundancy; there have even been reports of breakdowns and suicides. Competitivity also reduces the sense of trust and fraternity that might help weather the storm of commercialised academia (Raaper and Olssen, 2016). Universities have thus become like corporations with formulae, targets, and principles guided by the 'new managerialism' (Miller, 2010). In this manner, academics become entrepreneurs and the students become customers so that the university becomes a training institution where the aims, curriculum, and ethos of education are pre-determined. Intellectual activities outside of these realms have become marginal and peripheral (Lojdová, 2016).

Academia can therefore be viewed as a field of power dominated by an audit culture that exalts and promotes the 'competitive academic', adept at self-promotion through voluminous publication in top academic journals and the acquisition of grants (Sparkes, 2007). Spooner (2018, 895) in his analysis of academic audit culture argues contemporary audit culture is unique in the sense of the magnitude, depth, and ubiquity of audit culture's implementation and pervasiveness. Consequently, academics are depersonalised, quantified, and constrained in their scholarship, "via a suffocating array of metrics and technologies of governance". It has been said that the contemporary university has changed from a platonic academy to a commercial mall (Wood, 2010). In this marketplace, other academics become competitors – less inclined to acknowledge and respect the views and aspirations of their rivals, but also less likely to forge links with other researchers to create what can be described as an *emancipatory pedagogy,* inclusive of the wider community (Webb, 2018). In part, such distancing will be prompted by time and resource factors as the 'managed' academic and researcher race to complete the task within the agreed budget and time frame, but it will also be prompted by the desire to win contracts. Inclusive research which gives those being researched real voice is more likely to challenge the status quo and perceived wisdom of power-élites. In the commissioning of research though, policymakers are more likely to commission research shaped by notions of positivism and supposed scientific neutrality or tokenistic forms of engagement with researchers (Ryder, 2018).

The marketisation of the academy has created, in the opinion of some, an audit culture that limits the ability of academics to develop critical thought. Instead, the modern academic has to conform to performance-related managerialism where the focus is on sanitised and financially lucrative outputs (Brown, 2015). Hayek had argued that evolution and market principles would ensure the survival of efficient institutional forms and could bolster intellectual freedom. It would appear, however, that although universities invoke market principles, *new managerialism* is dependent on unprecedented bureaucratic interventions where academic freedom is weakened. The marketisation of academia has clear and profound implications for the academic environment of the university, with consequences for the inclusivity of research and propensity of academics to challenge and speak truth to power.

Populism and Culture War

In the present day, the terms 'populism' and 'culture war' are highly relevant to debates on academic freedom, especially in the context of Hungary. Brubaker (2017) may be right to contend that several independent crises have converged in recent years to create 'a perfect storm', a bi-product of which has been populism, a political phenomenon that can be said to thrive on crisis and emergency. A key catalyst to this storm was the financial crisis of 2008 ushering in a decade of austerity and accentuating a prevailing tendency for the rich to accrue even greater wealth and for the divide between rich and poor to become sharper (Piketty, 2014). A 'race to the bottom' of downward trends in wages and work conditions as countries sought desperately to gain competitiveness and economic advantage has contributed greatly to the crisis.

The crisis though is not solely economic, it has a cultural dimension. Giddens terms the present age as one of 'reflexive modernity' where ordinary social actors feel that society has changed rapidly and that the future is uncertain. We live in an age unlike the 'modernity' that was based on absolute truths and certainties (Giddens and Pearson, 1998). The catalyst to these anxieties has been globalisation and the increasing marketisation of society both of which have challenged and undermined old certainties and for some material well-being and the very cultural complexion of society. This has led to a cultural backlash.

Another argument presented regarding the rise of populism is that contemporary democracies have failed to provide a space and opportunity for alienated groups to express concerns and to be engaged with and persuaded to reorientate their views. In this sense, resentment towards political élites and hierarchies may have some validity. Mouffe (2005, 30) argues that constructive engagement and dialogue has been impeded by a neoliberal consensus and that instead there has been a confrontation between essentialist forms of identification or non-negotiable moral values: "When political frontiers become blurred, disaffection with political parties sets in and one witnesses the growth of other types of collective identities, around nationalist, religious or ethnic forms of identification".

The media has also been culpable in this political and cultural dissension. In a process Habermas (1989) described as the re-feudalisation of the public sphere, it was claimed that the media had failed to educate and inform and had instead been moved by a desire to maximise sales and profit, or alignment with reactive political agendas favoured by some media oligarchs who presented propaganda as fact. A dysfunctional media has increasingly stoked hysteria and discord. In addition, politicians have been inclined to 'surf' media-fuelled hysteria or orchestrate it themselves in what can be called a form of tabloid-based politics reliant on soundbites, slogans, and simplistic rhetoric (Wodak, 2015). With deadly effect, President Trump was able to demonstrate the effectiveness of such tactics by using his media platforms to sustain the false claim that he had been cheated of victory in the 2020 presidential election leading to the "stop the steal" rally and the storming of the US Capitol and House of Representatives.

It can be argued therefore that economic, cultural, and political factors have created constituencies of resentment that have spawned the rise of populism. The key traits of populism involve a desire for a strong charismatic leader, at times messianic, and willing to support issues popular with the masses while offending the political and cultural sensibilities of élites. Populism appeals to the masses through speech acts, which resonate with the emotions, including anger, of the masses and so-called 'common sense' thinking that disparages intellectualism. This can include forms of nativism and xenophobia. Populism can also present an appeal to folkloric traditions and a desire to preserve and maintain idealised notions of national identity, which often encompass jingoism and bombast such as the 'Make America Great Again' mantra of Trump. Populism also encompasses a form of paranoia where exaggeration, suspicion and conspiratorial fantasy are rife. Populism is an outlook, which it can be said lacks refinement and complexity, considered by some to be crude and simplistic. It voices the most base thoughts and anxieties of the masses that in previous times, might have been easily dismissed as demagoguery or opportunism. In this sense, it can be viewed as a re-politicisation of topics intentionally or unintentionally ignored by political élites and dismissed as being atavistic or reactionary. At the centre of the populist phenomenon is a critique of the establishment and adulation of '*the people*' portrayed as '*decent*' and '*hardworking*' whose collective positions must prevail in all policy decisions as *the will of the people*. The '*good people and values*' are defined in contrast to outsiders who present cultural and economic dangers, groups such as migrants and the political élite. The latter is deemed to be distant and privileged and furthering their interests at the expense of the masses (Mudde and Kaltwasser, 2017).

Populism, though, may take many forms and is evident on the 'Left' and the 'Right' of the political spectrum. It does not always threaten rights and freedoms (Halmai, 2019a). However, what can be described as authoritarian populism has been the most successful variant in recent years encompassing strong leaders, illiberalism, binary codes, and nativist conceptions of national identity. As noted earlier in the discussion, after the collapse of communism Fukuyama (1992) asserted an *End of History*, liberal democracies and economies, which would now triumph, as only such liberalism could satisfy an intrinsic human desire for dignity and recognition. However, this was not to be the case and developing nations like China, Russia, and the Gulf States were able to couple capitalism with authoritarianism (Foa, 2018). The period 2016–17 was a time of profound challenge centred on nationalist populism. It is clear that 'Brexit' (*British exit from the European Union*) features many of the characteristics of populism and was seen as a clarion call by the international populist far-right. Aside from the Brexit vote, there was the election of the populist Donald Trump to the presidency in the USA, and in Austria, the far-right nearly won the Presidency. There were fears that Kurt Wilders in the Netherlands and Marine Le Pen in France might triumph and join the radical right ascendancy that was at that stage well established in Hungary and Poland (Ryder, 2020).

Some communities and sections of society subject to profound socioeconomic and cultural change have undergone a process of 'cultural trauma' where a community feels they have been subjected to a profound trauma which leaves indelible marks upon their group consciousness, marking their memories forever and changing their future identity in fundamental and irrevocable ways (Alexander et al., 2004). Rapid change and trauma have fed a discourse of what has been described as 'moral panic' and a 'risk society'. 'Moral panics' and fear of 'folk devils' can help normalise hegemony, in other words, mainstream institutions and values, but it can also be a tool, especially in the hands of populists, to reorientate and change society. Hence, authoritarian populists have been adept at claiming that they represent the majority view based on tradition and/or established behaviour and they have castigated those (folk devils) who are deemed to deviate from convention. Successful panics and acts of collective hysteria can find resonance with deeper historical, cultural, and structural anxieties, which are also able to reinforce *boundary maintenance* in a neurotic form of 'us' and 'them' and thereby maintain the power of élites (Cohen, 2016).

These tensions have created a cleavage that can be described as a 'culture war' white men; ethnic majorities, the old, those on a low income, and the less educated have been the most susceptible to this cultural backlash, and the allure of authoritarian populism. For such groups, diverse forms of sexuality, LGBTQ rights, same-sex marriage, and varied family units, fluid gender identities, tolerance of migrants, refugees, foreigners, and support for multiculturalism are anathema and an affront to tradition. In this culture war that pitches *cosmopolitanism* against *monoculturalism* and tradition, authoritarian populist parties have been adept at articulating reactionary positions and mobilising their base (Inglehart and Norris, 2016).

These are notions and sentiments that have profound implications for intellectual freedom and the role and status of academic opinion in society. In some cases, populists have sought to frame academics as part of an intellectually confused and self-interested élite. The cynicism towards academia was evident in the UK referendum on leaving the EU in 2016 when Brexit supporting Conservative minister Michael Gove dismissed expert opinion that counselled against leaving by stating the public were "tired of experts" (Ryder, 2020). Attacks on academics should therefore be viewed as part of broader attacks on 'the establishment', leading to academics being perceived as privileged élites, as scapegoated by both politicians and right-wing media. Tufts and Thomas (2017, 4) describe the impact of these hostile perceptions of academia:

> Academic research is written off as obscure, inaccessible, and simply not up to the task of addressing society's real problems, or of providing students with the skills they need for the labour market.... Populist attacks extend into the realm of conspiracy, as universities are cast as breeding grounds for political correctness, the feminisation of society, and Marxist thought police.

Populism is an uncompromising politics with a propensity to metamorphose into an illiberalism that denies the existence of divisions of interests and opinions within *the people*, rejecting the legitimacy of opponents, both political and academic, and thus posing a real danger to academic freedom (Maiguashca, 2019). The precarious position of academics that speak out in authoritarian regimes is evidenced in Turkey, led by the authoritarian populist President Erdoğan. Since the failed coup attempt of 2016, more than 6,000 academics have been summarily dismissed from their university posts via emergency decrees, many of them accused by 'secret informers' of associating with terrorists, and therefore summarily banned from public service for life. Essentially recognised by the authorities as 'dead to the law', they are still living 'civil death' (Özdemir, 2021)[2]. This was a higher education sector deeply changed by market forces that eroded the power and prestige of academic voices, just one aspect in the transition to authoritarianism under Erdoğan. Could we be witnessing a similar chain of events in Hungary?

The discussion will return to the notion of academic freedom by chronicling the historic development of academic institutions and life in Hungary, but before doing that I seek to explore the historical development of authoritarianism in Hungary and to detail how it found expression in populist politics developed under Viktor Orbán.

---

2 Those who experience 'civil death' (sivil ölüm) are deprived of many basic civic rights: the right to presumption of innocence and a fair trial; to stand for election and work in the public sector; freedom of travel, speech and association.

Authoritarianism in Hungary

Given this book has a focus on higher education in Hungary, a country where authoritarian populism has established a hegemony, it is apt to explore in-depth the development of populism through the leadership of Hungarian prime minister Viktor Orbán. Hungary has been described as the EU's first non-democratic member state and it has been argued that alongside Turkey it presents the most extreme case of democratic regression in recent times. The media, civil society, and civil liberties have been significantly constrained in Hungary (Bódis, 2021, State Watch, 2020). To understand the cause and nature of the authoritarian populist regime headed by Orbán there is a need for a brief review of Hungarian history.

Hungary had been a major power in Europe during the late middle ages, especially during the reign of King Mátyás Corvinus (1443–1490), a noted promoter of renaissance values and style. Hungary's hegemony in central Europe though was undermined by its incorporation into the Austrian Habsburg monarchy and by the Turkish occupation. The Ottoman occupation of Hungary (1541–1699) gave Hungarians a sense of being the defender of Christian Europe. In addition, once Habsburg rule returned with the military defeat by them of the Ottomans, Hungary jostled with the Habsburgs for greater autonomy and rights leading to a serious uprising in 1848/9. Hungary also had a unique language with roots in the Uralic language family, a language not found elsewhere in the region, nor indeed anything remotely like it. Some would argue these factors forged a national identity that favoured independence and autonomy and to some degree defiance, traits still evident today according to some observers (Lendvai, 2014).

In 1867, as a consequence of nationalist pressure and economic challenges facing the very survival of the Empire, the Austrian Emperor agreed to make Hungary an equal partner in the Empire in what became known as the dual monarchy (1867–1918). The Austro-Hungarian Empire gave rise to a sense of Hungarian exceptionalism and bombast which meant they were enthusiastic supporters of World War One. Defeat, though, led to a profound crisis and the short-lived Communist revolution of Bela Kun in 1919, which was eventually repelled by Romanian soldiers. In 1920, though, Hungary lost two-thirds of its territory as a punishment for the war in the Treaty of Trianon (Wolin, 2011). The crisis in part explains the emergence of the regency of Admiral Horthy in the interwar period, a form of authoritarian leadership that gave Horthy the power to appoint and dismiss prime ministers. Although there was a multi-party system and a relatively free press, Hungary under Regent Horthy was a restricted democracy, with the landed aristocracy and church continuing to enjoy considerable power and privilege (Szegedy-Maszák, 1994).

Although the Treaty of Trianon was signed by the Hungarian government, during the period of Horthy's regency the huge anger it generated bolstered and shaped the Horthy administration. The regime became increasingly focused upon conservative and traditional values centred on Christian, conservative nationalism which derided bourgeois liberalism and radicalism, effectively marginalising them (Paxton, 2007). The regime was also antisemitic and passed anti-Jewish laws, also joining the axis powers under Hitler in fighting World War Two. By 1944, as the tide of war turned against the axis, Horthy became disillusioned with the war, leading to the German occupation of Hungary and an acceleration of the policy of extermination of Hungarian Jews and Roma (Braham, 2016). Subsequently, Horthy sought to broker a secret peace agreement with the allies, but before this could be concluded he was ousted as Regent by the German SS and the Hungarian Fascist Arrow Cross Party assumed power.

Hungary was occupied by the USSR in 1945 and the country fell into the Soviet sphere. Exiled Communist leaders returned from Moscow and introduced a Stalinist dictatorship with Mátyás Rákosi as its leader. The regime was based on the Soviet model in which the state had full control of the economy and a tight grip on society, including the world of academia (Kovai, 2016). However, disillusionment with Communism prompted the Hungarian Uprising of 1956 which was eventually quelled through the military occupation of Russian troops. The suppression of the Uprising led to a clampdown and imposition of a more authoritarian form of Communism, but from the 1960s under the leadership of Kádár, there was some relaxation, primarily in the economic sphere, which led to some liberalisation that allowed an element of private enterprise. With the collapse and disintegration of Communism from 1989, Hungary was transformed into a liberal democracy. In 1990, elections were staged with the Hungarian Democratic Forum (MDF), a nationalist Christian party taking power. From 1994 to 1998 the 'Reform' Communists (now democratic socialists, MSZP) and 'free democratic' party (SZDSZ) were in power, continuing to follow the 'neoliberal' trajectory set by their predecessors. From 1998 to 2002, Fidesz led a ruling coalition including the Christian Democrats and the Smallholders Party. This period of transition saw Hungary commit itself to membership of NATO and the EU, and there was a mood of optimism and a sense that such alignments would bring greater security and prosperity.

The constant political feature of the 1990s in Hungary was this alignment with neoliberal thinking, prompting rapid privatisation, economic change and new competitiveness, but it gave rise to structural decline, especially in heavy industries, which in turn greatly increased unemployment. Neoliberalism also fragmented the welfare safety net that had existed during Communism and consequently poverty and exclusion grew, especially for those located in the now de-industrialised urban centres, including minorities like the Roma who had relied heavily on unskilled employment in state industries (Ramet, 2007). As noted earlier, in 1998 Orbán led his first administration. This was an impressive achievement given the party had only been formed ten years earlier as *Fidesz* – an acronym of *Alliance of Young Democrats* in Hungarian, largely composed of dissident students like Orbán committed to liberalism and internationalism. By 1998 Fidesz was a more professional-led and centrist party committed to EU membership, secured in 2004. However, by 2006 the optimism of a society in transition was waning, and serious protests and demonstrations broke out following the release of a leaked recording. In the recording, the newly elected socialist Prime Minister Ference Gyurcsány, who had held a position in the communist youth organisation but who later as premier became committed to third way neoliberalism, stated to a group of fellow party members that the party had lied in the election about the extent of Hungary's economic woes, which he acknowledged were profound (McLaughlin, 2006). Under Gyurcsány the degree of economic difficulty facing Hungary became fully apparent and Hungary was compelled to request a loan from the *International Monetary Fund*, which prompted policies of austerity, leading to further hardship.

The Fidesz opposition party was able to effectively exploit these hardships but did so in a tone that was now markedly populist. In opposition, Orbán forged a new electoral alliance that shifted the party further away from centrist liberalism and instead sought to forge a conservative alliance centred on the church, family, and nation (Pap, 2018). Wilkin (2020) may be right to conclude that despite neoliberalism's professed commitment to reason and enlightenment values it is a system that has created social cleavages which have bolstered authoritarian and traditional belief systems and hierarchies. The Left in Hungary, as in many other European countries, now tamed and captive to the neoliberal order, offered little in terms of alternatives and solutions for the increasing numbers who felt disadvantaged in such a system. As a result, in 2010 Fidesz and their junior partner the Christian-Democratic People's Party (KDNP) was swept to power by a landslide that gave it a two-thirds majority in Parliament, enabling it to make sweeping constitutional changes (Lendvai, 2012).[3]

Over the last decade, Orbán's autocratic constitutional revolution has involved rewriting the constitution by making it compatible with autocratic gover-

---

[3] Fidesz and their partner the Christian-Democratic People's Party (KDNP) received more than 53 percent of the votes in 2010 and due to the disproportional election system – gained two-thirds of the parliamentary seats in the election. Fidesz made further revisions to the voting system that gave them further electoral advantage and again secured a two-thirds majority both in 2014 and 2018 with only 45 and 49 percent of the votes respectively.

nance, and through a stealth campaign of reform, he has captured or undermined state institutions of and national systems of checks and balances. This has included capturing the *Constitutional Court* and *the Judiciary* in general (senior judges were forced into early retirement and replaced with pro-government figures). These legal changes greatly limited the scope for a legal challenge. Added to this, the state or allies of Orbán gained control of most media outlets or used state regulatory instruments to marginalise or silence critical media voices. The constitutional revisions within a new *Fundamental Law* changed many cardinal laws, including election legislation, which was modified and largely passed without public consultation or inclusive dialogue. Fidesz's two-thirds parliamentary majority was not sufficient to adopt a new constitution. Making a new constitution required the votes of four-fifths of all members of parliament according to the 1989 Constitution, hence Fidesz removed this provision with their two-thirds majority in the Parliament and dismantled the liberal democracy established in transition. This transformation can be described as *autocratic legalism* where a political leader uses power to weaken institutions designed to check their authority in action: a democratically elected leader might first be suspected of autocratic legalism when they launch a concerted and sustained attack on institutions whose job it is to check their actions, thus weakening constitutional restraints on executive power (Bárd and Pech, 2019).

This new constitution contained a preamble committed to defending the intellectual and spiritual unity of the nation, which was 'hyped' as an attempt to turn the page of Hungary's Communist past and to transform the country into a nationalist Christian state. Under the new constitution, Hungary was proclaimed to be a Christian nation, and there were also commitments to traditional values related to foetal protection and marriage, which raised fears about the future rights of Hungary's atheists, non-Christians, homosexuals, and single-parent families. The constitutional change stipulated that in the future several key decisions would be subject to two-thirds majorities, restricting the autonomy of future governments. The new constitution also curbed the powers of the top courts on budget and tax matters. As part of the overhaul of the Constitutional Court, a majority of the places were given to Fidesz supporters who were generally favoured in wider appointments to the judiciary. Critics also complained that a culture of cronyism and corruption enabled business supporters of Orbán to gain considerable control of the economy and the media, which became increasingly deferential to the political agenda of Fidesz (Innes, 2015).

According to sociologist, former liberal politician and cabinet member Bálint Magyar (2016), Orbán is running a mafia-style operation. Magyar argues that Hungary should now be considered a "post-communist mafia state", with an elite grounded in family relationships or the adopted family fitting into a highly hierarchical order of subordination that has the head of the adopted political family, Orbán, at the top of this economic and political pyramid (Magyar 2016). Speaking of the reforms Wilkin (2020, 27) argues:

> Orbánization is to be understood as the transformation of Hungarian political culture into a form of illiberalism where the formal mechanisms of liberal politics remain (elections, a judiciary, a free press, the rule of law), but where the political system has been reorganised in a way that gives the Government authoritarian power on a variety of levels.

In 2014 at Băile Tuşnad, Romania, Orbán gave a speech that set the tone for the authoritarian populist agenda he seemed intent to follow when he described Hungary as an *"illiberal* democracy"*, where the state had strong powers unfettered by checks and balances. The German chancellor Angela Merkel was quick to highlight the contradiction of the term by posing the question of how illiberalism and democracy could be coupled (Halász, 2015). The nature of this *illiberal democracy* steered by a rampant form of *ethnonationalism* became more evident in the Syrian migration crisis in 2015, in which large numbers fled the civil war in Syria and sought refuge in Europe. Orbán sought to stem the passage of refugees through Hungary by building a reinforced border fence and measures to prevent refugees from obtaining asylum, such as bureaucratic hurdles and a refusal to allow refugees to enter transit zones along the border. Orbán 'securitised' the matter further by arguing that Hungary did not want to be burdened with the economic cost that migration would bring and that Muslim migrants settling in Hungary would lead to cultural tensions as Hungary was a Christian country. This in turn led to attacks on multiculturalism and the EU. Orbán claimed the EU was trying to force migrants into the country through its proposed migrant quota system. As part of Orbán's radical *Eurosceptic* invective, he has compared the EU to the Soviet Union. He has also complained about Soviet-style meddling, deeming the EU to be an external body trying to colonise Hungary and imposing values and laws that undermine Hungary's sovereignty, identity and traditions (Than, 2013).

Orbán also sought to cast George Soros, the Hungarian-born philanthropist, as the 'bogeyman' for the problems he was seeking to challenge and tackle. Soros had established a civil society network that promoted human rights and liberal democracy. Orbán accused Soros and his network of promoting migration into Europe as part of an identity-changing agenda and pledged to kick Soros out of Hungary as the country had done with the Ottomans, Habsburgs, and Soviets. In 2017 Orbán denounced what he described as a devious plan by Soros: "The [Soros] plan sounds like this: several hundred thousand, if possible a million migrants must be brought to the territory of the European Union from the Muslim world every year." (Orbán, 2017). In one speech in the run-up to the 2018 election Orbán denounced Soros with antisemitic rhetoric, playing upon Soros's Jewish ethnicity:

> We are fighting an enemy that is different from us. Not open, but hiding; not straightforward but crafty; not honest but base; not national but international; does not believe in working but speculates with money; does not have a homeland of its own but feels it owns the whole world... (cited in Walker, 2020).

Shanes (2019) has described this speech act as a textbook example of antisemitism, based above all on fear of global domination by an *international Jewish conspiracy*. Thus, Soros was depicted as a nefarious puppet master of forces that posed a political and cultural threat to Hungary (see the preface for Orbán's earlier opposition to antisemitism) (Walker, 2018). Reflecting this hostility, Orbán introduced the officially titled 'STOP Soros package of bills' which made the organisation of illegal immigration a criminal offence. Hungarian civil society groups claimed these measures were to intimidate them and that they would interfere with their legal and legitimate work supporting migrants and refugees. The Hungarian Helsinki Committee said in a statement that at that moment, the Hungarian government threatened to bring back "an era of fear, unheard of since the fall of the Communist dictatorship." (O'Grady, 2018). In response to these pressures, Soros relocated the headquarters of his Open Society network from Budapest to Berlin.

In 2020 Orbán's response to the Covid-19 pandemic was typically theatrical; an indefinite state of emergency was declared that accorded Orbán the right to rule by decree. The emergency measures also ruled that journalists distributing misleading information could be liable to punishment of up to five years imprisonment. In response to growing concerns, the European Commission threatened to make EU funds, including access to the recovery funds allocated in response to the pandemic, conditional on respect for rule-of-law criteria (Bayer, 2020). Hungary together with Poland, which had also found itself increasingly out of step with the rest of the EU, threatened to veto the EU budget. A veto could have delayed the distribution of the urgently needed recovery funds. However, Hungary and Poland were appeased by the decision that such conditionality would not be applied until after 2022 so that consequently, any serious disputes would not arise in all probability until after the 2022 election in Hungary. Soros (2020) derided the compromise, which according to him would allow Orbán to continue to funnel funds from public bodies into private "foundations controlled by his cronies" and could constrain the European Commission's ability to interpret and act on agreed EU legislation. Soros noted, "That is a dangerous precedent because it reduces the Commission's legal independence and may very well contravene the Treaty on European Union, at least in spirit".

The counter-Enlightenment tradition sees human rights as irrelevant and is rooted in national myths and legends, and blood connection to the homeland, (citizenship is not enough: blood supersedes citizenship). Action, emotion, and will, are paramount, hence there is a disdain for fact-based decision-making, intellectuals, the scrutiny of a free press, and enlightenment values of truth and transparency. Fascism is grounded in anti-enlightenment principles and threatens academic freedom with its obsessive cleansing of intellectual enemies. Such observations mean that we should be sensitive to the challenges to academic freedom in Hungary, as what may be described as *post-fascism* can alternate between, and fuse both conservative and fascist traditions. The co-existence of forms of democracy should not seduce us into a false sense of security since, if one party or group can dominate in a multi-party system, it could still create fascism (Ziegler, 2021a).

A brief review of Hungarian history indicates that the roots of democracy in this country are fragile and that for much of its recent history it has lapsed into forms of authoritarianism. In this sense, the ascendancy of Orbán should not surprise the reader. The rise of Orbán, as well as being a response and product of the growing socioeconomic cleavage in Hungary, is rooted in historical and cultural antecedents. An important question to pose is what plans and designs Orbán envisages for higher education and academic freedom. The next section details the history of academia in Hungary and provides an overview of Orbán's higher education reforms.

Higher Education in Hungary

The first Hungarian university, with faculties of law and medicine, was established in the town of Pécs in 1367, with the numbers increasing from the fifteenth century during a time when Hungary was considered an important political and military, but also cultural power in the region of Central Europe (Tarrósy, 2002). Eötvös Loránd University grew out of a Jesuit higher education institution founded in 1635.[4] By the nineteenth and early twentieth centuries, reflecting Hungary's prestige and power in the dual monarchy (discussed earlier), the

---

4 The university was originally based in Nagyszombat, then moved to Buda in 1777 and finally to Pest in 1784. More than sixty years ago the university was named after the world-famous physicist, Loránd Eötvös, who invented the torsion balance, and who served as Rector of the University and President of the Hungarian Academy of Sciences in the early twentieth century.

country had a vibrant network of universities and flourishing intellectual activity. Hungarian university students were active in the 1848 Uprising that sought to secure national autonomy from Hapsburg rule. Act XIX of 1848 was one of the achievements of the Revolution. This legal regulation provided a brief description of the fundamental features of higher education, including a commitment to the freedom of teaching and learning (Szögi, 2015). The failure of the 1848 Uprising and reimposition of Habsburg rule meant that the continued reform of higher education was controlled by the monarchy and was consequently shaped by a mix of liberal and conservative values, in part following the principles of Humboldt (discussed earlier).

By 1900 Budapest was the fastest growing city in Europe, and along with Vienna and Prague, it was considered an important centre of learning (Lukacs, 1990). By 1900, Budapest contained the world's largest urban Jewish population, more even than New York in 1900, of about 200.000, 23 % of the urban population. Some, not always in a hostile manner, referred to Budapest as 'Judapest' (Pronay, 2002). Jews were prominent in intellectual circles. Academics and intellectuals based in Hungary were also strongly integrated into the German-speaking intellectual lifeworld, and some participated in intellectual circles that sprung up such as 'Vasárnapi Kör' (Sunday Circle), advocating radical social reforms and positivism. Another intellectual circle was the 'Galilei Kör' (Galileo Circle) led by Karl Polányi, an anti-positivist radical thinker. As well as being the place of residence of brothers Karl and Michael Polányi, other notable thinkers lived and worked in Budapest, such as the philosopher György Lukács and the sociologist Karl Mannheim (Szokolszky, 2016).

In the short-lived Communist revolution of 1919 intellectuals were prominent in the new regime. Forms of tyranny portrayed as counter-revolutionary measures led to a loss of support for the Communists and its collapse led to a brief period of 'white' (anti-red) terror during the early part of the Horthy regime that included the dismissal of many academics who had aligned themselves with Communism. Some of these Left intellectuals were Jewish and their support for radicalism gave rise to the notion that a Jewish-Bolshevik conspiracy was at work in Hungary. After 1919, professors known to support conservative ideas came to take a dominant position in universities (Szögi, 2015). The political elite that supported the Horthy regime was centred on the aristocracy and industrial élites who, weakened by the war, had little inclination to shield Hungary's Jews from xenophobia as they had been willing to some extent to do in the pre-war period of expansion and modernisation. Christian Hungarian intellectuals and professionals saw Jews as their competitors and protested they were overrepresented in élite circles. After World War I, such views became more extreme as the myth of the *profiteer Jew* was popularised (Kovács 2012). These factors triggered growing hostility to Hungary's Jewish community. The Numerus Clausus Act of 1920 greatly restricted the number of Jews, irrespective of qualifications, to be admitted to universities (Kovács, 2012). Many Jewish, as well as radical thinkers, fled Hungary in the early 1920s (Nye, 2011). Among these intellectual refugees were the aforementioned Gyorgi Lukács, Karl Mannheim, and Michael Polányi (Hargittai, 2006).

During the Horthy regency, educational reforms were introduced by Kuno Klebelsberg in the 1920s, including the modernisation of universities and support for the Hungarian Academy of Sciences, by multiplying the number of research institutions (Szokolszky, 2016). As Hungary entered the 1930s, its politics became even more nationalistic and xenophobic. A law introduced in 1938 created a quota system to limit the participation of Jews in a range of professions and employment at any level of the Government was forbidden. An estimated quarter of a million Hungarian Jews lost their income (Patai, 1996). This led to a further wave of intellectuals and academics fleeing Hungary. Here it may be appropriate to note that Hungarian intellectual expatriates of the inter-war years were at the fore of intellectual achievement, so much so that many held positions at the most prestigious universities of the period: Cambridge, Princeton, Harvard and Yale among others. Some were involved in important research laboratories and research programmes of the age, like the nuclear programme at Los Alamos (Pronay, 2002).

In the aftermath of World War Two in Communist post-war Hungary, intellectual freedom remained blunted. Topics such as the Treaty of Trianon were not encouraged in academic discussion, neither was Hungarian participation in the Holocaust (Patai, 1996). Traditional conceptions of Hungarian history were erased from collective memory (Szokolszky, 2016). By the mid-1950s, a growing number of Communist intellectuals had become disillusioned with Communism in Hungary and were involved in the Petőfi Circle – a discussion group supporting Imre Nagy, the reformist Communist leader of Hungary (Litván, 1996). In the 1956 Uprising, Prime Minister Imre Nagy sought to secure for Hungary a greater degree of independence from the USSR. Students, through groups like the Revolutionary Student Committee, were active participants in the uprising. János Kádár, the new Communist Party leader initially reimposed strict Soviet-style rule and a 'reign of terror' that executed and imprisoned those who had been involved in the Uprising, including Imre Nagy. However, from the 1960s, Kádár allowed the liberalisation of the economic system and encouraged consumerism and some small level private enterprise in what became known as 'Goulash Communism' (Benczes, 2016). By the 1980s Hungary was considered the most westernised member of the Soviet bloc and although there was no real academic freedom, academics had some scope to depart from the Party line. Some notable research was conducted, for example, by socially-conscious researchers into the plight of the Roma, the findings of which challenged notions that poverty and disadvantage had been eradicated under Communism.

Only after the political transition in 1989 did meaningful intellectual freedom materialise in Hungary. The Law on Higher Education (1993) placed most higher education institutions under the supervision of the Ministry of Education. The Higher Education Act of 1993 also allowed non-state controlled (religious) higher education institutions to offer secular learning programmes. The number of church-run institutions tripled by 1993 and the number of private and foundation-maintained institutions rose (Harsányi and Vincze, 2012). Notable examples were the Central European University, founded by the philanthropist George Soros in 1991, and McDaniel College, established in Budapest in 1994 (an offshoot of McDaniel College in the US state of Maryland). Both of these international universities sought to bring to Hungary a liberal arts tradition of learning.

The Fidesz government (1998–2002) integrated higher education institutions; the number of state institutions was reduced from fifty-five to thirty (Tarrósy, 2002). This was a rather technocratic reform that did not herald any interference in academic freedom. Other reforms by successive governments sought to incorporate Hungary into the Bologna system, a system that seeks to create uniformity and cooperation across higher education in Europe regarding qualifications and academic principles. Successive governments have also sought to increase the efficiency of higher education administration and indeed the output of academics. A growing feature of the Hungarian academic landscape has been the introduction of what can be described as an *audit culture*, where academic outputs are counted and measured, and linked to pay and promotion (Toarniczky et al, 2019). Critics argue that such an audit culture presents a challenge to academic autonomy and freedom by steering academics to more mainstream subjects that might gather more funding and acclaim, conversely avoiding those subjects that are considered marginal (Ryder, 2020). However, it may be the case that such methods, in tandem with wider organisational and ideological reforms, have the propensity to fundamentally change higher education in Hungary.

In 2010 Fidesz was swept to power with a large majority, the causes of which were discussed earlier. As part of what became known as the Széll Kálmán Plan, an attempt to rein in public spending in the wake of the 2008 financial crisis, severe budgetary cuts were introduced from 2011 for higher education institutions. The 2012 government funding for higher education was only half of the 2008 figure and the cuts have been described as unprecedented (Harsányi and Vincze, 2012). Endowed with a two-thirds parliamentary majority, Fidesz was able to introduce some radical reforms that consolidated their control of the state, which, in the opinion of its critics, constituted a process of state capture, in other words, by authoritarian and *illiberal* forms of governance (see earlier discussion). At the centre of this consolidation of power was the *Fundamental Law* that enshrined in Hungary's constitution many measures and values to reflect the ideology of Fidesz. Article X section (3) of the Fundamental Law, stipulates that higher education institutions shall be autonomous in terms of the content and the methods of research and teaching. The Government is afforded the power to determine the rules governing the management of public institutes of higher education and supervise their management, such powers enshrined constitutionally are not to be found elsewhere in Europe. Furthermore, sufficient scope is provided to delimit (fix or define the limits) of the autonomy of state higher education institutions. Consequently, the Government was able to introduce the legal institution of chancellor and consistory (Rónay 2018).

In 2014 the Government introduced a new legal institution, the position of *Chancellor.* This meant the leadership position of *the Rector* was consigned to academic affairs and the Chancellor was given control of non-academic problems like finance, administration, informatics, etc. Neither the Senate nor Rector has the right to dismiss a Chancellor, whose only superior is the Minister responsible for higher education, and only they can give direct orders allowing the Government to intervene directly in the affairs of the universities. The Chancellors have to send the ministry monthly reports describing the key management actions, the financial situation, the progress of projects, and priority developments (Berács et al, 2017). In 2015 the Government established the legal institution of *the consistory* to oversee the operations of universities. The consistories perform no logistical functions and are only concerned with oversight. However, they have considerable powers to steer the activities of universities (Felix, 2015). It should be noted that during the rule of Queen Marie Theresa in the eighteenth century, the consistory was a mechanism to control the Hungarian university's operation directly (Keczer, 2009). To some, it seemed strange to revive such an antiquated term that had fallen out of usage (Rónay 2019).

In 2018, Orbán in his annual speech in Baile Tusnad ominously stated:

> An era is determined by cultural trends, collective beliefs, and social customs. This is now the task we are faced with: we must embed the political system in a cultural era. This is why it is logical – and in no way surprising – that it is precisely in the field of cultural policy that we have seen the explosion of what is currently the most intense debate (Orbán, 2018).

Orbán's statement reflected his ideological ambitions, as these were subsequently demonstrated in a series of bold reforms in higher education. The Fidesz government, through a series of measures, enacted some of its more ideological positions on higher education. In 2017, a new law was introduced, soon dubbed the 'Lex CEU', because it seemed to be directed at the Central European University. It stipulated that private/international universities operating in Hungary would now require an international agreement between the government of Hungary and a university's country of origin. In addition, the law also required that foreign universities wishing to operate in Hungary must conduct actual education activities in their home country. Most of these criteria only affected one institution, the CEU, as it was alone in such universities that were located in Budapest in not having a campus in its country of origin, namely the USA, where it is chartered. Zoltán Balog, the minister responsible for education defended the LEX CEU by stating "we are committed to using all legal means at our disposal to stop pseudo-civil society spy groups such as the ones funded by George Soros." (Byrne, 2017). The LEX CEU prompted the *European Commission* to initiate an infringement action and in 2020 the *European Court of Justice in Commission* v Hungary (C-66/18) ruled Hungary had breached the *Charter of Fundamental Rights of the European Union* "relating to academic freedom, the freedom to found higher education institutions and the freedom to conduct a business." The case of the Lex CEU is discussed in more depth in chapter three.

Why did Fidesz and Orbán seek to target the CEU? The CEU is committed to an *open society* and it can be argued that such principles are at odds with Orbán's desire to see Hungary cast as an illiberal democracy. Universities like the CEU are perceived, not just in Hungary but in other authoritarian states like Russia, as "intellectual boot camps of liberalism" (Enyedi, 2018). As well as presenting political challenges such universities are framed as posing a cultural threat, in what can be termed a *Culture War*. To reiterate points made earlier in the discussion, the concept of a 'culture war' as applied here, involves the perception that globalisation, forms of cosmopolitanism, even civil society and liberal ideals themselves present a challenge to more static and monocultural conceptions of national identity. This culture war is redolent of the populist tradition of framing perceived challenges as an emergency that needs to be met with resistance; it is a frame that particularly appeals to conservative-minded groups in society who feel threatened and besieged in a rapidly changing world. Universities in many countries have constituted a frontline in this culture war, and in Hungary, this prompted the Government decision in 2018 to no longer validate Gender Studies, a decision that impacted in particular on the CEU and ELTE universities, which both offered courses in this subject. Again, this measure was considered another affront to the principle of academic freedom and is considered in more depth in chapter four. The ideological ambition of the Orbán government is also revealed by its plans to turn state universities into foundations that will supposedly increase state autonomy. Critics have derided the promise of greater autonomy as the boards appointed to steer these foundations are dominated by government allies (see discussion in chapters six and seven).

Tusnádfürdő is the location for an annual Fidesz summer school where figures like Orbán seek to set the foundations for new turns of political thought. In the following extract Orbán (2020) lays out his thinking on academia:

> The struggle for spiritual sovereignty and intellectual freedom that we launched years ago in Tusnádfürdő is gradually bearing fruit. Rebellion against political correctness, against the dictates of loopy liberal doctrine, modes of expression, and style is flowing in an ever broader channel. Evermore people are showing increasing courage in freeing themselves from the shackles of the suffocatingly restrictive, single approved mode of speech, the only approved concept of democracy, and the only approved interpretation of Europe and the West. The escape attempt itself is not simple, and the risk of punishment is high: expulsion from academic life, loss of employment, stigmatisation, running the gauntlet at universities. Examples of this are becoming almost daily occurrences. But even if we manage to escape the systematic patrols of well-paid loopy liberal border guards, we must still struggle against the deeply embedded reflexes of ever so well-meaning public opinion.

It is evident therefore that Orbán sees his government's higher education reform as an integral part of a programme of national salvation, a struggle that warrants courage and bravery in the face of what he deems to be intellectual tyranny. This book seeks to map out the nature of, and rationale for those changes, but also the challenge and resistance to them.

Outline of the Book

Chapter One has provided a contextual overview of historic, cultural and political developments relevant to an understanding of academic freedom in Hungary. In Chapter Two, through a process of reflexivity, I explore my personal and emotional sentiments towards academic reforms in Hungary but also map out the methodology for the volume that is reliant on reflexivity, critical thinking, and dialogue, providing a framework to understand and measure resistance. Chapter Three provides an overview of the so-called 'Lex CEU' and government actions that pressured the CEU to relocate a large proportion of its operations from Budapest to Vienna. The chapter places this episode in the context of the broader campaign against Soros and the notion of an *open society*. Chapter Four discusses how Gender Studies was denounced as a pseudo-science and probes the Hungarian government's decision not to recognise and fund Gender Studies degrees. Chapter Five explores how in 2019 the Hungarian President, János Áder signed a law on giving the Government control over funding and key appointments of the *Hungarian Academy of Sciences* and goes on to reflect on the nature and impact of these reforms. Chapter Six explores the corporatisation of higher education by detailing the nature of reforms at *Corvinus University*. Chapter Seven explores how and why protests were triggered in response to making the *University of Theatre and Film Arts (SZFE)* a foundation. The chapter then returns to a discussion of the sociology and psychology of academic resistance to authoritarianism. Chapter Eight presents the reflective testimony of Peter Futo on educational experiences during Communism and that of Ferenc Krémer, a Hungarian sociologist, who some contend was one of the first victims of a clampdown against academic freedom. In addition, the sociologist Miklos Hadas reflects on the value of critical sociology in reimaging Hungary. Chapter Nine is a concluding chapter that sets out a vision of a renewed academia and presents the case for academic dissensus in academic institutions that welcome debate and dialogue. The chapter outlines how this could bolster deliberative forms of democracy and argues for an inclusive academy that moves away from neoliberal business models, by seeking to build bridges between academia and other communities, especially those at the margins. This renewed academia would complement more inclusive and civic notions of identity and citizenship.

Chapter Two
Reflections, Resilience, and Dignity

This chapter, through a process of reflectivity, provides the reader with some insights into my personal history and some of the key factors that motivated me to express dissent with reference to the erosion of academic freedom in Hungary. The chapter also provides insights into my methodological approach.

Reflexivity and Dialogue

In the preface, I outlined how reflexivity would have an important role in the book. Gross (2008) notes the narrative character of a self-conception is expressed and embodied through the stories an individual tells him/herself and others about the development of his/her life. It can provide an important tool to understand the mindset of an author, a useful aid in weighing and interpreting authorial assessments of intellectual ideas and philosophies and their relationship to the context of society. The book also has an interpretive dimension in the sense that the stories narrated in the book centred on interviews, dialogue, and key events in institutional change in higher education in Hungary are framed where possible with personal reflexive views of the self. The ethnographic data and collected stories are situated within personal experience and sense-making.

According to Adams and Herrmann (2020) autoethnography' comprises three interrelated components: 'auto,' 'ethno,' and 'graphy.' Hence, autoethnography uses selfhood, subjectivity, and personal experience (auto) to describe, interpret, and represent (graphy) beliefs, practices, and identities of a group or culture (ethno). Autoethnograpy is a research method that displays multiple layers of consciousness, connecting the personal to the cultural. Back and forth autoethnographers gaze and probe outward on social and cultural facets of the lifeworld as well as inward, exposing vulnerabilities and traces of submission and dissent (González-Calvo and Arias-Carballal, 2018). Autoethnography can be both evocative and analytical, indeed such a fruitful combination can enlarge the spectrum of autoethnographic research. Tedlock (2013) calls for the braiding of evocative with analytic autoethnography in ways that produce powerful writing about the self in the world in order to help change the world. These are principles that have influenced this book.

Autoethnography can be accomplished through the use of personal writing and reflection, the stories of others, and an understanding of the relevant liter-

https://doi.org/10.1515/9783110749816-004

ature and context (Wall, 2006). The starting point for autoethnography is the researcher's use of the subjective self. However, autoethnography has been derided for being narcissistic and too introspective, and disconnected from structure and society (Sparkes, 2000). This danger has been avoided in this volume with a contextual introductory chapter and factual overviews at the start of the chapters that detail the events related to a key moment of change and transition in Hungarian education where in most cases more than one actor is interviewed. Theory was emergent from discussion, reading of drafts, feedback, and revision. Compiling the book was a dialogic process. So as promised the first story I will tell is my own. In truth parts of this story are difficult to tell but have a bearing on my actions and position-taking on academia in Hungary, so I will be candid in narrating my story.

An Englishman Abroad

My relationship with higher education has been at times marked by hesitancy and wariness, a consequence of my background and my academic viewpoints and interests. I was the first in my family to attend university, my forebears were largely agricultural workers. My grandfather though established a small light engineering business initially connected to his work on steam engines, my father worked in the business. The business remained a modest enterprise for many years and even when it generated sufficient income to allow my father to see himself as middle class, he continued to work the lathes and machines with his brothers. At school, I was a very late developer. I failed the 11 plus (an exam to select pupils for grammar schools) and attended a secondary modern school designed to prepare me and others for the world of artisanal labour. I hated the school and curriculum and gained a reputation for defiance and misbehaviour.

At sixteen having failed my O-Levels (school exams) and shown no academic inclination, I decided to change my direction. This change was in part prompted by a serious accident after staggering into the path of a car after a night of heavy underage drinking. I sustained serious injuries and my long recuperation gave me time to reflect. The prospect of having to work in the family business of light engineering filled me with dread and also roused me to make some effort to secure a university place. This I achieved to the great surprise of my teachers and peers, such was my reputation for clowning around and my academic weakness. I had been motivated in the herculean task of becoming academically successful and gaining entry to university merely by a desire to escape the drudgery of working on engineering drills and lathes, work I knew well and despised through working in the family business from the age of eight during the holidays. A continual spur to my academic efforts was my father telling me that if I failed my exams, he had a job for me. The summer before going to university I worked in a scrapyard where my father had business connections. The scrapyard lacked what we would describe today as proper health and safety regulations. I and a co-worker handled a substance that potentially could have serious health issues in the future. Later in the day, we were alerted to the danger of what had happened. One of those days that change your life with a single action having consequences staying with you for the rest of your life.

Arriving at the university in 1984 and meeting people who had attended public (private) schools and who moved in a different cultural and intellectual milieu to mine came as something of a culture shock. Despite having no great love for academia, I led a full life at the small provincial university I found myself at, located in the small town of Lampeter in Mid Wales. I became highly active in Labour politics and the peace movement and in 1986 became known as one of the Carmarthen 17, a group of protestors threatened with the legal charge of tortious conspiracy. A local council threatened me and sixteen other protestors with a bill of 300.000 pounds because of the non-violent direct action protests we organised against the construction of a nuclear bunker in Carmarthen. The protests led to the council incurring the expense of hiring a private security firm to keep the protestors out of the construction site and hence a desire to reclaim the cost from protestors. On reflection, I can see that part of my militancy and activism was fuelled by the health scare experience in the scrapyard. It had traumatised me, but I had decided to channel my anger into efforts to challenge and change the world we then lived in. Once I finished my degree though I went onto teacher training and gave further academic pursuits little thought. At the time, becoming a teacher was for me the pinnacle of success. Teaching was also a challenging job, somehow the intensity of work helped me to forget about my health issues and my anger subsided as did my activism.

After five years of school teaching in the UK, whilst still in my 20s, I resolved to relocate abroad and live and teach in schools in the Czech Republic and then Hungary. I was tired of the UK. I had been through an Ofsted school inspection and was tired of the way in which the national curriculum was stifling teacher autonomy and overloading staff with administrative burdens.[1] Political life also seemed stale. The Conservatives had been in power since my teens and in

---

1 The Office for Standards in Education, Children's Services and Skills (Ofsted) is a non-ministerial department of the UK government, reporting to Parliament. Ofsted is responsible for inspecting a range of educational institutions.

the early 90s political change seemed a remote possibility. I taught in schools in central-eastern Europe and then taught with the British Council in Portugal with additional short contracts in a range of countries in North Africa/Middle East. In my final years with the British Council, I undertook a distance-learning MA centred on research. After my earlier lack of interest why did I resolve to undertake postgraduate study? As with my entry into undergraduate studies, I saw higher education as a means of escape. Postgraduate study offered a convenient escape route as I had a lack of imagination for alternative routes. I was tired of the increasingly regulated and audited world of teaching, especially in the corporate British Council that did not resonate with my interest in more open forms of learning. I also naively thought higher education teaching might be freer, more liberating. In this endeavour I decided to focus on Roma/Traveller educational inclusion as I had taught these communities whilst a teacher. This research in fact became a passionate interest in part because of the friendships I formed with Portuguese Roma and appreciation that social research could be a significant tool to change and improve people's lives; it prompted me to go further and take a PhD, this led to a return to the UK in 2001.

The sea change in my life was also prompted by a health scare I experienced in Portugal. A Portuguese doctor believed that I may have suffered some damage to my respiratory system as a consequence of my childhood/adolescent work experiences. It was in fact a misdiagnosis although it became clear in medical tests there was some damage to my respiratory system. Again, as in my adolescence, I experienced a profound feeling of trauma, especially acute at the time of the misdiagnosis. As with my activism at university, this seemed to spur a desire to change the world around me. I reasoned as to what else I could do: feel sorry for myself, bury my head in the sand through forms of escapism, or channel my pain and anger into an agenda that might bring about change and prevent what happened to me happening to others; this seemed the best and most logical course of action. I resolved that starting a PhD might facilitate this new life plan.

The PhD experience though was tortuous. After years of work, I was disorientated to be a student again and was alienated by some of the elitism of academics and disconnection to groups at the margins like the Roma, the focus of my research. After two years of research, I decided to defer, the decision to defer was prompted by a desire to more closely align myself to activism and social action. Also, a product of the doctoral research had been the establishment of a campaign network for Gypsies, Roma and Travellers, the Gypsy and Traveller Law Reform Coalition (GTLRC), that lobbied for more Traveller sites and social justice for these communities. Having invested a lot of time in establishing this network I decided to apply for the full-time post that was created of a policy development worker through a grant from the charity Comic Relief. I was successful in my application. The GTLRC went on to win the Liberty Human Rights Award and helped shape government policy. However, such was the intensity and pressure of the campaign I seriously delayed my PhD research and was not able to return to it for five years. By 2010 I had though completed my PhD and was suffering from the perennial problem of social movement activism, 'burnout'. I resolved to take my career in a new direction and leave the UK and return to Hungary where my partner is from and where I had lived happily before. I wrote to the Corvinus University Budapest and was lucky enough to secure some teaching in the sociology department. After a long break from teaching and now in my early 40s it seemed strange to be teaching again and to be an academic. In this new venture though I hoped to combine scholarship and activism through forms of critical thinking.

The Corvinus was originally established in 1934 as the Hungarian Royal Palatine Joseph University of Technology and Economics, renamed the Karl Marx University in 1953 under communism. It was known for producing the country's Marxist intellectual elite in the socialist era. Despite its links to communism, the institution became a hub for anti-communist dissent during the late Kádár regime. After the 'changes' in 1990, the university was renamed the Budapest Economics University, but in 2003 the university was again renamed after the fifteenth century King Matthias Corvinus. Corvinus was a great patron of arts and learning, in the tradition of the renaissance, so the new title seemed apt to the university leadership.

In this transition to the world of academia, I was helped by being located in a small friendly, and supportive department but also by a bureaucracy that seemed to exert little control and interference. With the British Council, I had witnessed how a large organisation could be corporatised and how staff could feel powerless at the hands of a marketised bureaucracy. In contrast, the Corvinus still in some respects seemed to be in a state of transition two decades after the changes. The bureaucracy seemed large and arcane, though the cumbersome bureaucracy could be frustrating it equally felt liberating not to have an ideological grand plan and ill-conceived micro-management imposed on unwilling staff. After two years at the Corvinus, I was able to secure a one-year fellowship at the University of Bristol. Here I was able to witness more directly the stories I had heard from friends working in UK academia of audit culture and the commodification of higher education. In this regime academic outputs are continuously assessed, audited, and linked to progression, promotion and remuneration. Some of the staff I met at Bristol felt it was like working in a business where profit, outputs, and student admission numbers were the paramount concern. Staff reasoned that it was right to have frameworks and plans to raise standards and to grow and develop but the current regime was too hierarchical and placed staff in particular under incredible pressure, with some staff working a 60 to 70 hour week to meet all the demands expected of them.

Returning to the more relaxed work environment of the Corvinus was thus welcome after my short sojourn in Bristol but that sense of relief was not to last long. Working life at the Corvinus had in truth already been made difficult by the relatively poor pay but also a lack of resources. The Corvinus was seen by some in the Fidesz government to be a 'hotbed' of radicalism, liberals, and critics of the Orbán government. Some staff charged the Government with intentionally trying to undermine the university through a lack of resources. Sometimes there was no money for even paper and ink for printing, at one point there were even fears as to whether the university had the money to heat the campus. The profile and standing of the university were further undermined when the Orbán government founded its own University of Public Services (Nemzeti Közszolgálati Egyetem), which incorporated some important and prestigious sections of the university.

Despite these difficulties, I was happy in my work and my teaching evaluations by students were positive, I was starting to publish with lead publishers, and my work to fuse activism and scholarship seemed to be progressing well. The Corvinus was becoming noted as a centre of critical Roma research, a number of emerging Romani Studies researchers/activists from the Roma community held visiting fellowships at the Corvinus. Through the university, I and my associates, also staged a series of Roma related international conferences and were active in lobbying for new forms of empowerment in Roma inclusion programmes centred on liberating empowerment. It was argued there was a need to avoid the tokenism of liberal approaches and instead through co-production, collectivity, and grassroots activism ensure those at the margins had voice and agency (Ryder, 2017).

An important landmark in terms of its commitment to social justice was the university's distancing from the controversial views of Géza Jeszenszky on the Roma. Jeszenszky was a Corvinus professor but prior to this, he had been foreign minister for the Hungarian government and an ambassador to the US. In 2005 a course textbook was published that was written by Jeszenszky and used for courses taught by him at the Corvinus University. In the textbook, there was a sentence that generated a great deal of debate and controversy. "The reason why many Roma are mentally ill is because in Roma culture it is permitted for sisters and brothers or cousins to marry each other or just to have sexual intercourse with each other" (Jeszenszky, 2005, 273). Following student and public protests in 2012 Zsolt Rostovanyi, the Corvinus rector, issued a statement that declared the Corvinus University did not agree with the sentence. The vice-rector Zoltan Szanto issued a public apology on behalf of the university to a largely

Roma audience. He also established a commission to provide an academic and scientific statement on the sentence with a view to seeking Jeszenszky's endorsement of the note and clarifying the actual expert opinion on these matters in order to diminish the damage caused by confusion and or acceptance of unsubstantiated claims. I led the commission. The commission concluded that Jeszenszky had used poor sources and had misunderstood some of the data to produce a statement that was incorrect and, in effect part of a racist trope against the Roma (Ryder et al, 2013). I was proud of the stand the university took on the Jeszenszky issue. Despite Jeszenszky's good connections to the Hungarian establishment the university was prepared to challenge his dangerous views on the Roma. Interestingly, in recent times Jeszenszky has engaged in some criticism of the Orbán government and distanced himself from his son, a Fidesz hardliner.

My happiness at the Corvinus though was to be broken. I noticed the university became more sensitive to government criticism. One of the first instances of a shifting mood was the decision to move the statue of Karl Marx. In the main hall of the university, a clear focal point was the seated statue of Karl Marx. The statue had been erected in 1956, the year of the Hungarian uprising, but in more recent times had become a point of nostalgia with former students recounting how they had received their university degree in the hall with Marx watching over proceedings. Others recounted how at Christmas they had dressed up Marx as Father Christmas and more than once I saw in the clenched hand of the statue a copy of Blikk a popular Hungarian tabloid newspaper similar to the Sun or a half-eaten sandwich. For some, the statue was more of a mascot than a philosophical totem. In defence of the university's commitment to plurality, the main hall contained a number of plaques and memorials dedicated to a wide range of thinkers across the political and philosophical spectrum. However, in 2014 protests against the statue were staged by the Young Christian Alliance, a group aligned with the ruling Fidesz Party's junior coalition partner the Christian Democratic People's Party (Tóth, 2014). Whilst the protest was being staged Milan Palfalvi, the deputy head of the student organisation involved in the protest informed the media outside the university building "It is unacceptable that Marx, who openly espoused anti-Semitic and racist views, should have a statue in Hungary" (Hungary News Today 2014). Cynics felt it had more to do with the animosity the Hungarian political centre-right had for the left which tried to tie the present-day centre-left with the undisputed excesses of Soviet Communism in Hungary. The Christian students called for the statue to be removed.

The Corvinus Rector Zsolt Rostovanyi responded in an open letter that reforms at the university and changing its communist-era name from the Karl Marx University to Corvinus had "clearly demonstrated a radical change in direction". Rostovanyi felt the statue was part of the university's history. He noted its removal had been proposed in the early 1990s, but the university's leadership felt at the time that "removing the statue would not change the past". Rostovanyi proceeded to argue that although Marx was controversial and that his ideas, especially their later interpretations, had paved the way for twentieth century dictatorships Marx remained a huge intellectual influence (Hungary Daily News, 2014). Several months later though some staff had a feeling of apprehension as the statue of Marx and all the other plaques and memorials were taken out of the main hall and placed in a new university museum. Had the university caved into political pressure?

Another important milestone was the appointment of András Lánczi as Corvinus rector in 2016; Lánczi is a conservative philosopher and political scientist closely aligned with Fidesz. In 2017 Lánczi issued a statement circulated to all university staff warning them of the importance of the code of conduct and ethics to be followed in expressing opinions in public. At this time Corvinus academics and students had organised a petition in support of the Central European University (CEU), its future operations in Budapest being at some risk due to Hungarian government reforms perceived to be motivated by political hostility. The letter from Lánczi emphasised the university code of ethics that expected staff to refrain from referring to the university when displaying their worldview and political preferences in their public appearances (Kasnyikm, 2017). The letter attracted some concern from staff who feared it was an attempt to stifle free speech and minimise acts of solidarity with the CEU. Concerned staff organised an open letter to the rector with points of clarification and implied criticism if the letter was intended to repress dissent. I signed the letter, but some staff members were critical of the challenging tone of the letter. One colleague who was part of the senior management team and who taught in sociology protested that the letter undermined the unity of the university through division and challenge. I felt though that it was the rector himself who had undermined collegiality through his statement and if the letter was intended to suppress dissent over the CEU then it was legitimate for academics to express their concern at limitations being placed on their freedom of speech. On reflection, this was a turning point.

In 2018 another rather sinister moment happened in the academic life of Hungary in the run-up to the 2018 election and reflective of the increasingly hostile invective from the Fidesz Party towards migrants. A colleague of mine in sociology, professor Melegh Attila, had comments he made on migrants distorted. He had tried to explain that migrants are often better educated than the average Hungarian and thus bring benefits to the country, but his words were grossly distorted. Claims were made that he had said 'migrants were better' than Hungarians. Orbán himself stated that it reflected well on the generosity of the Hungarian people that those like Melegh, who were scheming to promote the Soros plan, could live their lives unharmed and cheerful in Hungary (HVG, 2018). This was seen as an intimidating attack on an academic who was one of the lead experts on Hungarian migration. The matter was raised in a staff meeting of the Institute of Sociology at the Corvinus. A young colleague suggested that the institute should issue a public statement in support of Melegh, but the meeting shied away from this and instead started talking about how we could fight this kind of campaign and propaganda with educational events, where we talk about migration and the scientific results related to it (not that they organised any such event). On reflection, I think they were afraid. We were two months from the 2018 general election and in the middle of the campaign. I suppose they did not want to become targets themselves. This seemed like a classic act of self-censorship.

A more material change in the life of the Corvinus came about through the intensification of higher education audit culture, student evaluations and line manager assessments of academic outputs started to play a larger role in determining remuneration and promotion. This change did not cause me personally too many problems as my evaluations and academic outputs were sufficient to keep my wage at a relatively acceptable level. However, some colleagues found themselves receiving a wage close to the levels of the minimum wage; for experienced academics, some with families to support, such poor wages placed them in a difficult position.

The mood within Hungarian education also became more apprehensive as the Fidesz government appeared to take a more active interest in the sector through the 2017 Lex CEU (amendment to the Law on Higher Education). The legislation stipulated that any foreign-funded university institution in Hungary could only operate in the country once the Government of the source country and Hungary had signed an intergovernmental agreement, while the legislation also specifies that the given university must have operations in its source country. Critics derided the reform and claimed it was designed to force out the Central European University (CEU) from Hungary because its liberal/critical stance was at odds with the Orbán administration. Furthermore, relations between the Fidesz administration and chief patron and supporter of the CEU the philanthropist George Soros had greatly deteriorated from 2015 with the Syrian refugee crisis. Prime Minister Orbán accused Soros of being part of a plan to promote migration and transform the cultural and political complexion of Europe. Such criticism was part of Orbán's agenda to challenge what he considered the scourge of multiculturalism and desire to protect Hungary's Christian identity which he deemed could be threatened by religious and demographic diversity (See chapter one).

I felt deeply alarmed by these developments, I found the tone of the rhetoric highly disturbing. What could and should I do? In general, I had avoided Hungarian politics and focused on pan-European Roma-related research and activism. On reflection, I think I had for a number of years 'buried my head in the sand' with regards to the democratic decline of Hungary. However, it was becoming impossible to ignore the political excesses now taking place in Hungary. In the reports and research I was commissioned to undertake, I could not ignore the Hungarian government's manipulation of Roma politics, my own area of expertise, that allowed a pro-Fidesz grouping Lungo Drom to dominate the Roma agenda. Accusations of cronyism and corruption were rife. Furthermore, the Hungarian government seemed to bolster the educational segregation of Roma children by allowing religious schools to maintain schools and classes specifically for Roma.

My concerns regarding Hungary were deepened by Brexit, the UK's exit from the European Union. The referendum on EU membership had taken place in 2016 and signalled a fundamental shift in how British politics operated with the Conservative Government increasingly aligning itself with authoritarian populism and nativism. In my mind, political, cultural, and social parallels could be drawn between Hungary and the UK. Both countries seemed to be in the grip of forms of political demagoguery which played upon national pride and exceptionalism, that eroded political checks and balances, and for whom fact and reality came second to emotion and stridency. I decided to try and make a small contribution by writing a book on Brexit. The book sought to understand the Brexit phenomenon through critical discourse analysis, basically a study of political rhetoric (Ryder, 2020). This mammoth task was hugely challenging. Brexit dragged on with key deadlines being missed. Also, British politics was becoming more polarised. At the end of the task of producing a book, my fears and concerns regarding both Hungary and the UK being gripped by dangerous forms of authoritarian and nationalist populism became more pronounced. A sense of apprehension that was intensified by the wave of populism that appeared to be in vogue, as evident by the electoral success of Trump in the USA, Modi in India, and Erdoğan in Turkey. A key step in my more public expression of concern regarding the political situation in Hungary was my teaching at what became known as the Szabad Egyetem 'Free university' in 2018 (See chapter three). As part of student protests about the Lex CEU measure to force the university out of Hungary, a free university was set up in tents on the square beside Hungary's parliament that offered free lectures, music, and other cultural events (McLaughlin, 2018).

Change within the Corvinus accelerated with the announcement in 2018 that the Corvinus University was to be transformed into a foundation that in theory was set to give the university greater autonomy. Critics felt though that in practice the reforms seemed to be preparing the ground to make the university more aligned and submissive to the Government's agenda as the board leading the foundation was closely aligned with the Government (See chapter six). A mood of anxiety and pessimism became evident among many of my colleagues. I started to consider my position. Should I stay or find a job at another university? Should I stay in Hungary?

My sense of insecurity was also aggravated by my associations with the Roma Education Fund (REF). REF is a lead international NGO working to promote the educational inclusion of the Roma, a key supporter and funder is the philanthropist George Soros. In 2018 I joined the board of REF in a moment of crisis. The hostility directed towards Soros by the political right in Hungary including the Government was ramped up by what became known as the 'Stop Soros bill'. The law would allow the interior ministry to ban an NGO that deals with immigration if it posed a "national security risk". The Bill also proposed a 25 percent tax on foreign donations to NGOs that support migration (DW, 2018). It was decided that the Soros-supported NGOs in Hungary should relocate. One of the largest civil society entities to relocate was the Open Society Foundation (OSF). The President of OSF Patrick Gaspard justified the move to Berlin:

> The government of Hungary has denigrated and misrepresented our work and repressed civil society for the sake of political gain, using tactics unprecedented in the history of the European Union...It has become impossible to protect the security of our operations and our staff in Hungary from arbitrary government interference (Open Society, 2018).

It was decided that REF would be moved to Serbia. Initially, as a board member I opposed that decision as I felt leaving sent out the wrong signal and would embolden the Orbán government to undermine broader civil society. Later I came to accept the wisdom of that decision. My involvement with REF had a sense of irony for in my writing I had been a critic of what I deemed to be NGOisation, the managerialism and hierarchicalism of civil society, traits I argued were evident in Soros Roma NGOs (Cemlyn and Ryder, 2017). However, I accepted the invitation to join REF as I recognised the deep importance of their mission and felt that I could assist in improving REF's connections to the grassroots because of my history of such work.

At the start of 2020 I seemed to be overloaded, I was finishing the final draft of my book on Brexit and was contracted to start another on the Roma and Social Europe (Ryder et al, 2020). I also had several research projects to finish and the care duties for my autistic child. I was spending 20 hours a week taking my child to a special school located at the edge of Budapest in the countryside an hour away from my home/workplace, so two round trips a day took four hours. I was struggling and felt I was nearing the stage I had experienced previously when I suffered from extreme exhaustion and fatigue in the NGO sector (discussed above). In January reports of a new virus were emerging in China and its potential to spread to Europe accentuated the gloom. The impact of the virus became very apparent to me as my Chinese students who had returned home for the Christmas vacation started to write to me to inform me that they would be delayed in returning because they lived in a part of China in quarantine or on their eventual arrival in Hungary would need to spend ten days in quarantine. In March 2020 Hungary and many other European states entered into what became known as 'lockdown', a restrictive policy to restrain peoples' movements and interactions in order to limit the number of Covid 19 infections.

The Covid Pandemic

The intense lockdown meant that I and my family did not leave the flat for three months. Both my partner and I and our child had underlying health problems that made us vulnerable during the pandemic, so we had to be extra cautious and vigilant. At the time the number of infections in Hungary was low compared to the UK, Italy, and Spain. However, the feeling of fear and concern was rightfully deep. A key question on the minds of many was, how would the greatly underfunded and under-resourced Hungarian health system cope with the huge wave of infections, that in all probability, would eventually reach Hungary. The lockdown presented further challenges as over half of my students were international students and they now found themselves far from home and isolated, some were completely alone in their apartments. The Corvinus University, as is typical of many universities in the region, had limited welfare and counselling services. Thus, I and other staff without instruction or guidance from the management, did what we could to fill the vacuum and maintain the mental and physical welfare of our students by making one-to-one tutorials more frequent and using that time to assess how the students were coping.

By June the lockdown was relaxed and the university even reopened for the final exams, where I was able to meet face to face some of my students and colleagues. However, the joy this brief respite offered was deflated over the retirement of my colleague Miklos Hadas. Hadas had established himself as a lead critical thinker in Hungary with research specialisms in masculinity and the writings of Bourdieu, he had also become a prominent critic within the Corvinus University of the reforms taking place. In the summer of 2020 Hadas was due to re-

tire and I was surprised to hear that Hadas would not be offered an emeritus pro-
fessorship as was the general custom for long-serving Corvinus professors.
Hadas could sometimes be blunt and emotive in his statements, traits that
some would frame as the actions of a committed critical sociologist, but at
times grated on some of my colleagues. I suspect this irritation was the reason
not to give him the award. I and other colleagues reasoned that given he had
taught at Corvinus for many decades, held senior positions, and was an ac-
claimed teacher and researcher that it was appropriate for him to end his career
with this award. It was decided though to ignore the appeals for a rethink on this
matter and the award was not given.

The summer in Budapest was glorious as some degree of normality returned
to the city, infections were initially low. The Hungarian government had had the
sense to initiate an early lockdown, avoiding the health disaster of other countries like Italy. However, Hungary now went into reverse with a policy of opening
up the economy. Eager to avert severe economic crisis the Government encouraged businesses to reopen, for bars and restaurants to reopen, and even for
large outdoor events to be staged. However, by late August the number of infections inevitably began to rise. I felt a deep sense of apprehension at the prospect
of teaching again, fearing not just the dangers of the pandemic but also what
appeared to be a more rapid process of organisational change at the Corvinus.

The start to the academic year was not portentous for a trouble-free academic year. The staff meeting we were summoned to at the start of September was
held in a windowless hall with the air conditioning switched on. Forty of us
sat in the hall wearing the masks we had been told to wear and listened to
the organisational instructions we were given for the coming year by our line
manager. From my reading on health and safety connected to Covid 19 I realised
the staging of the meeting, in particular the use of air ventilation in a windowless room, could spread the virus. Despite, this I sat in the hall with the others
and said nothing. I reasoned that to have alerted the line manager in the room to
these apparent dangers would appear rude and maybe alarmist. Even though I
could not understand the instructions the line manager was giving because it
was in Hungarian, I felt I should show solidarity with my colleagues and be
in the meeting. I sat for 60 minutes in the room listening to Pink Floyd on my
headphones to calm me down but sat there politely and quietly. Later I felt
angry at my submissive behaviour and resolved I would not make the same mistake again.

The night before the start of the teaching semester felt strange. I was like
many other teachers expected to transition from a state where we maintained
strict social distancing to one where we would spend 90 minutes per class in
the company of large numbers of young people. Such was my anxiety I decided

to meet a couple of other teachers the night before teaching started and get drunk in a local park. We needed the chance to express our anxieties and to steel ourselves for what lay ahead. My concerns regarding health and safety were confirmed once the semester started, students pleased to see their peers again had difficulty in maintaining social distancing. Large groups gathered in the corridors and students would sit in lecture rooms waiting for staff to arrive and only then put on their masks. The weather was still warm and many teachers had air conditioning on in their offices, no warnings on the dangers of this had been issued.

All classes above 40 were to be taught online but for smaller groups in-person teaching would take place, this was described as a hybrid approach as we were expected to stream the class live via Microsoft Teams for students still abroad and unable to return to Budapest or self-isolating. On my first day I had contact with nearly 100 students having taught three classes that day. The tension in the lecture room was palpable and communication was hampered by mask wearing which at times made me and my non-native speaker students inaudible. The first day was an experience that left me agitated and troubled. After a week of such teaching, I resolved to change my teaching approach. I negotiated my own hybrid model with my students that involved sending students video lectures and having online discussions based on the lecture. In addition, I organised weekly field trips that supplemented the lectures and discussions. For example, one of the courses touched upon populism so I organised a field trip to the nearby square of the Hungarian parliament where we looked at how the Orbán government had reorganised the square, removing some statues associated with the communist and liberal past of Hungary and restoring statues that had stood in the square during the inter-war period, the time of the national leadership of Admiral Horthy. The Horthy administration, discussed in the introduction, based itself on what can be considered as an authoritarian nationalist Christian outlook and allied Hungary with Nazi Germany during the second world war. Despite the controversy surrounding Horthy Orbán had sought to rehabilitate the reputation of this infamous leader. The redesign of the parliament square to reflect its appearance in the time of Horthy was part of the culture war Orbán was conducting as part of his nationalist Christian agenda. The aforementioned square and other locations in Budapest proved to be excellent locations to bring to life academic discussions not only on culture war but also other topics such as genocide and diversity.

I found that organising classes in such a way and moving away from the lecture hall reduced formal and static teacher-centred approaches, and instead greater informality, conversational opportunities, and spontaneity were injected into learning experiences. Not all students attended the field trips, so the numbers were never too large. Some students were in fact deeply apprehensive about attending offline/in-person classes and becoming sick. As international students, they had no family in Budapest to rely upon in the event of becoming ill. In fact, some of my students were deeply anxious, some had only just arrived from far and distant countries in Africa, the Middle East, and South East Asia. For some, it was their first time away from home and as I knew from experience coming to a new country and taking up a new role could be highly stressful, but to do so in a pandemic greatly increased the propensity for culture shock and trauma.

Some of my colleagues also seemed to be traumatised by the experience of in-person teaching. Many like me were in their 50s or older and had family members who were vulnerable and who had underlying health problems. Some had serious health problems. However, the university had no clear formal policy of shielding vulnerable staff but professors over 65 were exempted from teaching in-person. One of the university line managers sent to staff in their department an email hectoring them because allegedly, students had come into the general office saying that some classes with under 40 students were being held online contrary to the university regulations. Some staff in private objected to the message. They felt they were being pushed into a dangerous situation and that the university needed a clear policy of shielding. Later I learnt the Ministry of Education was taking a close interest in the correlation between offline and online classes in Hungarian universities, this might explain the line manager's zealous position. I am not sure whether staff were defying the regulations, if they were I suspected they had good health reasons for avoiding the classroom. I reasoned that my highly hybrid approach of video lectures, online discussion, and field trips maximised the safety of me and my students but also offered the chance to meet in-person and interact. I and many other teachers did the best we could to educate our students and give them some emotional support in hugely challenging circumstances.

I raised the various concerns I had with colleagues and after collecting their views resolved to summarise health and safety concerns and review UK government guidance on how to manage the pandemic and highlight guidance that might be usefully applied in Hungary. Although a member of the teachers' union I resolved to send my discussion paper to the university leadership and not go through the union, although they were sent a draft for comment. The reason for this was that relations between the university leadership and union were so bad that if the discussion paper had come from the union it would be discarded. It was reasoned by some of my associates that given the university leadership wanted to make the university into an 'elite' institution and become one of the top 200 universities in the world and aimed to recruit a large number of foreign staff, receiving such a discussion paper from an English professor who had taught at the Corvinus for a decade might have some impact.

One of the recommendations of the discussion paper was for the university to adopt a 'Deliberative Risk Assessment Plan for the Pandemic'. The university had established a Presidential Committee on the reduction of risks related to the spread of the coronavirus, but this appeared to be opaque and top-down. It was not clear how the committee functioned or engaged with the wider university community in formulating health and safety measures. The trade union was not represented on the committee. Risk assessment is the act of determining the probability that a risk will occur and the impact that event would have, should it occur. Risk management is an ongoing process that continues through the life of a project/crisis. It includes processes for risk management planning, identification, analysis, monitoring, and control. Many of these processes are updated throughout the project life cycle as new risks can be identified at any time. I reasoned in my discussion paper that a risk assessment plan would provide a detailed overview of parts of the Corvinus campus and behaviour and the risks that are evident and assess the probability of risk.

The deliberative risk assessment plan I proposed would have built within it communication channels to collect and analyse data based on the experiences of staff (teaching and support) and students. Staff meetings and departmental student liaison events should have a health and safety item on the agenda to facilitate feedback on the effectiveness of protective measures and updates on innovations in those measures. I also reasoned teachers should be encouraged to assess the mood and experiences of students in the pandemic and draw students' attention to changes in the university regulations for the pandemic. Data could also be collected via an online discussion forum, data collection point in the form of an online submission form as well as via information relayed by institute, faculty, staff, and student representatives. The information flow I argued could also be facilitated by regular stakeholder meetings between management, staff, and students centred on the pandemic. I noted that the UK Health and Safety Executive guidance (2020) calls for the involvement of workers in completing risk assessments so they can help identify potential problems and identify solutions.

I argued in the discussion paper that a deliberative risk assessment plan would be a fluid and 'living' document. A deliberative approach nurtures understanding and a sense of ownership through dialogue and may go some way in overcoming student and staff misunderstanding and/ or non-compliance with health and safety rules during the pandemic. I also noted in the paper that based on the experiences of the first wave of the pandemic staff were concerned about the mental welfare of students, especially foreign students who were more prone to isolation not having family support networks nearby. I appealed for staff guidance on welfare support and a mental health plan for students. Indeed, mental health experts have called for policies and guidelines made about students to involve meaningful co-production and open lines of communication with students and experts in student mental health (Tressler, 2020).

Part of me wanted to appeal in the discussion paper for all teaching to go online but I knew despite the merits of such an action that this could lead to the university leadership rejecting all the points in the paper. I sent the discussion paper in mid-October to the university president, rector, and the vice-rector who dealt with teaching and asked if it might be possible to discuss. The president responded that he would be interested in meeting. We did not meet but shortly afterwards I had an email from someone in the administration saying they would be in contact. I was told some efforts were made by phone to contact me, but we did not talk. Three weeks later I wrote to the president again informing him that I had so far not been able to speak with anyone. Several more weeks passed and I asked the trade union for advice and they raised the matter with the university administration. At the end of November, I was telephoned by the administrator who had emailed me earlier. It had taken six weeks to reach this point. I made a number of points on the phone that were summarised in a follow-up email. The key points were:

1) A policy/guidance to line managers to discuss with, counsel, and shield staff with underlying health problems if offline teaching returns.
2) A deliberative dimension to Corvinus's Covid 19 strategy. Students, teachers, and non-teaching staff and their representatives need to be directly involved in strategic discussions and given scope to express their concerns and propose improvements.
3) Many staff are deeply worried about the mental health support for students and staff and fear the university does not have enough resources and counsellors to meet the challenge. International students are particularly vulnerable during the winter holiday at Christmas – some have not been in Hungary for long, have limited social networks, and might alone during the winter holiday. Urgent action is needed to get advice and support to these people.

I asked if the points I raised could be discussed at what I was told would be a meeting the following week to review the university's response to the pandemic. I asked to be updated on the outcome of the meeting, but I heard nothing and none of the key suggestions in the paper were adopted as far as I could see, although I was told an email was sent to students before the Christmas vacation reminding them of the welfare support services available. The lack of engagement the university had with my proposals has some irony given the university leadership is a major proponent of business approaches in higher education. In large organisations and businesses, the top managers define the general behavioural guidelines and boundaries but 'emergent strategies' can evolve within these frameworks. Front-line staff who have more direct links with the client base and who are at the forefront of service delivery are well informed as to the strengths and weaknesses of operations and are well-positioned to contribute to emergent strategies, good business practice suggests effective senior leaders take heed of such inputs and assessments and consequently adapt operations (Bodwell and Chermack 2010). I felt my direct experience of working with students during the pandemic and that of my colleagues was not appreciated or valued, and that this was counter-productive to our educational and welfare commitments during the pandemic. A compassionate organisation appreciates and understands that workplace wellness and mental health are a priority. Clear communication and dialogue are important means of anticipating and understanding and supporting employees' emotional responses to the crisis. With reference to the pandemic, good practice expertise asserts that if employees are fearful of coming to work, they should be listened to and concerns should not be dismissed or silenced. Such managerial tactics run the risk of increasing burnout, anxiety, and depression (Riess, 2021).

Some of the tension of the situation was alleviated on account of the fact that from the first week of November 2020 the Hungarian state ruled higher education teaching should go online. However, there would continue to be extreme mental health challenges, in particular for students. Somehow, I was deeply traumatised and affected by Corvinus University's leadership's failure to effectively engage in meaningful dialogue on this matter. At the end of the semester, I decided to take a sabbatical (leave). I had had enough! I also wanted the flexibility to either take my son to the UK for medical treatment for his severe epilepsy as the Hungarian health system seemed to be struggling to find an effective medicine to limit/control the affliction. If the pandemic made such a temporary move difficult, I would postpone this plan and try and take up a teaching position at another university in Hungary. This I did by taking up a position at Eötvös Loránd University in Budapest in February 2021.

Part of me felt a deep sadness at leaving the Corvinus, it felt comparable to a divorce such was the emotion of the split. The incident regarding the health and safety measures related to Covid and the rebuff of my overtures to the university leadership made me feel that the university was no longer one that I wished to be associated with. I also feared that given the political complexion of sections of the university leadership that the university would gravitate increasingly towards the political and cultural agenda of the Orbán regime and that a genuine commitment to equality would be undermined through an increasing audit culture orientated regime within the university. Some of my colleagues and associates though believed in staying and trying to defend more critical forms of thinking. Some older colleagues reasoned they had lived through communism in various institutions, including the Corvinus, and had found ways to work around it and bide their time and wait for better days to come. I was not so sure of this strategy. I had one decade of teaching left in me until retirement and preferred to spend that, hopefully in a university in Hungary, working in an environment supportive of my ideals rather than being passive or engaged in a running battle.

I also felt the Corvinus staff had been too passive in their opposition to the Government higher education reforms unlike at the University of Theatre and Film Arts where the opposition had been bold and included student occupations and demonstrations (see chapter seven). I somehow felt inspired by their action but also ashamed. I like many of my colleagues had been too passive and submissive when the Government reforms had first been introduced at the Corvinus, we had shown our group agency to be weak. I wanted to make amends somehow for my passivity and felt that somehow writing this book might be part of that process. However, writing the book would inevitably bring me into conflict with the Corvinus management given my concern about changes within the university and more broadly Hungarian higher education policy. It would be better to write such a book I felt outside of Corvinus University, I would be under less pressure and free to write what I felt.

Resilience and Dignity

My resignation from the Corvinus and decision to write this book was also symptomatic of a pattern of behaviour in my life in response to trauma. Trauma is a comprehensive, fundamental, and unexpected painful shock for the social and particularly cultural tissue of society and or individual (Sztompka, 2020). Profound shock and change can create what Emile Durkheim described as anomie (normative chaos), a form of dislocation that can encourage new departures and reorientation. Robert Merton (1996) as part of his sociology of deviance classified responses to social trauma and social change with four typical adaptations; innovation, rebellion, ritualism, and retreatism (Merton, 1996). It is evident to me that in moments of trauma that I have faced as an individual I have been compelled to follow the path of rebellion. This seemed more constructive than the other options, at least affording a chance to change and alter the forces that had impacted on me, maybe there was also a sense of 'getting even'. The experience in the scrapyard, the medical misdiagnosis, and the Covid crisis had spurred within me intense spurts of activism that have greatly shaped my life in generally positive ways. In some respects, I view these cyclical moments in my life as the most meaningful and productive in part because of the value of clearly identifying an adversary and appreciating the value of individual and collective agency and resilience. Such struggles taught me the value of the warmth and fraternity of comradeship and collective struggle and the joy of what Freire (1994) described as the 'pedagogy of hope', the belief we can bring about change and better the world we live in. I think such a response is also connected to resilience.

Resilience generally arises in crisis situations and adversity and grants the vulnerable coping strategies to avoid breakdown and facilitates an escape strategy from a deepening spiral of crisis. In an increasingly complex and precarious world, it is a resource that many rely upon to alleviate the problems confronting them (Dunn et al, 2015). Resilience offers a conceptual means to understand society as constantly shifting and in a state of disequilibrium (Walker and Cooper, 2011). It is a mindset that recognises that predictability is not the norm, in that sense, it has some transformative potential as if the world is not constant there is scope for adaptation and change. However, it is also a concept that has been harnessed by neoliberalism, a means by which the state can 'pass the buck' and rather than intervene can place action on the shoulders of the vulnerable through responsibilisation (Hagmann and Dunn Cavelty, 2012). Thus, neoliberalism individualises resilience and can shift the blame for crisis and disequilibrium onto the individual. The reasoning is that individuals are either lazy or unwilling to 'bounce back' from adversity, that those people who are not resilient have to pay the price of their inability to develop resilience. In the neoliberal mind it can be a tool to be instrumentalised for the optimisation of organisational productivity. However, in contrast, we can interpret resilience through the lens of 'dignity'. A dignity paradigm in the workplace and other environments stresses the value of dialogue, democracy and, empowerment. A dignity-rooted conception of resilience affords greater opportunity for collective rather than individual action in upholding dignity (Bal et al, 2020). Collectivity is the antithesis and the antidote to neoliberalism and indeed authoritarianism. I have seen the power and dignity of resilience in the Roma community where group identity and intense social networks have sustained community members to survive and cope despite the wave of prejudice and exclusion facing them (Ryder, 2017). Hence, through the voices of dissent profiled in this book and their review of the chapters they were involved with, I hope the production of this book has been a collective endeavour.

Academic Dissent

The chapter outlines my trajectory and journey towards resistance. The other chapters and stories will do the same for other participants in this issue. The strategies employed and motivations are not always the same, but all the actors profiled chose to 'speak out', all, like me, experienced cognitive dissonance. Cognitive dissonance is when you have two or more cognitions that are in conflict and tension with one another – when our behaviour or other reactions appear to conflict with our self-image, we try and reduce the dissonance, by taking some action, changing our behaviour. We can choose to resist (Huemer, 2013). A process of what Durkheim (1972) described as 'anomie', an internal war of doubt and question, can be prompted when we find ourselves confronted with change that challenges values central to our self-conception. In fact, changes and challenges at odds with our self-concept can bolster pre-existing attitudes (Sherman and Golkin, 1980). The theory of psychological reactance contends that humans have an innate desire for autonomy and when they feel it is threatened resist (Rains, 2013). Such forms of resistance can encompass 'empowerment strategies' that involve empowering or strengthening the self or one's existing attitudes to reduce one's vulnerability to external influence attempts.

In such strategies, people seek to confirm their confidence in existing beliefs or themselves. Compliance or failure to act can sometimes be harmful to our self-conception, these are dilemmas laden with moral questions. In becoming an activist it sometimes feels like one has no choice, that the unreasonable actions of those in power have compelled one to take action. Of course, there is the option to do nothing, getting on with life and keeping one's head down. Doing nothing though has a price in terms of the damage to our self-concept, the realisation that one is failing to live in accordance with the principles one has set. A feeling that one has been intimidated into submission, a feeling that one has complied and bent to the force of power by being silent (Rodríguez-Dorans et al, 2021). Doing something also has a price in terms of pressure, anxiety, and a stunted career path and that is why some prefer inactivity and passivity. However, such stratagems can be subtle, grey, fluid, and shifting.

Foucault (1977) is right to assert that where there is power there is resistance, it can take many forms being spontaneous, scattered, solitary, collective, and situational, in the sense that in some contexts actors resist in others they acquiesce. During times of institutional and political change, people will reposition themselves on the continuum between compliance and resistance (Di Napoli, 2014). In fact, in the academic context, we should not underestimate how feelings of fatalism, fear, and cynicism can be aroused in moments of change and challenge. Academic resistance in fact might be something of a rarity and for some might be largely confined to knowledge outputs in the form of publications and classroom discussion (Bowes-Catton et al, 2020). Of course, critical writing and teaching can incur for academics risk and sanction, but cases of more overt challenges are less common.

Dissent stems from dissonance, and rejection of a state of affairs that we feel to be wrong, it is a first step in changing the world (Holloway, 2005). Dissent can be said to be an important indicator of whether the state or another party is transgressing what are deemed to be central values and norms. Blokker (2017) notes that although populism can be situated within a modern democratic tradition of constitutionalism, it distorts and perverts that system and can transform into a democratic dictatorship. The need for dissent in Hungary is thus of paramount importance. Furthermore, the university is not just an institution shaped by governmental controls, it is a crucial site where wider social struggles can be won and lost. It can be a crucible of dissent where counter-narratives and new directions can be envisaged, framed, and gained (Caffentzis and Federici, 2011).

The testimony of academic dissenters in this volume will give some record of the degree to which Hungary is taking a trajectory that Blokker warns could end meaningful democracy. The testimonies also give valuable insights into a re-envisioning of Hungary. By presenting personal testimonies in this book the narrative can be seen in the critical and feminist tradition as waging a struggle against injustice and advocating transformation. Furthermore, subjectivity is seen as a site of power and agency, where hermeneutical conceptions of subjectivity foreground the influence of a number of forces – from our unconscious selves to our emotions to our everyday experiences – enabling dissenters to see the possibility of resistance (Maiguashca, 2019).

The changes and challenges profiled in this book and the threat they pose to academic freedom are not just tied to the authoritarian populist transition in Hungary but are also connected to what can be termed as academic capitalism (Collyer, 2015). The commodified and neoliberal nature of the modern university steered by the new managerialism that promotes amoral and atomising power regimes, as noted in the introduction, presents profound challenges to the vision and cherished ideals of some academics. It is a regime of audit culture and the fetishisation of indicators and evaluations, where the students are products and the staff machines (Courpasson et al, 2021). Atomised and isolated in such regimes where competivity and profitability is at the core of institutional thinking the scope and opportunity for resistance might be limited. Given the increasing appliance of new managerialism and audit culture in Hungary, the book will also seek to assess resistance to academic capitalism.

Dissent also plays a role in prompting change and can be viewed as a positive dynamic in society. Dissenters can also go on to become the architects of the future they desire and move from the margins to the centre of decision-making and knowledge production. In the context of the university, such institutions could have a utopian role in providing a dress rehearsal for an alternative world (Neary, 2010). The response to dissenters also provides profound insights into the political nature of the regime being challenged. In the heavily corporatised world of the modern university though it might be naive to aspire to such goals (Webb, 2018). All of these factors give reason and rationale to explore resistance to Hungarian higher education reforms through personal testimony.

According to Dahl's (1998) pluralistic democratic theory, democracy can only exist when it is rooted in shared mass values concerning rights and liberties. But what happens when the state seeks to shift and redesign those values to consolidate power and a particular worldview? How should dissent be voiced? Is there a chance that dissent might be able to stem such change or reorientate change in a direction more compatible with democratic values? The rest of the book seeks to provide insights into those questions with reference to higher education by profiling the experiences of a number of Hungarian academic dissenters.

Chapter Three
The Central European University and the Quest for an Open Society

The Central European University (CEU) was established in 1991, its formation was conceived by the Hungarian-born philanthropist George Soros and a number of dissident intellectuals from the Central Eastern Europe region in the dying days of communism. It was seen as a tool that would facilitate what became known as transition society, a move towards market economies and liberal democracy. It was envisaged that the CEU could play a pivotal role in training the technocracy for this 'brave new world' (Foer, 2019). Interestingly such philanthropy included support for the Fidesz Party and Victor Orbán himself was the beneficiary of a scholarship that took him to Oxford University for a year.

A guiding principle in this work was the notion of 'Open Society'. Soros had been one of the Jews fortunate enough to survive the Holocaust in Hungary during world war two and had had to go into hiding with forged identity papers. Soros, as with many European Jews, sought to turn a page in his life and relocate to a new country where the horrors and memories of war were less marked. He thus found himself studying as a young man at the London School of Economics where one of his teachers was the Austrian philosopher Karl Popper, a teacher who was to have a profound influence on the young Soros. Popper was the author of the seminal book the 'Open Society and Its Enemies'.

The term open society had originally been devised by the French philosopher Henri Bergson in 1932, the concept is centred on moral universalism, a form of meta-ethics, and notion that a universal set of moral values can be applied to everyone. In contrast to the open society, Bergson framed the term 'closed society', a static, exclusionary, and polarising society. Popper (2006) was to take the concept of open society further arguing that the Ancient Greeks had played a pivotal role in transitioning from the closed society of tribalism to one where tradition could be critiqued and challenged and where universal norms and values could regulate the polis, a demographically larger unit than the tribe and thus a more depersonalised world less dependent on personal interaction and close ties. For Popper, the momentum of the open society with its quest for humanitarianism and the application of universal moral values was unstoppable, although he realised the allure of the closed society and regressive tradition was still potent in particular during times of crisis. For Popper, this reversion had been espe-

https://doi.org/10.1515/9783110749816-005

cially evident during the troubled and chaotic 1930s, a decade marked by totalitarianism.

The CEU originally had campuses in Budapest, Prague, and Warsaw, with the majority of activities in Prague. However, the neo-liberal Czech Premier Vaclav Klaus was deeply suspicious of Soros, fearing the influence of his open society idealism that grated with Klaus's nationalism and neoliberal fundamentalism and thus sought to make life difficult for the CEU in Prague (Stepan, 2009). Klaus's hostility to the institution persuaded Soros to make Budapest the central point of his new university (Gessen, 2018). The CEU soon emerged as a major institutional force in the academic world. With time the university drew students from beyond Central Eastern Europe, admitting students from Africa, Latin America, and the Middle East, and beyond, creating a global profile. According to the QS Top University Rankings of 2020, several CEU departments such as History, Politics, Philosophy, and Sociology are in the top 100 ranking.

The Lex CEU

Despite the political shifts that had taken place under the Orbán administration many were shocked and surprised shortly after the twenty-fifth anniversary of the CEU to see a series of measures introduced by the Hungarian government that was dubbed the 'Lex CEU' that ostensibly appeared to be designed to push the CEU out of Hungary.

On the 31st of March 2017, the Minister of Human Resources Zoltán Balog proposed an amendment to the Higher Education Act of 2011. The most important aspect of the law was a new requirement regarding bilateral agreements between Hungary and non-European Economic Area (EEA) countries of origin of higher education institutions that stipulated the need for higher education institutions to provide educational services also in the country of origin. The vote was fast-tracked and days later on the 4th April, the Hungarian Parliament adopted the measure (EC, 2017). The measure acquired the label 'Lex CEU' from its critics as this university seemed to be targeted by the provision as it was the only higher education institution in Hungary lacking a campus in the country where it was chartered, the US in the case of the CEU (Deák, 2017). The CEU rector Michael Ignatieff described the measure as a "masterpiece of legal mugging" (Foer, 2019). As noted, although the legislation did not mention CEU it appeared to be its single target. It should be noted that the CEU was chartered in the state of New York, but it had no campus there. The law laid out that the national government of the CEU, namely the Federal Government, would need to enter into a bilateral accreditation agreement with Hungary. However, in the U.S., accreditation agreements are under the jurisdiction of the states, not the federal government.

Some speculated as to whether this provision was to bring the matter to the attention of President Trump, a political figure noted for his hostility to Soros and the ideals of his Open Society Network. Others speculated on possible Russian influence. Balázs Trencsényi, a professor of history at the CEU noted that two months after Putin's 2015 visit to Hungary there was an intensification of the Russian government's campaign against George Soros and his network. This Russian campaign included the emergence of a 'STOP Soros' movement in Macedonia sympathetic to the Russian-backed Macedonian leader Nikola Gruevski. The campaign is reported to have used the emails of the Brussels office of the Open Society Foundation that had been hacked in 2016 by the same hacker team that hacked the US Democrats' internal correspondence. Two weeks before the introduction of the Lex CEU, a Russian undercover TV crew entered into the CEU campus in Budapest and unveiled a supposed conspiracy orchestrated by Soros. It was claimed that Soros used NGOs to topple nationalist-oriented governments and impose his cosmopolitan values on the world (Trencsényi et al, 2017).

Interestingly in the run-up to the 2018 election Orbán himself organised a 'Stop Soros' campaign in Hungary accusing Soros of backing mass migration to Europe and providing support to civic groups that give legal aid to asylum-seekers and refugees. Soros was framed as the leader of a secretive network aiming to subvert national identities by coaxing millions of migrants and refugees into Europe, the so-called 'Soros Plan' (Etl, 2020). Orbán referred to the Soros network as a "mafia-style operation" (Hungarian Government 2017 – see introduction chapter for a wider contextual discussion). Another parallel between Hungary and Russia is that Hungary emulated Russia in the introduction of new stricter rules on NGOs. The new measures introduced in 2017 are strikingly similar to measures introduced in Russia in 2015, NGOs were required to register with the authorities if they receive an annual foreign income of at least (£19.240; $24.700). Such NGOs were compelled under the measure to put the label 'foreign-funded organisation' on their publications. Russian NGOs have to call themselves "foreign agents" if they get any foreign funding (Boldyrev and Benke, 2017). Orbán's assault on civil society thus came in the form of legalistic maneuvers designed to subvert and intimidate institutions that might challenge his authority. It should therefore not surprise the reader that such tactics were employed with an institution such as the CEU.

The US ambassador to Hungary, David Cornstein an octagenarian jewelry magnate and friend of Trump, was involved in negotiating a solution that would have allowed CEU to remain in Hungary. Cornstein though was hesitant to criticise Orbán for creating the situation, and criticised Soros for not developing a better relationship with the Hungarian prime minister, describing the conflict as a personal dispute between the two men rather than one centred on academic freedom. Cornstein compared the university's situation to his experience owning jewelry shops within a department store. "I was a guest in another guy's store," he said. "The university is in another country. It would pay to work with the government" (Witte, 2018). Cornstein even set up a personal meeting between Orbán and Trump in the White House and frequently downplayed concerns about Hungarian corruption, antisemitism, and the erosion of democracy. At a lavish gala party Cornstein hosted in Budapest with 800 guests, Cornstein had the singer Paul Anka serenade Orbán the special guest of honour with the song 'My way' (Apuzzo and Novak, 2019).

Mark Toner, Acting Spokesperson of U.S. Department of State did urge the Hungarian Government to suspend implementation of the higher education law affecting the Central European University, but in general American diplomacy seemed to be far from robust on this matter and its tacit support for the Government no doubt emboldened Orbán. In contrast, in April 2017 the European Commission concluded the Lex CEU was not compatible with the Charter of Fundamental Rights of the European Union and would take legal action against Hungary; announcing infringement proceedings. The European Commission concluded:

> ...the law is not compatible with the fundamental international market freedoms, notably the freedom to provide services and the freedom of establishment but also with the right of academic freedom, the right to education and the freedom to conduct a business as provided by the Charter of Fundamental Rights of the European Union, as well as with the Union's legal obligations under international trade law (EC, 2017).

In October 2017 the Hungarian government did announce a one-year extension to the Lex CEU, leaving the CEU's case unresolved. In a press statement, the CEU noted that an agreement between the State of New York and the Government of Hungary guaranteeing CEU's existence was ready to be signed. The CEU also conformed to the provisions of the Lex CEU by entering into an agreement with Bard College to undertake 'educational activities' in the State of New York, thus the CEU could now be said to stage educational work in its country of origin. The Press statement noted that Hungary had already signed an agreement with the State of Maryland concerning McDaniel College, a US liberal arts college based in Hungary with its mother institution based in Maryland. The statement noted "Failure to sign an agreement with the State of New York in relation to CEU can only be perceived as discriminatory" (CEU Press Statement, 2017). Frustrated by a lack of response the CEU declared that unless the Hungarian government signed the agreement by the 1st of December 2018 it would move out of Hungary. The Hungarian government failed to respond to this deadline and the decision was taken to relocate most of the CEU's teaching operations to Vienna (Redden, 2018).

In October 2020 the European Court of Justice ruled that the Lex CEU' violated Hungary's commitments under the rules of the World Trade Organisation, and infringes the provisions of the Charter of Fundamental Rights of the European Union relating to academic freedom (C-66/18). The CEU Rector and President Michael Ignatieff stated that the ruling was a vindication of the CEU's position and that he hoped the landmark judgment would strengthen the legal protections for academic freedom across Europe. (Statement from the Office of the CEU President and Rector, 2020). Despite the victory, some observers felt the decision had come too late, for Orbán appeared to have won in forcing the CEU out of Hungary, a factor that some observers might conclude reflects badly not only on the speed and ability of the EU to enforce the rule of law, but also the resolve and strategic nous of the CEU leadership (Scheppele et al, 2021, Inotai, 2020). The chapter will return to these points later in the discussion.

The Rationale for the Lex CEU

Given the academic success and ranking of the CEU, many capital cities would welcome the presence of a centre of learning like the CEU, indeed the city of Vienna was extremely open and accommodating to the proposal to relocate CEU teaching operations to Vienna. The Hungarian government's desire to eject the CEU stemmed from ideological considerations which are described in chapter one and encompassed the framing of Soros and his civil society network and university as a challenge to the conception of an illiberal democracy aspired to by the Orbán administration. Zoltan Kovacs Hungarian spokesman and the lead communication voice of the Hungarian government stated bluntly "We do have a problem with George Soros – or rather George Soros has a problem with us. He's been using his money and influence – through his NGOs – to put pressure on Hungary" (BBC, 2017).

Orbán claimed that the controversial measures his government had introduced, coined the Lex CEU, merely abolished privileges and loopholes and distributed rights across universities in an equal fashion. An assertion the CEU challenged and asked Orbán to name the specific privileges it possessed, a question the Prime Minister failed to answer (The Office of the CEU President and Rector, 2017). In similar vein, Justice Minister Judit Varga posted on Facebook "The government finds double standards unacceptable. All universities in Hungary must comply with the law equally. It is not possible to create a law that puts Soros university in a more advantageous position than Hungarian universities". A comment that seemingly ignored the fact that it was her government that had changed the law to make the CEU non-compliant and in effect placed it at a disadvantage (Inotai, 2020). Lajos Kósa, the then leader of the Fidesz parliamentary group portrayed it as a "phantom university" and asserted many had been scammed by "Uncle Georgie's" tricks (Hirado.hu 2017).

Some of the key figures around Orbán though furnished more ideological justifications as to the rationale for the Lex CEU. Mária Schmidt, a Hungarian historian and university lecturer, Director-General of the Twenty-First Century Institute and the House of Terror Museum, a key cultural stalwart of the Orbán administration, described the CEU as "George Soros's forward garrison in Europe" (Walker, 2019a). For some on the political right, the CEU was an exercise in political engineering, offering degrees in what they deemed were the politicised social sciences rather than the real sciences (Baskerville, 2019). Zoltán Balog, then Minister of Human Resources stated in the Hungarian Parliament: "The existence of a strong, autonomous and internationally-recognised university is in Hungary's interests. But it is not in our interests to have players in the background who are conspiring against the democratically elected government or for example to support Soros-organisations. Soros's organisations are not above the law." According to Balog, Soros was involved in a "worldwide smear campaign" against Hungary (BBC, 2017). Providing some insights into such statements Cass Mudde (2017a), a political scientist and lead authority on populism, notes the CEU represents the antithesis of Orbán's values being critical, global, independent, and multicultural. The CEU thus represented an intellectual citadel that needed to be vanquished and its departure added to the strongman image Orbán was keen to cultivate, both at home and abroad.

Resistance

Aside from the European Commission's stance discussed earlier, condemnation of the Lex CEU was vocal within Hungary and abroad. Over 500 prominent U.S. and European academics, including 20 Nobel Laureates signed an open letter in support of Central European University in Budapest (CEU Press Release, 2017). A number of Jean Monnet academic chair holders wrote to the European Commission (Presidents Juncker, Tajani, and Tusk).

> Because we share a commitment to a European Union based on democratic values, we are writing to you to express our profound disappointment and outrage about the EU's failure to respond more robustly to recent developments in Hungary. On the 1st December 2018, after a long-running campaign of egregious harassment, the Hungarian government forced the Central European University to leave Hungary. The fact that an independent university could be expelled from an EU member state is a galling attack on academic freedom that contravenes the Union's core democratic values. Sadly, we are accustomed to seeing such attacks on academic freedom in authoritarian regimes such as Russia and Turkey, but the fact that this could occur within the EU is a truly shameful moment in the history of European integration (Jean Monnet chair holders, 2018).

In April 2017 a day before the Hungarian President Janos Ader was to sign into law the measures labelled Lex CEU, an estimated 80,000 people took to the streets of Budapest to protest, some commentators believed it was the biggest ever demonstration against the Government since the start of Orbán's second tenure as prime minister that started in 2010 (BBC, 2017). Another landmark event took place in November 2018, where for a week, Kossuth Square, the square where the Hungarian Parliament is located, was turned into 'Szabad Egyetem' (Free University). The Szabad Egyetem hosted classes, public lectures, performances, and discussions. The occupation started after the march for Academic Freedom on the 24th of November, a week before the 1st of December deadline for the Hungarian government to sign the agreement that would allow CEU to stay in Hungary (See earlier discussion).

I gave a lecture at the Szabad Egyetem on Brexit and populism and remember clearly the pain of teaching in the bitterly cold conditions, at the end of the session I could no longer feel my toes. Despite the discomfort, I felt invigorated, I had a feeling of 'having crossed the Rubicon'. Although I had critiqued the Orbán government in my academic writing on issues like the segregation of Roma I did not feel such work had brought me into direct conflict with the Government. As one academic colleague reasoned in 2015 "We academics, to a degree, are fairly safe, the Hungarian Government does not take an active interest in what we say in academic publications. It's when you challenge them in the media and gather large audiences that you are then perceived as a threat". As evidenced by this chapter in recent years that disinterest in the world of academia had been radically reversed, but to return to the point of my vignette of life as an academic activist I felt that by being at Szabad Egyetem I was taking a stand that would have fundamental consequences for my life in Hungary. This turned out to be true given I was to resign from the Corvinus University in part because of concerns about the future of academic freedom and later started on the process of writing this book (See chapter two). Young people and academics at 'Szabad

Egyetem' also felt enthused by this sense of idealism and hope. One student declared with reference to her support for the Szabad Egyetem:

> I am joining the protest and am going to occupy Kossuth Tér, because I feel that supporting academic freedom is the right choice. If we fail in having freedom in academia, we will fail in freedom of speech in our countries. And since academic freedom affects every single person, I believe that not only students and faculty members, but every citizen should stand for Hungarian universities. If we give up there, we will give up everywhere (Gawkowski, 2018).

The protests centred around the Szabad Egyetem were to form the nucleus of a cross-university network that was able to resist further challenges to academic freedom in Hungary. Some though were hesitant to take such action. One of the organisers of Szabad Egyetem, Imre Szijarto a student at the CEU found it hard to recruit other Hungarian students, who worried that their CEU degree might be a 'scarlet letter', a mark of activism that would lead to them being marked out by the authorities as untrustworthy or as a troublemaker. Some were influenced by more careerist concerns and argued protesting would only make their chances of landing a good job harder (Gawkowski, 2018).

Caution was also evident in the actions of the CEU leadership. The Rector Ignatieff believed it would be counter-productive to feed Orbán's hunger for confrontation. Instead, Ignatieff sought to rein in the fervour of the CEU community. Ignatieff stated, "I explicitly gave the order that we cannot be associated with street protests. It's not what universities should do." (Foer, 2019). The CEU board discussed how best to respond to the serious crisis it was confronted with, apparently, some board members wanted the CEU to make a defiant stand and remain in Hungary. However, Soros it has been reported felt that what can be described as a game of 'cat and mouse' was undermining the future of the university and interrupting the education of students and that it was for the best to transfer most of the teaching operations to Vienna (Foer, 2019). As noted later in the chapter some students and human rights activists were deeply disappointed with this caution feeling that it undermined the mission of the CEU (See Voices of Dissent). Was the caution of the CEU leadership astute or was it a case of appeasing authoritarianism? These are questions that will be returned to later in the discussion. One thing that became clear was the move to Vienna did not necessarily mean the end of the CEU's problems. In Vienna students from outside of the European Union complained of a procedural labyrinth of bureaucracy in terms of securing residency permits, with reported allegations of bias from the authorities and even a lack of support and help from the CEU (TRT-World, 2021).

Voices of Dissent

In this section of the chapter former students at the CEU provide testimony as to their experiences of the impact of the Lex CEU and the resulting student protests and formation of the Szabad Egyetem. Through discussions with several Szabad Egyetem activists, I learnt many of the students involved in the Szabad Egyetem had been involved in activism before they came to the CEU and this was one of the factors that had attracted them to the CEU, where they hoped to find an academic experience that was more philosophically critical than what they had experienced in their BA studies. Students from Central and Eastern Europe were especially critical of the staid and formal learning experiences they had experienced at BA level, poorly paid and demoralised teaching staff, sometimes imbued with teacher-centred approaches to learning had for some sapped their joy in learning and constrained the potential for innovative and challenging thinking and learning. However, students from western countries had been dismayed by universities operating like businesses with large class sizes and high tuition fees and demoralised teaching staff drained by audit cultures, organisational traits that universities in Central Eastern Europe seemed keen to emulate. Many of the students I spoke to were to find aspects of the CEU experience matched the aspirations they held but there was also disappointment. A number of students described the excitement of a learning environment that was stimulating and open, with high-level teaching staff creating open learning environments in relatively small classes. Staff were also said to have a lower teaching workload than other universities giving them more time, not just for research and publications, but also to give support to students. Also meeting other students from other countries and hearing in and outside of class about how their cultural and political experiences had shaped their experiences and worldviews, added another valuable aspect to being at the CEU.

The revocation of Gender Studies MAs by the Hungarian state and the Lex CEU were seen as direct challenges to the CEU and the notion of academic freedom. A general assembly was formed to take ideas forward, this was to evolve into what became known as the Szabad Egyetem. In the following testimony, supporters of the Szabad Egyetem describes their experiences.

Katalin

Katalin is Hungarian and no longer lives in Hungary.

Coming to study at the CEU as a postgraduate student was the fulfilment of a longstanding dream, and it seemed a logical conclusion of events in my life. A turning point in my life occurred during the primary school years in Hungary, I formed a close attachment with a Roma boy and this led to bullying and ostracism on the part of my peers, even the teachers seemed to challenge me. Fortunately, my parents supported me, but the experience gave me early insights into the closed minds of a certain Hungarian mindset. I went to a progressive high school, where open debate was encouraged, I had space to express myself and be myself. One day students from the CEU came to the school to talk about their experiences. I was impressed with how they spoke about their commitment to progressive causes and their accounts of learning at the CEU. This sparked within me a desire to attend this university one day for my postgraduate studies. This desire seemed to become more intense as the Hungarian state university I attended for undergraduate study, typical of so many in the country, seemed staid, formal, and tired. I felt isolated. In 2018 I won a scholarship to study for an MA at the CEU, I felt a sense of euphoria and remember the tears of joy when I told my mother. This was a critical time for the CEU as the Hungarian government seemed intent on forcing it out of the country. Students at the CEU organised resistance to these measures, but this mood was not uniform. Some seemed uninterested or passive, some were not recipients of scholarships and their families had paid the high tuition fees, coming to the CEU for them it appeared was the chance to receive an elite education in a fun city rather than a bond and affinity to radicalism. Only some students actively supported the Szabad Egyetem.

I felt deeply that the CEU should stay in Budapest, but I and other students felt frustrated that the decision-making on this matter was not in our hands. The CEU leadership seemed to place too much emphasis on diplomacy and was vacillating and at times timid. Some students and staff felt CEU leadership should have done a better job. The CEU left without any fight! That was embarrassing for all those who believed in human rights, freedom and an open society! I was part of the year group that spent my second year of study in Vienna after the university decided to transfer its teaching operations. Many students did not want to go and their fears about the cost of living and bureaucratic hurdles for non EU citizens securing residency proved to be correct. The new campus in Vienna, a former bank, seemed characterless and devoid of the vibrancy of the old CEU.

As a Hungarian I can say there seem to have been so many crazy moments in the country, my mum and others have hope that the election in 2022 may bring change. They believe it is our last chance to save the country. I had this feeling in 2018 though. It now feels for me like the 'end of the end' of the process of Hungary's transition to authoritarianism. Fifteen of my twenty-six years have been spent under Fidesz administrations, I hope for change, but it seems a distant dream.

Imre Szijarto

Imre Szijarto was a prominent student activist during the counter campaign to the Lex CEU (see earlier discussion), he now lives in Germany.

I was raised in the suburbs of Budapest and was schooled in Hungary but left the country to study Politics and European Studies at University College London (UCL). I have done some work with the corporate sector and now reside in Berlin. I had an MA from UCL but decided to register at the Central European University in part because I was told I would need another MA to start doctoral studies. I also felt drawn to the CEU as it was struggling for its survival in Budapest because of the pressures being exerted on it by the Orbán administration. The chance to be taught by academics like Tamás Gáspár was also an additional attraction to studying at the CEU.[1]

To some degree I had mixed feelings about life in the CEU. I did not like the Anglo-Saxon corporate management style and the emphasis in some courses on a positivist and quantitative approach to knowledge production. These traits seemed to be juxtaposed, and in contradiction to the dimensions of the CEU that did animate me, namely its commitment to an open society and the vision of Karl Popper as well as its diversity and the radicalism of some of its students and subjects like Gender Studies and Sociology.

The autumn term of 2018 was the final decisive moment of whether the university should stay. Some of the students started to organise discussions and brainstorming as to what could be done. Some of the students had established activist backgrounds, having been involved in G20 protest, Occupy and similar type movements that had a culture of anarchism and horizontal approaches. A general assembly was formed to take these ideas forward, at first it was called 'Students for CEU' and a facebook group was formed. We organised a demonstration a week before the deadline the CEU had set for the Hungarian government to resolve the uncertainty created by the Lex CEU. I was partly drawn into the centre of this activity because some of the leading voices in the campaign were foreign students and not Hungarian speakers. I found myself helping to liaise with the media on behalf of the campaign.

Dissent was evident at other university campuses. The Corvinus was facing privatisation, the autonomy of the Hungarian Academy of Sciences had been restricted so the campaign broadened to include these other institutions with a focus on academic freedom. Around this time there was also tension over what became known as the 'Slave Labour Law'. The law increased the overtime

---

1 Gáspár is a public intellectual who is highly critical of the Orbán administration.

employers could demand from 250 to 400 hours, while payment could be delayed by three years. This prompted a series of major demonstrations. I have clear memories of Tamás Gáspár speaking at one event organised against the law calling upon workers and intellectuals to unite given the supreme challenges they now faced from an increasingly authoritarian government. It felt like a critical moment and this prompted some of us to organise the occupation, 'Szabad Egyetem' at Kossuth Ter. As a symbolic act we invited trade unions to participate, I was pleasantly surprised to see lead trade union leaders participate in the action. Sections of the mainstream media derided us as Soros agents or LGBTQ activists all with the intent of challenging and undermining Christian values. We wanted the CEU to stay in Budapest, but it was also a deeper question about what kind of country Hungary was becoming.

The decision by the CEU to transfer most of its teaching to Vienna seemed inevitable. I would have preferred it if it had stayed until the last possible moment, even if the police had to come in to force it out. Of course, a university like the CEU cannot operate like that, it was managed with an elite management approach, it was run like a business based on a US business model where it saw itself as a supplier that had to deliver to its customers. Despite its reputation for radicalism, it is a university with a significant customer base with high tuition fees. It had to be in a position to continue to deliver its service. Also, Orbán seemed determined to oust the CEU and Hungary is now the kind of country where the will of Orbán is paramount. However, to have remained would have created a unique learning experience, being a university under siege. The European Court of Justice of course did rule that Hungary had broken the law and that the CEU had the right to operate in the country several years after the move to Vienna.

Balduino

Balduino is from Portugal and took a BA in sociology between 2014 and 17. Balduino was active in the young Greens and came to the CEU to study Gender Studies in the Fall of 2017.

I have a longstanding interest in social justice, when I studied political science in Portugal it was more focused on economic justice issues but my interest in gender issues grew. I did an elective course in my BA on gender and in the final year spent a semester at a university in the USA where I studied 'Women's Studies'. Such was my interest in this area my final thesis was on marriage. I had heard about the CEU and knew it was one of the leading centres in Europe on Gender Studies. After I applied to do an MA in Gender Studies, I learnt the

CEU was in a precarious situation with the Hungarian government seemingly trying to push the CEU out of the country. When I arrived in Hungary you could feel the tension in the university, but nothing seemed to happen. In the summer of 2018, it was the end of my first year at CEU and I was on vacation in Portugal. I heard in the media about the Hungarian government's decision to ban Gender Studies. It took the Gender Studies Department a long time to respond and update us on the announcement. but I think this was a result of the fact they did not know much about it themselves. The Government had been neither clear nor transparent in this matter, the Government notification was in a single sentence in a large document sent to the universities in August. On one level I was worried about whether I would be able to finish the MA, on another level, I was concerned about academic freedom but more broadly the movement by Hungary towards a very conservative nationalism. The ban on Gender Studies needs to be seen in the context of the Hungarian government's actions on refugees that included the construction of a border fence and nativist rhetoric. Also, there was an increasing number of polemical attacks against Soros. The Gender Studies ban was just one aspect of this wider development. I wanted to take a stand.

The CEU board seemed reserved and docile on the Lex CEU, so students like me thought we should do something. As part of this growing mood of militancy, a number of actions were staged in formal lectures. In 2017 the rector Michael Ignatieff invited the British philosopher Sir Roger Scruton to address the university on the concept of an open society.[2] Ignatieff argued that it was important to hear both sides of the argument, but Scruton was a controversial speaker to many students he stood for everything we were against in Hungary. I and several students were involved in a collective walkout.

The CEU was cautious in its dealings with the Hungarian government. I understand to some degree why they feel they needed to be careful, they wanted to wait and see what could be achieved through legal structures and I guess hoped it all might 'blow over'. However, students like me looked at it from a political perspective and felt more robust action was needed. A student association existed but it was rather technical, so we organised a student collective. One aim was to push the CEU board towards a more critical position.

In October 2018 the CEU president Ignatieff invited the US ambassador David Cornstein to speak at the CEU.[3] It seemed at the time the CEU board was relying upon and hoping the ambassador, a Trump appointee and personal friend of the

---

2 https://www.ceu.edu/article/2017-11-20/trust-belonging-duty-necessary-sustaining-free-society-scruton-says.

3 https://www.ceu.edu/article/2018-06-28/ceu-welcomes-us-ambassador-cornstein-campus.

president who also enjoyed a close friendship with Orbán, would find a way out of the impasse. There was some discussion about this on social media and I posted a message saying we should protest. The Dean of students heard about this and sent me an urgent request to meet. The Dean advised me and other students considering protest to be careful as the university was hoping the ambassador could help. However, I still wanted to make a protest and the Dean recognised I had a right to do so. Other students who had been considering taking action decided to drop their planned action. I and others from the collective planned to hand out leaflets when the ambassador came. An hour before the lecture a friend texted me to tell me that she saw my picture at the security desk of the CEU. I went to the ambassador's lecture but the CEU security stopped me and would not let me enter the building. Later a staff member helped me enter the building and I was able to hand out the leaflets. Later I spoke to the CEU provost on this matter and he recognised that the ambassador did little to help the CEU. Ignatieff set the Hungarian government a deadline of the 1st December 2018 to resolve the legal dispute with the CEU and this deadline became an important focus of protest for us. I was involved in the student occupation at Kossuth Ter (the parliament) 'Szabad Egyetem', where an occupation and lectures were staged. The CEU leadership did show some support for this, some of them visited the occupation.

Why did I do it? Part of my personality is one of always pushing forward, not backing down, and not giving up. I think my activism was also formed through the close links we formed within the student body, many of the international students were in a kind of bubble, we were a cohesive group. I feel this involvement was a valuable learning experience. I had been involved in party politics, but in Portugal Green politics is at the border of mainstream political activity. Regarding the CEU issue, I entered into what can be described as civil disobedience to influence the CEU board and then the Hungarian government. The actions I was involved with at the CEU presented the first forms of activism I had organised outside of institutional structures. Maybe some might say it was naïve and idealistic, but we did generate media interest that made many in Hungary and beyond aware of what was happening. We gained global coverage from media outlets like the BBC and Al Jazeera among others, we did not leave in silence and we fostered an atmosphere of protest that is still evident in Hungary today.

In the end, the deadline passed, and the Hungarian Government chose not to resolve the matter and the CEU relocated most of its operations to Vienna. I suppose the university had few options, but I was pleased to see the CEU would not leave the country entirely and would continue to have at least some presence in Budapest. In 2019 we had a weekend retreat with the core group of activists and discussed how to move forward. We discussed activism in connection to gender identity and critical theory, there were some disagreements, one participant was accused of being a Leninist and walked out. There was also a discussion of privilege in activism. I was able to take the actions I did because I was Portuguese and could return home but those from less democratic countries had to be more wary and cautious. Others had had previous experiences with oppressive regimes in their home countries. As someone from Portugal, I was a little naive and blinded by my privilege of nationality when it came to the risks that such actions involved.

On reflection, I can see it was a mistake to protest in the way we did at a Nazi gathering 'the Day of Honour' where fascists commemorate world war two. At this event, we got too close to the fascists, with the police separating us. Later some of the fascists surprised us in the backstreets and intimidated us. In 2019 Jordan Peterson a Toronto based professor and clinical psychologist came to Budapest, he is a controversial figure who is critical of identity politics and argues that 'political correctness' creates a form of tyranny.[4] To interrupt his talk and visit we blew whistles, which made us feel good, but I am not sure how productive it was.

Often direct action ignores the broader societal structures in which the object that the direct action addresses is situated. It is based on the assumption that both this object and the direct action itself can be seen as separate and unbound from these structures, and therefore the single action is presumed to be able to change what it aims to. It is often intertwined with masculinity in the sense that such a simplified perspective of the world can only be taken from a position that bears the masculine privilege to ignore underlying gender relations. Often it also involves taking certain risks that one can (better) afford because of male privilege, e.g. physical risks or risks when it comes to how one is treated by the authorities. Some of these thoughts are inspired by a few journal publications I read from Coleman and Bassi, such as their articles "Deconstructing Militant Manhood: Masculinities in the disciplining of anti-globalization politics" and "Militant Manhood Revisited".

However, not all direct action ignores such underlying structures by definition. There are ways of embedding direct action within a broader strategy that takes into account such structures. I think my brief experience with Extinction Rebellion in 2019 showed me how this could work, although not always perfectly. For example, by involving a focus on regenerative culture, mental health, and openly discussing the layers of privilege that play a part during activism.

---

4 https://hungarytoday.hu/orban-meets-jordan-peterson-in-budapest/.

The strategy towards Peterson was an example of how direct action can sometimes be blind to the underlying structures. It was improvised in the very spur of the moment: simply because a friend of mine had a whistle with her, three of us decided to walk down to the talk and attempted to interrupt it. We didn't do any well-considered risk-calculation and just went on with our first thought. The lack of risk-calculation showed at the very moment I got assaulted by one of the audience members. Furthermore, it was also very much focused on the person of Peterson, rather than on challenging the underlying ideas and discourses he and many others are taking part in. That is not to say that one shouldn't protest such an individual event, but rather that such a thing should always be calculated and embedded in a larger strategy that addresses the broader discourse.

The value of pragmatism and planning in activism is elaborated upon in the concluding chapter.

Transforming the Ivory Tower

Academic freedom, the pursuit of truth, and openness should be viewed as part of the long tradition of intellectual dissent that has been a central catalyst in knowledge production but also a safeguard that challenges and warns of infringements to liberty and equality. It is for such reasons that authoritarian and totalitarian regimes have often swiftly moved to suppress academic freedom and dissent. Within the academy though there are conservative forces that Bourdieu (1988) described as academic orthodoxy who sacrilise their positions through status and arcane traditions, but also seeks to marginalise the 'heretics', those who challenge the conservatism of the academy. The strategies of the orthodox elite can be viewed as a form of cultural reproduction which, for Bourdieu, leads to 'misrecognition' where power relations are perceived not for what they are objectively, but instead in a form which depicts them as legitimate in the eyes of the beholder (Jenkins, 2007, see chapter one). Such contestation and struggles have been a marked feature of academic life for decades and it should not surprise the reader to learn that such features were evident in the life of the CEU. The final section of the chapter gives an overview of the innovative contributions the CEU has made to academic life and practice that can be said to have striven to transform the ivory tower into an open and inclusive learning environment, welcoming of those at the margins and giving such communities voice. It will become evident though that there were times when such innovation was subverted by traditional conceptions of academia and even by timidity.

Dissident academics have been prominent in nurturing oppositional ideologies encompassing variants of Marxism, feminism, critical race theory, intersectionality, queer theory, and post-colonialism that offer serious challenges to inequality and oppression (Stockdill and Yu Danico, 2012). These traditions have been evident in some of the pioneering work of the CEU and were innovative in the sense that despite the increased interest in such critical research methodologies they are still at the margins of the academic world and receive little mention in most research methods textbooks. Indeed, those at the margins have been the objects but rarely the authors of research, and the discomfort that those on the margins feel about adopting traditional research processes and knowledge creation has been interpreted as their personal inability or failings (Brown and Strega, 2005).

When I relocated from London to Budapest in 2010 I sought out like-minded activists and researchers and established the Roma Research and Empowerment Network (RREN), it promoted participatory research and grassroots activism by hosting seminars and conferences in community venues. If staged within universities, such events were open to, and targeted , a mixed audience of researchers and community workers. The Network provided a platform and vehicle for a range of civil society workers and academics sometimes constrained in their activism by institutional limitations created within large NGOs and universities. A high point of the RREN was 'Nothing About Us Without Us?' seminar and conference in 2014 that provided an important deliberative event for critical and emerging activist-researchers. The papers and ideas presented were further explored and elaborated upon in an open-access special edition of the European Roma Rights Journal (Ryder et al, 2015). This special edition of the journal sought to make academic writing accessible to a wider audience than standard publications. The aforementioned conference and journal provided an important platform for discussion as to the role Roma should play in radical social movements and research. The journal included calls for decision-makers and civil society to genuinely connect with Roma communities. It also called for a more intersectional agenda embracing feminism and LGBTQ rights and radical conceptions of social justice in the campaign for Roma rights (Ryder, 2017). The RREN was to form the nucleus of a new initiative at the CEU on Roma studies.

The CEU had a long track record of organising Roma educational programmes. One of its programmes established in 2004, which has supported around 200 Romani students, was the Roma Access Programme that trained and prepared young Roma undergraduates for MA studies by improving their English, but also by training them in human rights and advocacy, helping to produce a new cadre of Roma intellectuals and activists. In this sense, the programme reflected the philosophy of Paulo Freire (1972) teaching students not only theories, concepts, and academic skills, but also how to apply them to effect change. Another initiative was the CEU summer school, for many years organised by the British academic Michael Stewart that provided opportunities for postgraduates to learn more about Roma issues from leading experts in Romani studies. The first formal Romani Studies event I ever attended was a summer school session organised by Stewart in 1998. From around 2014 though members of the RREN became critical of the summer school as few, if any, experts of Romani origin were selected to present their work. A mood of frustration was accentuated by the fact that an EU and Council of Europe initiative to establish a European Academic Network on Romani Studies in 2012 had resulted in a committee being elected with no Roma. Activist scholars felt this was redolent of academic elitism which seemed to marginalise critical Romani thinkers (Ryder et al, 2015).

Responding to these concerns the CEU established in 2017 the Romani Studies programme at the CEU, an independent academic unit that according to its mission statement aims to engage scholars, policymakers, and activists in interdisciplinary knowledge production and debate on Roma identity and activism; antigypsyism; social justice and policy-making; gender politics; and structural inequality (CEU website). The ambitious aims of the Romani Studies Programme can be viewed as critical and intersectional. The Romani Studies Programme was led by Roma academics and a new journal 'Critical Romani Studies' was established as well as a new summer school. The positions created by this initiative were filled by members of the RREN. The activities and locus of the RREN had been transformed from an informal network to one of a major academic institution. Alongside this development, a growing number of Roma PhD holders were emerging and asserting that Romani Studies needed to radically change and move away from the stifling academic traditions, hierarchy, and self-interest that had created dissonance between academia and Romani communities.

This major shift in the direction and leadership of Romani Studies was met with some hostility. One lead, non-Roma, expert Yaron Matras (2015, para. 3) denounced the new cadre of Romani intellectuals, claiming they were:

> hoping to fast-track their careers by getting influential jobs on the basis of their self-declared Romani ancestry, without having to produce a track record of many years of either leadership in human rights campaigns or contributions to scholarship. They wish to benefit from the stream of European funding for Roma-projects for years to come, and they want to be able to mimic the recognised scholarly authority of eminent researchers.

Matras (2017, 119) also derided the establishment of the Romani Studies Programme at the CEU with its alleged emphasis on political empowerment that in his opinion was turning the CEU into a "sponsored advocacy centre". Such a statement it could be argued fails to acknowledge the important contribution of ethnic and indigenous-focused departments in universities in Canada, the USA, Australia, and New Zealand which the CEU it could be said was bravely emulating.

Stewart (2017, 141) was sceptical with reference to the intersectionality of critical Romani Studies which was an important feature of the Romani Studies Programme at CEU, arguing that it constituted a "tragic cul-de-sac" with a "framework of one-sided descriptions of historical persecution and lamentations of white hegemony". Stewart though fails to appreciate that such intersectionality, despite his dismissive interpretation, could be a nuanced tool that could garner fresh and valid insights into race, class, and gender and the interplay between these variables. Intersectionality can also be viewed as a central factor in the strength of the new critical Romani studies allowing for a critique of internal group oppressions as opposed to idolising tradition facilitating the Roma in aligning with intersectional and broad movements for transformative change that challenge the cultural and structural causes of marginalisation in the twenty-first century. It allows critical researchers to gain insights into the crisis within neoliberalism and its efforts to reorient its path through alliances with radical conceptions of nationalism in the form of authoritarian populism, but also the manipulation of identities to support or challenge hegemony. Critical activism sometimes leads to the introduction of new frames to communities and debates and deliberation as to how to interpret identity, in part, this can contribute to what Spivak terms as 'strategic essentialism', the finding of common ground and forging of alliances. Intersectionality thus allows for dialogue, flexibility, and reflection and are qualities that are essential for inclusive identity formation. Critics of intersectionality run the risk of repeating the mistakes of the Gypsylorists of the nineteenth century by insinuating change and adaptation is redolent of decline and the dilution of Romani identity.

The intense and at times acrimonious debates and tensions within and around Romani Studies reflect the longstanding antagonisms between scientism and critical research. Smith (2003) has observed that, according to Descartes, knowledge was based on a form of dualism, the knowing subject and the known object, an enlightenment philosophy labelled by some as scientism. Scientism glorifies "objectivity," and thus the tenets of this approach stipulate that research should be detached from the researched. Conversely, embodied knowledge is a research approach grounded in the reality of everyday life. Debates have raged as to the legitimacy of traditional notions of hierarchies of knowledge, which place the expert as the filter and shaper of what is perceived as knowledge and wisdom at the summit of the hierarchy. Critics argue this is an elitist stance that reduces the value and recognition of grounded and localised knowledge (Weiler, 2009). Critical researchers believe, in what has been termed standpoint theory, that research should be situated in the concerns of marginalised people (Harding, 2 1991).

Despite my active involvement in the RREN, I did not take an active part in the Romani Studies Programme at CEU, although I did present papers at two of the CEU summer schools, these were historic events as most of the presenters were of Romani origin. I declined an invitation to join the editorial board of the CEU journal of Critical Romani Studies. My reticence stemmed from the fact that despite the radical mission statement of the CEU Romani Studies Programme I had some concerns that it might fail to forge new connections with wider Romani communities, this had been a key goal of the RREN, I feared that the Romani Studies Programme might be emulating too much conventional academic practices by staging international conferences which attracted a primarily academic audience. Also, although the journal of Critical Romani Studies Journal was open access, I feared the articles, primarily by academics, would not resonate with community activists and only appeal to a narrow academic audience. In part I was also aggrieved, it felt like the CEU was taking over the important work of the RREN and this had been done without sufficient dialogue. I supported a proposal for the new journal to be managed by a consortia of universities with an active interest in Roma issues and NGOs, reflecting the composition and operation of the RREN. I was disappointed to be told that the CEU wanted and expected to have overall control of the journal.

The core of researchers and activists at the centre of critical Romani Studies at the CEU could be described as proponents of affirmative sabotage, basically using the master's tools or machine to dismantle/ruin the master's house/machine. Such a course of action could be described as making change and presenting challenges from the inside. In terms of Roma academics such a strategy could be comparable to the process within Indigenous Studies in North America, Australia, and New Zealand, where indigenous community members took up academic positions and worked within the academic system. However, such a strategy could be fraught with risk. The Black lesbian feminist writer Audre Lorde (2007) felt there was a danger of tokenism in such a stratagem and it might not bring about concrete change for they were working in parallel and in tandem with existing structures of power that could subvert transformative change. My views and concerns about Romani Studies at the CEU may be churlish for despite my reservations the work of the Romani Studies Programme was taking a radical departure from established convention in Romani Studies as is evidenced by the hostility it drew from established white Romani Studies academics, as outlined above. Instead, though I chose to work closely as a contracted consultant with another CEU programme 'The Roma Civil Monitor'.

The CEU Roma Civil Monitor (RCM) has played an important role in the EU Framework for National Integration Strategies that was initiated in 2011. The Framework obliged EU member states to develop national action plans that needed to be assessed and monitored. To facilitate such assessment the EU funded the CEU RCM to coordinate the formation of civil society national coalitions to undertake evaluation (2017–2020), this has included extensive training and capacity building and the involvement of Roma activists in survey template design and data analysis. In total 101 different local NGOs participated in the project as its direct beneficiaries. Out of them, 66 were Roma-led local NGOs (or individual experts declaring their Roma ethnicity). Although guided from a central point of coordination national coalitions and participants in the CEU RCM have steadily been handed more responsibility and have been afforded freedom to shape the direction of the evaluations. For example, the RCM (2020) synthesis report that I edited 'Identifying blind spots in Roma inclusion policy', asked local NGOs to identify and discuss the issues they consider crucial for successful Roma inclusion. Hence, through this more 'bottom-up' approach, a series of case studies were presented that were based on research plans devised by national coalitions with guidance from the RCM that whilst not giving the more uniform overview of previous reports presented valuable insights into persistent or undetected problems facing too many Roma. Some NGO coalitions involved in the CEU RCM developed meaningful and effective methods of involvement of grassroots NGOs with limited skills and experiences in monitoring. In some cases, partnerships between established NGOs and small/informal grassroots organisation in several countries effectively divided tasks, grassroots NGOs collected and provided local data to a national-level coordinating organisation skilled in analysis and reporting. Thus, national-level and local-level NGOs learnt from each other. The CEU RCM constitutes a diverse civil society network and demonstrates such networks can work together in a European Commission funded project across all EU member states producing monitoring reports, capacity building, and transnational dialogue and understanding among Roma activists across Europe (Ryder, 2021).

Conventionally, monitoring and evaluation have involved outside experts coming in to measure performance against pre-set indicators, using standardised procedures and tools. In contrast, the work of the CEU RCM has created a unique partnership between Roma communities, civil society, and academics. For me this work felt more aligned to the ideals of the RREN, bringing what Gramsci coined as 'organic intellectuals' into a dynamic partnership with the academy. I hope that this important and innovative work by CEU RCM will prepare the foundation for even more participatory and egalitarian forms of research and evaluation where community members are actively involved in the design, data collection, and analysis of research, principles in tune with radical definitions of academic freedom.

Another example of innovative and ground-breaking work at the CEU in Budapest was the Open Learning Initiative (OLIve) established in 2016, a series of education initiatives for asylum seekers and refugees. A key catalyst to the establishment of the course was the refugee crisis in 2015 that brought many thousands of Syrian refugees to Budapest. CEU students felt compelled to press the university to offer educational support to the refugees and out of their concern OLIve was born. The course was based on the Roma Access Programme (discussed above) and that experience including the deployment of core staff was instrumental in establishing OLIve. A core philosophical value in Olive was the principle that regardless of their perceived status within society migrants and refugees have a right to education and this is viewed as an integral part of the CEU's mission of being a socially-engaged university. However, the CEU suspended the OLIve programme in 2018 as a result of the so-called 'Stop Soros' law that proposed extra taxes on organisations that help refugees and migrants enter Hungary (Balla, 2018). To be more precise a tax of 25 % of revenue (with the exception of humanitarian aid) was proposed to be levied on all funds sourced from abroad (Immigration Funding Fee). Individuals or groups that help illegal migrants gain status to stay in Hungary would be liable to prison terms under the provisions of the law (Boros, 2018). The legislation was defined in a way that appeared to threaten prison sentences for entirely legitimate legal and humanitarian work. In 2020 the Court of Justice of the European Union ruled that the controversial measures in the law were stigmatizing, harmful and in breach of EU law. The Hungarian government withdrew the measures.

Another important initiative that involves the CEU is the Open Society University Network (OSUN). OSUN is a global partnership of educational institutions dedicated to expanding access to higher education for systematically disadvantaged and minority populations and to nurture critical thinking, amid the resurgence of authoritarianism. A central aim is to build a new model of global higher education premised on the principles of an open society. Soros has endowed the network with one billion dollars ($1 billion (OSUN, 2020). OSUN will include the 'Threatened Scholars Integration Initiative' to support academics at risk of persecution, war, or other life and work-threatening circumstances. This initiative will provide extremely important and much needed support to academics making a stand for academic freedom and freedom of speech where such stances can incur heavy penalties.

Conclusion

This overview of the work of the CEU and its response to the authoritarianism of Orbán has not been uncritical. At times caution, timidity and adherence to conventional academic tradition and practice have it can be argued blunted its efforts to nurture innovation and resist challenges to academic freedom. Despite such criticism, it cannot be denied that the CEU, in particular through some of its pioneering work, as outlined in this chapter, has sought to make academia and knowledge production more inclusive. By providing, space, recognition, and platforms for marginalised groups the CEU has helped challenge the elitism of academia. The CEU can also be said to have resisted the commodification of academia, which holds the notion higher education should serve the needs of the labour market rather than society. A testimony to the value of the CEU is that an insecure and confrontational national leader felt threatened by its critical discourse and sought to diminish and sever its influence in Hungary.

With some poignancy Professor Joseph Stiglitz, nobel prize winning economist warned at the final degree award giving ceremony at the CEU in Budapest that "an assault on anyone's human rights is an assault on everyone's human rights". Nothing, he said, is more symbolic of an open society than academic freedom and free media, both of which are now under threat from the self-described "illiberal democracy" of Hungarian president Viktor Orbán. (CEU, 2019). Soros was not to return to Hungary, a fear of attack from a fanatical Orbán supporter being one reason (Walker, 2019a). It is difficult to imagine the impression the whole episode of the Lex CEU and Stop Soros Law must have had on a man who in his youth in Hungary had narrowly escaped the Nazi concentration camp, an experience that had prompted him to champion the ideals of an open society, ideals at odds with the vision of a closed society that Orbán now propounded.

Chapter Four
Gender Studies and Culture War

Central and Eastern European feminism was somehow disrupted in its development by communism and its interpretation of state feminism. State feminism can
be defined as a gendered view of state action. In other words, the state should
promote women's status and rights in relation to men's, and democracies can
and should be feminist (McBride and Mazur, 2013). However, under communism,
a form of state feminism meant women experienced what became known as the
'double burden' where women found themselves suffering from the demands of
being both a worker and a mother. State feminism in socialist states like Hungary, despite state declarations to support gender equality, did little to challenge
patriarchy in reality. Today the former communist bloc remains at the economic
periphery between the advanced and developing economies, a "bridging, yoking
position between hegemonic feminisms and the feminisms of the poor women of
the world" (Bodó, 2015). Since the change of system in 1989 new approaches to
and conceptions of gender equality have gained traction.

Gender Studies courses started to appear in universities in Central Eastern
Europe in the 1990s, in part as a response to the marginalisation of women's
rights in the communist period. The expansion of Gender Studies courses was
in part attributable to US foundations and institutions. The MacArthur Foundation was a major funder for such programmes in the Russian Federation, as was
the philanthropist George Soros through the Open Society network across Central
Eastern Europe. In Hungary, the Central European University and the University
of Szeged were offering Gender Studies courses by the mid-1990s. Gender Studies
was framed by some as a symbolic marker of the westernisation of Central Eastern Europe and its transformation from communism to a liberal democratic market democracy (Zimmermann, 2005). Gender Studies is now being challenged in
the region, as in other parts of the world, by the radical right and nationalists in
what has been termed a culture war (see chapter one for a fuller discussion of
the concept).

As part of a backlash to globalisation and the demise of class-orientated politics, nationalism has remained a persistent feature of the political landscape
and its characteristics have been accentuated through what can be described
as cultural nativism, part of the culture war discussed in the introduction of
this book. It is a conservative revolution that sees its mission as preserving
and protecting insular and rigid conceptions of identity rooted in history and tradition (Sayan-Cengiz and Tekin, 2019). It is in this context that the reader should

https://doi.org/10.1515/9783110749816-006

consider how and why the Orbán government chose to revoke its recognition of Gender Studies degrees in Hungary.

Revoking Gender Studies Degrees

In 2018, members of the Hungarian Rectors' Conference received an email from the Hungarian Ministry of Human Capacities requesting comment on a draft decree. They had less than 24 hours to respond. This was surprising given it was August, a month when universities are closed and many are on vacation. What was more startling though, was the fact that within the large document, Subchapter 16 to be precise, there was a clause that in effect revoked all permissions given to postgraduate Master's programmes in Gender Studies (Pető, 2018). The decision impacted on two universities in Hungary, one being the Central European University (CEU), a private university financed by the philanthropy of George Soros, which had been offering an MA in Gender Studies for over two decades. The other university impacted by the decision was Eötvös Loránd Tudományegyetem (ELTE), a state university that had started to offer an MA in Gender Studies two years earlier.

The Government justified this measure in a response to an independent MP who posed the question 'Who does the MA in Gender Studies harm?' The Ministry reasoned there was no demand for the MA degree in Gender Studies on the job market and it was thus unsustainable. The popularity of the two courses and career success of alumni, some of whom had remained in Hungary and had carved out successful careers related to their studies, refute such a claim. However, the ministry also argued that the subject could not be considered an academic discipline, but was an ideology and was not appropriate for university-level education. In addition, the ministry felt the course was not compatible with the Government's conception of human nature (Barát, 2020, Hungarian Ministry, 2018). This ideological justification was clearly at the crux of the decision and will be elaborated on later in the discussion.

The Hungarian Accreditation Committee, which gives advice and guidance on study programmes, stated that it had not been party to the drafting of the Government proposal and did not endorse the professional and academic arguments used to justify the proposal (HAC, 2018). Outside of Hungary the Political Studies Association, an organisation that supports social science research, stated in a letter to the Hungarian Ministry of Education:

> The Political Studies Association is alarmed by the Hungarian government's proposal to ban Gender Studies programmes within its higher education institutions. This represents,

we believe, a serious attack upon academic freedom and the spirit and ethos of the university as a centre of learning and expertise (PSA, 2018).

The European University Association (2018) felt that the decision by the Hungarian Government signalled an unprecedented case of state intervention in higher education in the EU and declared:

> Such a ban would pose a serious threat to academic freedom and institutional autonomy in Hungary and would confirm the trend towards increased state control that began with legal reforms in 2014, which have already undermined institutional autonomy in Hungary's universities.

EU education commissioner Tibor Navracsics, a member of the Hungarian ruling party Fidesz and former cabinet member, defended the decision by stating, "The whole case has been absolutely misinterpreted". According to Navracsics, the decision of the Government was administrative, and only revoked the right to issue diplomas in Gender Studies. Research or courses on gender, and the right of the CEU to award US-accredited diplomas in Gender Studies, would be untouched (Zubaşcu, 2019). Such an argument was disingenuous: although the CEU offered double degrees validated by Hungary and the US, it was under pressure from the Hungarian government about its legal status, a pressure that would lead to its relocation of teaching operations to Vienna (See Chapter three). Furthermore, Navracsics failed to appreciate that with the revocation of Gender Studies degrees no state university would be offering Gender Studies specific degrees, and the end of such programmes would undermine the ability of academics to work solely in this study area, to develop research interests, to train and nurture future researchers and teachers.

The Moral Crusade on Gender and the Family

Gergely Gulyas, Prime Minister Orbán's chief of staff, informed the Reuters news agency "The Hungarian government is of the clear view that people are born either men or women. They lead their lives the way they think best, but beyond this, the Hungarian state does not wish to spend public funds on education in this area" (Reuters, 2018a). The Deputy Prime Minister Zsolt Semjén stated that Gender Studies "has no business in universities" because it is "an ideology, not a science" (Oppenheim, 2018). To understand these comments and the rationale to revoke the state recognition of Gender Studies degrees, there is a need to place the comments in the social, cultural, political, and historical context of Hungary.

Hungary can be viewed as epitomising a traditional male-dominated society. The European Institute of Gender Equality (2020) has ranked Hungary as 27th in the gender equality index with 53.0 out of 100 points. In the Hungarian Parliament following the 2018 election, there were 174 men and 25 women, representing 12.56% of MPs. Hungary has the lowest parliamentary representation of women in Europe, currently globally in 158th place out of 189 in the respective list of the Inter-Parliamentary Union (2021). European survey data indicates that Hungarians are one of the nations that most highly regard the value of family (Horn and Keller, 2015). A 2017 Eurobarometer survey of the 28 EU member states found in all countries surveyed with the exception of Sweden, that the majority of respondents believe that women are more likely than men to make decisions based on their emotions. Hungary had the highest proportion supporting this view (87%). In the same survey, Hungary was the second-highest European country to believe the most important role of women is to look after the family and home (81%).

Such patriarchal and family-focused tendencies may thus explain the Hungarian government's hostility towards Gender Studies. Such gender conservatism on the part of the Fidesz government had been evident before the decision to revoke recognition of Gender Studies degrees in 2018. In 2010 the Hungarian government started the process of radically revising the constitution (The Fundamental Law of Hungary 2012). The constitution revealed its religious and social conservatism by declaring "the institution of marriage as between a man and a woman" as "the basis of the family and national survival". A clause also seeks to enshrine the fundamental human right to life from the moment of conception, a pro-life viewpoint strongly aligned with anti-abortion, Christian fundamentalist and radical right interest groups. In 2013 the constitution was further revised to define marriage and family as a union between man and woman and stated "family ties are based on marriage" seemingly discarding the validity of same-sex spouses as well as other forms of cohabiting families (Felix, 2015, 57). In 2010 the Government decree on the national curriculum of kindergarten education was amended and diluted references to avoiding gender stereotypes and justified this action by asserting there was a need to promote the moral and mental development of children and the need to limit the spread of "gender ideology" (European Parliament, 2018, 31). In 2012 a new Family Protection Act reinforced the heteronormative conception of marriage. The school national curriculum was also modified by emphasising the biological nature of gender roles/differences (Vida, 2019).

In 2020, the Hungarian Parliament refused to ratify the Istanbul Convention that aims at combating violence against women, arguing that it promotes gender ideologies and illegal migration (Agence France-Presse, 2020). Furthermore, a draft amendment submitted to the Hungarian parliament by Justice Minister Judit Varga declares that children must be guaranteed an upbringing based on values stemming from Hungary's Christian culture. The amendment asserts "The basis for family relations is marriage...The mother is a woman, the father is a man." The amendment also stipulates that it seeks to "protect children's right to the gender identity they were born with". Deputy Prime Minister Zsolt Semjén stated that gays should not be allowed to adopt children and start families (Reuters, 2020). Hungary's parliament also passed a law in 2020 making it impossible for transgender or intersex people to legally change their gender (Knight and Gall, 2020, Barát, 2021).

In 2021, Hungary's parliament inserted a clause into a law that addressed paedophilia, banning gay people from featuring in school educational materials or TV shows for under-18-year-olds. Critics accused the Government of conflating paedophilia and LGBTQ people. Leading human rights advocates across Europe castigated the reform as an affront against the rights and identities of LGBTQ persons (Rankin, 2021). If we accept the view that homophobic attitudes and legal measures are a litmus test for democracy and sexual minority rights (Takács and Szalma, 2020), then this legislative act should be viewed with deep concern.

It is evident from this overview of gender-related social policy that the decision on Gender Studies degree recognition forms part of a wider framework of social conservatism. The factors propelling this conservatism are explored in more depth in the next section

The Conservative Cultural Revolution

Within the politics of Orbán, as with other authoritarian leaders, there is a strong seam of patriarchy in the sense that such politics normalises obedience to a 'strongman'. A strongman who will be the father to the nation in a time of crisis, resolutely and decisively delivering conservative and traditionalist remedies to cure the ills of the nation (Galasso, 2019), representing a macho and combative leadership in search of enemies to be vanquished.

The hostility of the Orbán government to Gender Studies, same-sex adoption, the depiction of LGBTQ people in the media, and transgender identity reflects the gender binary frames that are central aspects of authoritarian populist movements in many countries. Hence, radical right parties like Fidesz frame the role of women as primarily a spouse and mother and exalt traditional conceptions of the family (Mayer 2015). Elsewhere other radical right parties and figures have taken similar positions on Gender Studies. For example, 'Alternative for Germany', the first far-right party to enter the German Parliament since the Second World War, has stated it would cease all gender-studies funding, university appointments, and research if it were to attain power. In Poland, the radical right has successfully deployed anti-abortion, anti-LGBTQ, and anti-gender rights rhetoric to mobilise its political base. In his inauguration speech in 2019, the populist Brazilian president Bolsonaro pledged to "liberate" Brazil from "gender ideology", "political correctness", and "ideology that defends bandits".

Mudde (2007) notes that radical right parties reflect a "natural differences" mindset with reference to women and men, consequently as women are the only sex that can give birth and are thus essential to the demographic survival of the nation, it is argued this role must be defended. Indeed, following the 2018 election Orbán bemoaned Hungary's declining population and outlined how the family would be a central feature of government social policy in an attempt to increase the birth rate for a nation whose leaders were hesitant to reverse a declining population through inward migration. Orbán offered a series of financial rewards and incentives to those having children, which included the non-payment of tax for those women having four or more children (Kingsley, 2019). Loans are offered to women under 40 who marry, and progressive debt reduction with the birth of children, and debt cancellation with the birth of the third child. In addition, state-subsidised mortgages were offered with deductions for married couples who have at least three children, while a more recent reform reduces the commitment to two children (Geva, 2021).

A report prepared by the European Parliament Committee on Women's Rights and Gender Equality (European Parliament, 2018) expresses a number of concerns as to how this conservative approach is negatively impacting on women's rights. In particular, the report notes that Hungary does not have a specific law on gender equality and that the general law on equal treatment does not sufficiently address discrimination against women. In addition, the report notes there is poor political representation (discussed above) and that senior political figures have made sexist comments, many of whom are within the governing party. Vida (2019, 15) provides an overview of the Hungarian government's gender policy:

> Hungarian women are held up primarily as wives and mothers, regarding them as reproductive citizens of the nation against the demographic deficit of the country or in favour of Christian family values. Through the recreation of a nationalist, conservative, heteronormative family-supporting patriarchal discourse, which is also anti-gender and against LGBTQ rights, the Government seeks to undermine liberal democratic values, as well as the global and European human rights agenda.

The family-centric and socially conservative policies of the Orbán government have to be considered in the context of the conservative revolution or culture war, as it can be termed, discussed elsewhere in this book. There are also economic, political, and religious factors within this matrix that are worth considering.

The transition from 1989, the change from communism to a liberal free market, had a major impact on gender relations. Many women lost their jobs as industries were privatised and/or streamlined and welfare state cutbacks meant fewer childcare places and a reduced value in state benefits for children and families. However, transition did enable a more autonomous feminist movement to emerge in Hungary and for debates to materialise on issues like domestic violence and patriarchy (Fodor, 2013). For some men, the emergence of a more vocal feminist movement and culture in Hungarian society has presented a challenge to a traditionalist and patriarchal worldview. Such a sense of challenge may have been especially acute for uneducated and unskilled men who experienced a severe loss of status and economic power in the process of the Hungarian transition. It is such men at the social and economic periphery with profound economic and cultural grievances who are said to form a major constituency of support for radical right populist parties in Hungary and other countries. Care though should be taken not to reify working-class men in this respect (Maiguashca, 2019).

Gender studies, with a more fluid conception of gender roles and identities, challenges and recognises gender as something shaped and interpreted by societal norms, values and forms of hegemony that can be reorientated and challenged, and should not be seen as immutable biological facts. Such a transformative worldview presents a profound challenge to the static and insular conception of gender roles as espoused by authoritarian populists (Apperly, 2019). Hence, gender equality is derided as an 'ideology' and/or 'theory', and its critics accuse it of propagating propaganda for LGBTQ rights, for reproductive rights, and sexual and equality education (Kováts and Põim, 2015). Such motivation was evident in the Hungarian government's decision to revoke recognition of Gender Studies degrees and espouse a position that perceives women's and men's roles as complementary rather than equal, with women consigned to motherhood and the reproduction of the nation through childbirth and reproductive labour (Serughetti, 2019).

So, Gender Studies has been disparaged as not being a legitimate academic discipline but is seen as a mendacious ideology whose adherents wish to undermine and subvert the nation and its traditional identity, with a political agenda that does not constitute legitimate scholarship (Coffé, 2018). Such thought was evident in a speech by the Hungarian Government Deputy Prime Minister Zsolt

Semjén, who stated the main problem with "gender ideology" is that "it got a huge support from Brussels" and these "tiny, but loud lobby groups" want to "force their deviant view to the world" (Cited in Felix, 2015, 69). Hostility to Gender Studies is also shaped by the communist past of countries like Hungary where Soviet policy on gender has been perceived by its radical right critics as 'state feminism' that forced 'social engineering'. In the minds of such critics, Gender Studies and feminist movements are the residues of such Soviet-era mindsets (Hall, 2019). Authoritarian populism also contains an element of anti-intellectualism that reveres the so-called 'common sense' thinking of the people and seeks to cast the thinking of feminists in particular as tainted by 'cultural marxism', agitational politics and, forms of 'political correctness' that create an intellectual tyranny (Grzebalska, et al, 2017). This new conception of common sense also demonises liberal democracy and human rights, in effect a consensus on equality issues that has been highly influential in Europe and North America since 1945 (Pető, 2020). Evidence of the Government's ban being ideologically motivated is revealed in the Hungarian government's decision to introduce a new MA in 'Family Policies and Social Policies' at Corvinus University (Barát, 2020). Interestingly the programme was not launched in 2019 because of insufficient student demand.

Having mapped out the historic, socioeconomic, cultural, and political motivation for the Hungarian government's hostility towards Gender Studies, the next section of the chapter presents personal testimony from a number of actors directly impacted by the decision to revoke recognition of Gender Studies. It furnishes insights into resistance strategies and reflects upon the impact of the Government's decision on academic freedom in Hungary.

Voices of Dissent

In the following section, testimony from important figures in Hungarian Gender Studies research is presented. Two students of Gender Studies also detail their views on the revocation of the Gender Studies degrees.

Erzsébet Barát

Erzsébet Barát is an Associate Professor in the Department of English, at the University of Szeged and since 2000 Recurring Visiting Professor in the Gender Studies Department at CEU (Central European University). She holds a PhD in Linguistics from the Social Sciences Faculty, Lancaster University, UK.

I started my career as a gimnázium (high school) teacher of English and Hungarian in 1982. Six years later I moved into teaching English as a foreign language at the medical school in Szeged for an academic year, waiting for a post-opening in the English Department at my old alma mater, JATE (József Attila University in 1990, which is where I have been employed ever since. In 2000, as part of the transition changes, various colleges and universities, including JATE were merged into the single unit of the University of Szeged.

At the beginning of the transition period, the US was sending EFL teachers and some academics to Central Eastern Europe as Peace Corps volunteers to help develop English language skills. One US colleague arrived at the same time as me in the Department. She had a degree in creative writing and taught courses on Black women's writing in the US. We were on the same wavelength and this generated my interest in Gender Studies. In addition, at the university in Szeged we developed Gender Studies by creating a module of ten different courses. In those days, a university degree took five years and ended with what you call now an MA; BA degrees were issued by colleges and they took four years. The module system was very effective, students could have the final two years to select the relevant courses and write their thesis in the scholarly field as well; there was great scope for such modules.

From 1992 to 1994 I went to the University of Queensland on a scholarship by the Australian Government where I could study Gender Studies related topics more intensely. Such was my interest in the subject I decided to start a PhD by research at the University of Lancaster. The British Council helped with the tuition fees for three years but only after I covered the fee for the first academic year of my PhD. I decided to use my savings from Australia to finance the research that was not available in Hungary at the time. I did not see this as a sacrifice, although it was. It was a conscious decision and I felt lucky to do something I felt passionate about. I wanted to ensure that I had the very best training and support in my area of interest. I felt that as a high school teacher, I had been in my element, and by studying in the UK I believed I could be in the same position in higher education. The University of Lancaster had the first BA and MA programmes launched in Gender Studies in the UK during my studies. They launched the programmes through an incredible one-week conference. I could go along and see all the key figures in the field of scholarship in a single event, like Judith Butler, Elspeth Probyn, Gayatry-Spivak who were leaders in the field, It was a great place to be. I gained my PhD in 2000.

The Gender Studies module is a specialisation in the Bologna-type two-year MA in English Studies at Szeged, and as such it was not directly affected by the Government's decision to revoke the MA in Gender Studies. Besides, the three semesters of the specialisation are more like a feminist cultural/literary studies programme, while the ban concerned a four-semester MA with a social science orientation. So, the Government decision did not ban our specialisation module. Our Gender Studies Research Group (TNT), in addition to teaching the programme, organises an annual Gender Studies conference, we have a website, and publish a blind peer-reviewed online journal 'TNTeF: Interdisciplinary e-Journal of Gender Studies'. The journal is the only Gender Studies journal in Hungary that publishes scholarship on Hungary in Hungarian (with the odd English language contributions). All of this work continues – pro bono.

The Government's revocation of Gender Studies degrees stemmed from their view that the subject is not a science, but rather is an ideological and political tool. I think that the Government was not entitled to make such a decision. Sadly, the Hungarian Accreditation Committee and the Rectors' Conference were not 'up in arms' about all of this, they had nothing to really say when seeing the Government's interference in academic autonomy and freedom. This inertia by lead academic bodies reveals a wider problem in Hungary of institutional sexism, they just did not care at the end of the day and were relatively passive. Institutional sexism is a serious problem: when it comes to promotion, or looking for a head of department, many universities simply do not think of/consider women. The university where I work has an official anti-discrimination document. I tried to put it into practice when a female colleague was applying for a head of department position in competition with her male colleague (who already was head of institute and deputy dean!!! – this can be seen as a grabbing of decision-making positions). Both candidates had equal support and standing in the faculty, but I could not use the anti-discrimination policy to ensure the position went to a female candidate in this case. Institutional sexism is evident beyond Hungary and with the hegemony of neoliberalism and growth of dictatorial regimes we see growing hostility to academic subjects like Gender Studies that are critical of hegemony and how they (ab)use power.

Sometimes EU surveys appear in which people are asked what women's place should be in society. I always ask why such surveys do not ask what place men should have in society, such a question seems to problematise women's visibility in the public space, leaving men's visibility a natural entitlement. But to return to the point, such surveys reveal a very high level of conservativism towards gender relations in Hungary. In the future, I hope a new Hungarian government will again recognise Gender Studies as an MA course. However, wider changes are needed so that women have a more equal chance of promotion in higher education and access to research funds. Gender Studies should produce critical scholarship in existing gender relations of power that prioritize hegemonic masculinity, the central value of the sex-gender system. Today it is needed in Hungary to expose the disappearance of explicit gender policies and their reconfiguration as "family policies" (meaning white, educated, middle-class hetero families preferably married).

A vivid memory that I have that gives important insights into the situation in Hungary is when Orbán came to Szeged as his last stop on the eve of one of the elections: elderly women were treading on each other in order to be able to see him and kissing his hand, almost worshipping him as if he was a religious figure. This is a global phenomenon, Erdoğan manipulates Islam, Modi Hinduism, and Orbán uses and weaponises Christianity in the same way. This is why he put his controversial provisions on gender relations and identity into the so-called Fundamental Law.

A lot of painful and distressing conversations are needed in higher education and beyond. Patriarchy and radical conservatism are connected to Orbán, these forces shape his behaviour on a daily basis. Some have the assumption that this is a demographic issue reflecting the values of older and often rural people, but I don't think so. I have some very conservative students, for instance. We live in an increasingly precarious world where your situation can change suddenly and those who lose their work find there is little support for them. This fuels anxiety and scapegoating.

In Hungary, there is a culture of fear. Within Orbán's rhetoric there are numerous examples of combative and racist language, he constantly looks for enemies and has to be the victor, he loves to engage in a fight. The fear people have is not without reason, for you can be punished. Some people would say Hungary is not autocratic and that you can express your views but doing this has consequences in work and access to resources. You don't want to 'set yourself on fire'; if you do so, will it change the system? We need collective resistance. Sadly though, the trade unions in academia and elsewhere are weak. Collective resistance takes a long and committed struggle and a strong sense of self-worth. It is easier for me to speak out as I have tenure and retire soon but I am also the kind of person who likes to be open and express an opinion at public fora, it's the way I am. I cannot afford to change who I am without losing my cultural capital. If I held back, my sense of self would be damaged and discredited. I do understand the fear some have but at the same time, I do not understand why they are not fearful about what might happen if they do nothing! This is my fear, the fear that fear of power emboldens and nourishes autocracy.

Judit Takács

Judit is a Hungarian sociologist. She is a Doctor of the Hungarian Academy of Sciences and works as a Research Professor at the Institute of Sociology of the Centre for Social Sciences. Her main research interests are social attitudes, family practices, childlessness, community engagement, and the social history of homosexuality.

Gender Studies has been a part of the intellectual life of Hungary for many years; it was and is more than the two MA courses at the CEU and ELTE. Other universities have also made important contributions, including a Gender Studies research centre at Corvinus University and there is an important network of researchers at Szeged University. However, the decision to not recognise the MA courses at CEU and ELTE was not right. People should have the freedom to choose what they want to study. One of the main arguments from the Government was that there was no demand for such a subject in the labour market. However, there are many people who studied humanities working in international companies. Such studies provide workers with useful analytical tools and the ability to contemplate deeply about the nature of society. However, if we look at the converse argument that studies should ideally be linked to specific jobs, it can be seen that there are many jobs where such skills are needed and Gender Studies is an academic field of study that can nurture these skills. If one follows the logic of the Government, we might end up banning subjects like, say, Phoenician studies. How many study that? This market-led thinking and belief that education must precisely serve the needs of the economy and be useful and practical are reminiscent of Soviet thinking (see chapter two).

Of course, there were more ideological reasons on the part of Orbán supporters to oppose Gender Studies; for them such study is indoctrination of young minds and bodies. Such thinking is reminiscent of the classic conservative argument used against sex education, namely that it can fill young minds with dangerous thoughts. There is this thinking that if you learn about gay people, you run the risk of becoming gay. In the past when I was interviewed in the media I and others would try and understand what these opponents were angry and upset about. Sometimes in the face of blatant propaganda and prejudiced views, it was difficult to keep one's 'cool'. I did my best though to stay calm and tried to accept they had something to say. Getting angry would have meant losing them forever and never changing their minds. However, there are some fanatical homophobes who, like anti-vaxxers, will never be persuaded, such is their irrationality. Yet there are some who do not totally believe these things who might be capable of entering into a dialogue and have the capacity to embrace a more open-minded viewpoint. The media has not helped; it is not possible to have such debates in the media. On Hungarian television channels, supposed to provide public service, there were programmes discussing the merits of reparative therapy, actually giving a platform to those who support reparative therapy, instead of merely presenting neutral reportage highlighting the dangers of such an approach to homosexuality.[1] Arguments in the media that claim studying Gender Studies will turn your son into your daughter seem to work. The question of how we can reach ordinary Hungarians is an important one. I have to follow the rules of academia and produce books and articles that will be referenced and used to support constructive arguments and hopefully provide support and impetus for policy change. Sometimes, though, I enjoy acting as a traditional activist in the sense that sometimes moving away from the academic and legal arguments, as important as they are, it is good to show personal empathy.

The rising mood of homophobia has impacted negatively on some colleagues. I have had a number of colleagues who did LGBTQ-related research who have left Hungary because they felt uncomfortable. One was on the list of academics named by Figyelő, a now pro-Orbán weekly magazine, which attacked well-known progressive academic researchers. For him this was the last straw. I was also listed in the Figyelő article (See chapter five). Academic freedom is not well in Hungary. You can witness negative developments in the changing structure of how universities function. Things were different in the past. In 2003 the Equal Treatment Act was introduced, and Hungary became the first country in the whole world where gender identity was protected and to have the right enshrined in national law. During that time there was a great team of experts and activists working together in Hungary who were highly effective in their LGBTQ rights advocacy work. Of course, back then Hungary hoped to enter the EU and we Hungarians had to prove our commitment to liberal values. I remember in 2007, which was the 'Year of Equal Opportunities' you could apply to the Ministry of Labour and Social Affairs for small research grants related to equality, and there was scope to conduct research on LGBTQ issues but now this does not happen. It is a warning that you should not take things for granted. Rights are not safe for perpetuity, they need to be defended. Orbán has been adept at interpreting efforts to give groups rights as an attempt to take rights from others, hence he talks a lot about the need to protect families and to protect them from cultural threats supposedly presented by feminists and LGBTQ people.

---

1 Reparative therapy is a form of pseudoscientific treatment, that encompasses conversion therapy. Proponents argue it can overcome or mitigate homosexual desires and replace them with heterosexual ones. Sometimes such therapy is aligned with fundamentalist religious views.

Lubomir

Lubomir was an MA Gender Studies student at the Central European University.

My entry into CEU life came after a number of years of personal struggle. I had been a prominent LGBTQ activist in my native Belarus, but this had led to surveillance and harassment for me and my family. Getting a scholarship to study Gender Studies at the CEU gave me valuable respite from the troubles I had faced in my homeland. Studying at the CEU was also an eye-opening and revelatory experience. In my studies I was exposed to new theories and paradigms such as Queer theory. These were revelations for me, giving me insights into the potential for new forms of activism that might one day be deployed in my homeland. My classmates came from a wide and diverse set of backgrounds and nationalities and it was invaluable to learn about their personal experiences, which in some cases mirrored my own in terms of victimisation. This sense of fraternity was strengthened through the students in the group frequently discussing the challenges now facing the university, for the Hungarian government from 2017 seemed to be embarking on a campaign against the CEU, by refusing to validate Gender Studies and the so-called Lex CEU (See chapter three). The tensions of the time and the frame of the Hungarian government had something of the prosecution of Socrates to it, the CEU was perceived by the state to be 'corrupting the minds of the youth'.

Boglárka Tóth

Boglárka is a Hungarian PhD student and was a student in Gender Studies on the MA programme at ELTE.

I was raised in the 17th district of Budapest, in the suburbs. My upbringing was conventional, and my father worked in more working-class occupations like bus driver and handyman. My mother had a higher level of education and income and worked in the health/food/communication sector. It was a family typical of transition Hungary, traditional roles were changing. It was a family that was more class conscious than gender-conscious and the challenges to many working-class families were not easy during this time. My father comes from a very rural village and spent most of his life in absolute poverty, so getting these jobs in the first place was a step up for him. He was just happy to provide as much as he could both for himself and us, at least that's how it felt. My father told stories about how they did not have a bathroom at all when he was a child for example. My family in general was more on the poor-side, lower-middle-class

I would say. Money was always a concern. That's why the class and money element was always stronger, I think.

I did my first degree in social sciences at ELTE and chose the Gender Studies MA as it was always a topic I was interested in. I remember in my BA studies I took a course on Gender Studies. It was a bit strange, as the teacher they employed for sexual minorities was a psychologist who interviewed LGBTQ people for psychological assessments. The teacher seemed to believe that most gay people are sad, so the focus was on suffering, and not on what being part of the LGBTQ community is like. I think most of the time the teacher's personal views did not feel like they made an impact on what they taught. There were cases when it did of course, but that was less common. They usually focused on the less 'radical' topics of Gender Studies, however, mostly because they are the base to understand feminism, but I also think they tried to show how reasonable Gender Studies is, and what exactly it is "used" for.

I had always had an interest in these issues and would discuss them with my brother at the dinner table. I was concerned how women are treated. Even in high school, I started to notice that girls and boys are treated differently, especially since I went to a Christian high school. I also remember asking my mother if she knew more about this, so she told me about how she is often "sexualised" in her workplace because of her body, and how her superiors at the time made dirty jokes at her expense from time to time. It was very heart-breaking for me to hear this. In choosing to study Gender Studies I had some sense that something was not right and it was good through these studies to have numbers and theories that I could tie to the issue and help me understand. My mother was a bit concerned about the choice of the MA but only because she feared such a course might present limited career opportunities.

I started the MA in Gender Studies in 2018 and shortly after this, the Government decided to stop validating the course. I was not shocked by the decision given the political climate of the time; this was around the time of an election and the 'Stop Soros Bill'. Propaganda claimed that Gender Studies was dangerous because it could make people LGBTQ. There was a kind of hysteria. I think it's very complicated as to why this hysteria arose. But to a degree, I also think it is because people have this sense, that the world is unfair, or they are struggling maybe financially. And they are looking for someone to blame for that, but instead of trying to find the "truth" or trying to be critical of capitalism, for example, they pick a mysterious group of people whom they claim secretly control society and make everything worse for everybody else. I think for some that's easier to accept than thinking about how the roots of their issues might come from the current structure of society. I think this is common in places where religious fundamentalism is popular. Most major religions don't believe that being gay could be within the range of the "natural" human experience. I also think hegemonic masculinity has something to do with it; gay men are threatening because they are both more "feminine", threatening the ideal of what a man can be like, but they also imagine that gay men view them the same way as they view women, so they are afraid that these men will be violent and take advantage. Lesbians on the other hand are the "forbidden fruit" to a degree, and for a man who feels entitled to have sex with any woman, the existence of women who are just not interested in men is going to be infuriating. Lesbians also have a different idea of "beauty" in a sense, so they are sometimes less feminine and people who are very strict about gender might get angry just from that. In general, I think the question of why people are homophobic is very hard to answer because this is a complex issue, but I still feel religion has a lot to do with it (and here I mostly mean Christianity and Islam). The issue with the Hungarian government is that they push certain agendas to stay in power. They try and present things in a binary way that fires up peoples' emotions and passions. The attack on Gender Studies is an example of them trying to enrage people with false claims that through Gender Studies women will stop shaving and become lesbians.

I became involved in activism for the first time by getting involved in actions to save Gender Studies. There were many meetings and events at ELTE to protest against the decision to not validate Gender Studies. I was involved in the day of action where classes, at ELTE and other universities, were staged on the theme of Gender Studies. I was surprised at the level of support we received, including from a Jewish university, I guess they felt a sense of solidarity because of their historical experiences. This was the first time I was involved in a protest, maybe I was one of those 'ivory tower' types not so good at taking action but able to think an issue through and come to a position. Also, it was a 90-minute bus journey to get into the campus from the suburbs and I had to work, so time for activism was limited. I got involved though because I felt inspired. I think we Hungarians, in general, do not like protests much but I felt a real need to do something. As well as being involved in the campaign to save Gender Studies, I became involved with an NGO as an intern/volunteer working with them on lesbian identity issues.

Protests come in waves and they have lifespans, but people get tired. I am very interested in the work of Black Lives Matter – they have schedules where they plan out not only activism but how to support others so they can be free to offer support and time to a campaign. Activism needs networks of support to stop people from getting tired. Interestingly the feeling of protest did not subside at ELTE, many students from the Gender studies class became more drawn into activism and campaigns. Everyone started to participate or keep an eye out for already existing NGOs and there was a growing mood to no longer let injustice against women slide in their personal lives.

The Need for Painful and Distressing Conversations

Erzsébet Barát notes that there may be a need for a 'painful and distressing' conversation to be had about patriarchy in Hungary and the degree to which it is ingrained in Hungarian society, a sexism that Boglárka Tóth found deeply distressing when her mother confided in her as to the extent and scale of the problem and how she is sexualised in her workplace. A sensitive but moot point is to consider why in the 2018 election in Hungary 52 percent of women voted for Fidesz-KDNP, compared to 46 percent of men. How did this come about?

In identifying the roots of patriarchy in Hungary we may need to go deeper than the current administration in identifying its source. Under communism, there was a so-called 'dual morality', which meant that people had to stay silent on political issues, and in exchange, their private lives were respected by those in power. Consequently, gender issues were under-developed and many women had little enthusiasm for raising challenging questions as they accepted the sacrosanct nature of the private sphere under communism that was prized as one of the few freedoms people felt they had (Papp, 2019). Thus, in the former countries of Central Eastern Europe, communist egalitarianism erased notions of difference, and women were compelled to be good workers and good mothers. In this context, the public sphere became a space of oppression and aroused women's distrust. Within the private space, traditional hierarchies were maintained and women were charged with nurturing and caring for the family, the man being the central breadwinner and political voice in the public sphere. These are sentiments and positions that still have pertinence today. Part of the legacy of communism also meant that some women are suspicious of feminism, as it is deemed to conflict with the traditional family-centred socialisation that they received. Soviet-era propaganda denounced feminist ideology as a bourgeois distraction to the real challenges facing the socialist state. Feminism, with its emphasis on individual as well as group emancipation and its propensity as a critical philosophy to challenge and overturn oppressive conventions and practices, was seen as a threat by the communist elite (Temkina and Zdravomyslova, 2014). The same perception has shaped the Orbán administration's stance and strategy towards the feminist movement and hence their decision to ban Gender Studies and castigate and demonise those who seek to promote gender equality.

The testimony reveals that at best the senior academic leadership's protests at gender injustice in Hungary including the ban on Gender Studies have been half-hearted, probably reflecting what Barát called in her testimony 'institutional sexism'. Globally, successful academics are overwhelmingly white and male with a westernised epistemology that exalts and privileges 'western imperial knowledge', which is often masculinised, competitive, and hierarchical (Lynch and Ivancheva, 2015). Men have tended to dominate university leadership positions and their adherence to the tenets of Fidesz politics and Hungarian patriarchy and possibly in many instances both have reduced the incidence of serious challenges to institutional sexism. Of course, there are cases of women reaching senior positions but in some situations that has involved embracing masculinised mindsets.

The testimony provided by the Gender Studies practitioners and students in this book touches upon the economic woes that beset Hungary in the time of transition, challenging and undermining, in some cases, traditional conceptions of gender relations. In her testimony, Tóth depicts the disorientation in her family where her father became the secondary breadwinner in an economy that favours and rewards skilled and educated workers above manual. Tóth's father seems to have come to terms with such changes, but other men have not. A significant body of men have, because of the lack of clear and credible political and economic alternatives, been drawn into the politics of resentment, blaming outsiders and external forces for their predicament, and seeing tradition and conservative values as the best route out of the series of woes, real and imagined, that beset their lives. Such positions serve hegemony by deflecting blame from the structural factors that have made life increasingly difficult for many in Central Eastern Europe.

Eszter Kováts (2018) cautions against casting hostility to Gender Studies and equality as a mere regression that frames these tensions as a binary of past versus the future and closed-mindedness versus open-mindedness. Kováts argues that a neoliberal and human rights consensus with its emphasis on individualism, identity politics, and liberal rights has failed to fundamentally challenge a range of inequalities and injustices that have a structural foundation. In other words, anodyne politics has emerged that fails to offer a serious challenge to neoliberalism, a state of affairs that bolsters the economic and political elite as well as patriarchy. It is argued that authoritarian populist leaders have been able to use gender to forge broad coalitions of support that unifies religious, conservative, authoritarianism and the aggrieved (those alienated economically and culturally who span the class divide) against a common enemy, namely feminism. In other words, the issue of gender can be perceived as a 'symbolic glue' integrating anti-EU, anti-liberal, anti-communist, and homophobic attitudes, which can galvanise and mobilise electoral support for authoritarian populists (Grzebalska, et al, 2017). Such mobilisation can be seen as a product of post-transition democracy where a neoliberal politics has marginalised debates on class and inequality and instead spawned forms of identity politics that fail to speak to many, in particular the white working class at the periphery. Frustrated and feeling ignored, such constituencies have been attracted to the radicalism of authoritarian populism (Kováts, 2018). However, neglect of class issues is also argued to be attributable to the rise of identity politics where, according to Fraser (1995), recognition rather than redistribution has become a primary driver of social movements. Some would argue that feminism has dovetailed too neatly with neoliberalism in propounding social and political agendas that do not challenge neoliberalism but can even bolster it (Kováts, 2019).

Such arguments, though, need to be balanced against and contrasted with strands of critical gender thought. For example, Barát (2021) argues that the struggle to challenge Orbán's attack on gender equality is undermined if it is framed by some feminists as the "hidden ideology of the gay lobby". In other words, a claim that the present situation stems from the depoliticising agenda of contemporary trans politics that places cultural issues above economic. It has been argued that such fissures in the gender equality movement run the risk of bolstering the radical right's attempt to frame gender-critical views as extreme. Critical gender thinkers such as Barát contend that neoliberalism should be challenged, but such critique should not be confined to what can be described as 'structural criticism' of a self-contained political economy as the precondition for changing non-economic aspects of gender relations. Barát (2020) advocates de-centring the concept of gender as grounded in biology and thus challenges the ideology of heteronormativity grounded in an essentialised biological sex.

The discussions centred on recognition or redistribution as priorities, and whether gender roles are fixed and biologically determined or whether such roles are fluid and open to reinterpretation and reorientation has been emotive and difficult in recent years. Such tensions are evident in many countries including Hungary. However, through deliberation and negotiation, new understandings and alliances might be formed. Barát (2021) alludes to such alliances by proposing a radical left coalition around an inclusionary empty signifier of "feminist people" that spans and encompasses trans, queer, and feminist interests and is open to negotiation, part of the 'difficult conversation' that needs to be had.

As part of the new transformative politics of gender equality, "difficult discussions" may need to also reflect on the failings of liberal feminism. Liberal feminism has sought to feminise social hierarchy rather than eradicating it. A liberal feminist 'equal-opportunity' paradigm has created imaginaries and notions of the possibility of a kind of meritocratic gender equality. The achievements of a small and tokenised female elite who have broken the glass ceiling and risen to the top cannot disguise the fact that many women remain highly exploited and at the margins (Galasso, 2019). Disillusionment with liberal feminism might be propitious for the formation of a new radical consensus on gender that can offer an effective challenge to authoritarianism. However, it has been argued that identity-focused campaigns have, to some degree, failed to resonate with the wider public. It can be said that to date the progressive voices ranged against the forces of reaction that clamour for bans of Gender Studies, reflecting the politics of misogyny and homophobia, have lost a number of battles in this culture war (Pető, 2020). How can the gender equality movement more effectively mobilise against authoritarianism?

These 'lost battles' it has been claimed could be attributable to false binaries created by some critical activists using cultural frames (positional fundamentalism) to demonise groups and individuals who themselves may be victims of neoliberalism and oppression (Kováts, 2020). It is argued that such stridency, dogmatism, and self-righteousness drive some at the margins into support for the radical right. As a self-proclaimed critical social justice activist-scholar, I need to reflect carefully on such charges, I do recognise such charges have a foundation and should not be rejected. However, I do believe that it is possible for critical and feminist movements to avoid deep schism and internal fracturing, simultaneously addressing economic and cultural marginalisation and offering an effective challenge in broad-based campaigns. The popularisation, growth, and in some respects, adaptation of the Black Lives Matter social movement perhaps proves this point. I will return to this extremely important discussion in the concluding chapter of the book, but part of that discussion will rely on a vision of intersectionality that challenges neoliberalism. Intersectional understandings of exclusion recognise class, gender, race, and temporal positions can be interconnected in producing forms of exclusion with multifaceted dimensions (Weldon, 2008). Such notions and perceptions of marginality might be more effective in shaping broad and transformative coalitions that challenge economic and cultural hegemony. Intersectionality has been a key driving force in the activism of Black Lives Matter in the US, and through transnational intersectionality in the global south, oppressions centred on class, gender, race, caste, and global capitalism have been challenged.

Debates or what could be described as 'painful and distressing' conversations are being staged on the significance of biology in gender identification and rights. Higher education is proving to be an important forum for these intellectual exchanges. At times these debates have been fraught with tension and discord. Controversial speakers have been met with protests, boycotts, and 'non-platforming' where institutions are encouraged to withdraw invitations to speakers and/or where speakers are disparaged to the extent they suffer reputational damage (Norris, 2020). These intense debates about biology, culture, and the economic system and their relevance to gender need to be had, but care must be taken to avoid deep schism that might permanently fracture the gender equality movement, and which could undermine freedom of speech within higher education if contestation is not properly articulated and protected. Correspondingly, academics need to be attentive, when availing themselves of the academic right to free speech, to the pain and suffering that might come from positions they take on issues such as transgender rights that might bolster the prejudices directed at such groups. A careful balance will need to be mediated between these two positions through academic dissensus and deliberation in the quest for a radical consensus within the gender equality movement. Regarding the gender equality movement, there are networks and alliances that have long existed between different strands of feminist and LGBTQ activism, and have managed to work together despite different perspectives. If the gender equality movement can find its way to achieving a radical and unifying consensus, then such a powerful lobby might more effectively be able to advance the gender transformation of higher education, a process that would challenge institutional sexism and patriarchy in the academy as well as the masculinised competitivity of audit culture. Such changes would have profound consequences for academic freedom in the context of gender inclusivity.

Chapter Five
The Hungarian Academy of Sciences:
The Triad of Academia, the State and Business

After introducing measures that impacted on the Central European University and Gender Studies, that were discussed in the previous chapters, the Orbán government revealed the ambition and scope of the radical vision it held for academia and knowledge production in Hungary with its plans for the Hungarian Academy of Sciences (HAS). Critics argued that the reforms unveiled in 2018 would stifle the autonomy of the HAS and presented a serious challenge to academic freedom. This chapter details the history of the HAS and the manner and nature of the reforms the Government introduced which radically reformed the management and financing of the HAS as well as its relationship with the state. The chapter also explores the rationale of this reorganisation and the resistance posed to it by the academic community. The chapter concludes by considering the broader question of the relationship between academia, power, and the wider public.

History of the Academy

The HAS was established in 1825, in part as a response to the perceived decline of the Hungarian language and culture. Important acts included the standardisation of the Hungarian language and publications on orthography, grammar, and a dictionary. The HAS was financed primarily through a major contribution from Count István Széchenyi who offered one year's proceeds from his estates to this cause. The establishment of the HAS can also be seen as a reflection of a growing sense of nationalism in Hungary that wished to see greater autonomy for the country within the Habsburg Empire and the ability to express a sense of nationhood (Pótó and Fónagy, 2016). These sentiments found expression in the failed war of independence of 1848–49. However, with the establishment of the dual monarchy in 1867 (see chapter one) the HAS started to receive state subsidies. Its ties with the state were further bolstered by the fact that many of its presidents were also ministers of Hungarian governments and its board was dominated by the aristocracy. The HAS by the turn of the twentieth century was a prominent part of the Hungarian intellectual establishment, albeit a conservative one (Körtvélyesi, 2017).

https://doi.org/10.1515/9783110749816-007

The conservativism of the HAS prompted the People's Commissariat for Public Education of the short-lived communist revolution in Hungary (1919) to suspend the operation of the HAS with the intention of major restructuring. However, this reform never materialised and under the authoritarian leadership of Admiral Horthy, the HAS was financed through a state subsidy administered by the educationalist Count Kunó Klebelsberg who believed culture and science could play an important role in the reconstruction of the country. In the inter-war years, the conservatism of the HAS was evident in its relative disinterest in natural sciences like chemistry and physics which in countries like the USSR and Germany were being greatly promoted and seen as the engine of a brave new world of technological advance (Graham, 2004).

Post-war Hungarian communism transformed the HAS in 1949 into a Soviet-type academy that witnessed an increase in the representation of natural sciences and the creation of the Academy's network of research institutes in the 1950s and 1960s (Pótó and Fónagy, 2016). Despite becoming a centralised communist research institution integral and subservient to the five-year plan cycle of the Hungarian socialist economy the HAS is said to have also become a refuge for researchers critical of the regime who could work without having a direct influence on university students through teaching (Körtvélyesi, 2017).

After the regime change, the HAS rehabilitated academics who had been proscribed and excluded under communism and the institution was financed through state funding and grants. Supporters of the HAS claim its present-day prestige stems from the fact that after the regime change in 1989 scientific merit rather than political loyalty became the primary criterion for being elected as a member of the HAS (Nolan, 2018). The HAS remained an important voice in the intellectual life of the nation and continued to function as a society of distinguished scientists and intellectuals, alongside a broad research network of 15 institutes and 150 research groups comprising about 5,000 scientific researchers and administrative staff up to the period of reform in 2018/19 (Walker, 2019b). Perhaps though the latent conservatism of the HAS is reflected by the fact that in 2016 it was estimated that only 35.3% of researchers employed by the HAS were women (MTA/HAS, 2016).

Political interference in the HAS and its use as a platform to frame national identity have been prominent features of this organisation's historical development, and it is thus not surprising that in 2018 the Orbán government unveiled plans for the HAS that critics argue reflect a major intellectual and cultural reorientation of its role, these are outlined in the next section.

Reform of the Hungarian Academy of Sciences

In 2018 the Minister of Technology and Innovation, László Palkovics announced the Government planned a new network of research institutes within the HAS under the supervision of the Eötvös Loránd Research Network (ELKH). Six of the thirteen ELKH board members are appointed by the HAS and six by the Ministry of Innovation and Technology, with the head of the board appointed by the ministry and holding the casting vote. The ministry will also be responsible for the bulk of the HAS institutes' funding (Gardner, 2019). The reforms were criticised as an attack on the autonomy of the HAS and it was feared that only pro-government research would be funded.

The timing could be viewed as audacious as it came after the European Commission had referred Hungary to the Court of Justice of the European Union on account of how it had dealt with the Central European University. The commission had expressed concerns about the right to academic freedom in Hungary. The HAS reform meant in effect that the minister Palkovics would become the arbiter of policy-making on research, development, and innovation. Palkovics gave the HAS's president László Lovász, a world-famous mathematician, just 54 minutes to comment on the proposal sent to him via email. The bill implementing the proposal passed in the Parliament in a matter of days in 2019. For Lovász it was reported the aggressive and improper manner in which the changes were communicated and the Government's approach to negotiations had eroded trust between the HAS and government on this matter (Walker, 2019b). As was outlined in the state budget framework presented by the Ministry of Finance, 28 billion forints (87.5 million euros) out of the total amount of 40 billion forints (125 million euros) allocated to the division of the Hungarian Academy of Sciences in the state budget would be transferred to the control of the Ministry of Innovation and Technology in 2019 (HAS, 2018)

Palkovics decided to withhold the disbursement of subsidies covering material expenses of research centres for 2019 and threatened to withhold the salaries of employees in an effort to force the Presidium of the HAS to agree to the handover of its research network to the Government. As a result, the HAS lost financial control over its budget (i.e. its financial autonomy), and became unable to make binding contracts for the whole year or longer, causing great instability within the HAS (HASF et al, 2019).

The Rationale behind Reform

In terms of justifying the reforms to the HAS the Hungarian Government reasoned that the measures lay the foundations of a new regulatory and financing framework for science and innovation policy, focused on applied research. In a statement, the Government declared it wanted to see more research done, with more government funding. According to the Government, the reform of the HAS was part of broader efforts to increase research that supports Hungary's economy. According to a government official "Every forint of state funding spent on research must generate concrete returns for the Hungarian economy and eventually for Hungarian society" (Zubașcu, 2019).

The Government's plan for the HAS was explicit in articulating a vision of scientific research contributing to innovation and enhancing economic competitiveness. The rationale for this reform was the allegation that Hungary's main economic problem was poor performance in innovation, and the weaknesses of universities and small and medium-sized enterprises, weaknesses that it was claimed were primarily responsible for poor economic performance. Consequently, the centralisation of research resources was seen by the Government as a necessary means to improve innovation and to increase Hungarian patents (Szűcs, 2019). In a statement issued by Hungarian holders of European Research Council grants, it was argued that:

> Success in innovation will only come if basic research is pursued on a high level. Genuine scientific breakthroughs are not produced to seek immediate answers to today's innovation challenges. They are designed rather to widen the scope for future solutions to these, lay the foundations for emerging fields of science, or highlight unexplored trends in our societies. Any approach suggesting that the sole purpose of basic research is to provide the key to today's innovation challenges can only be deemed short-sighted. Therefore it is essential that scientific excellence remain the only criterion for funding decisions at the only Hungarian institution dedicated to basic research. It is also essential that the funding for basic research should not be reduced at the expense of industry-driven applied sciences (ERC grantees, 2018).

Critics also noted that research institutes external to the HAS can submit grant proposals to the new research fund that was once in the control of the HAS. It is feared that the money taken away from the HAS will be available to research institutes established by the Orbán government and its allies, which serve political purposes (Hungarian Spectrum, 2019). Some critics argued the measures were motivated by a desire to funnel EU research grants into pro-government research institutes (Halmai, 2019b).

It is also important to view the reform of the HAS in the context of how the largely pro Orbán media accuses academics and research institutes of serving a liberal agenda and wasting taxpayers' money on studies that embarrass the Government, such as Gender Studies (Halmai, 2019b). Such bias and framing were evident in an article published by Hungarian pro-government magazine Figyelő, with the headline "Immigration, homosexual rights, and gender science – these topics occupy the researchers of the Academy". The article claimed that the research topics of the Centre for Social Sciences of the Hungarian Academy of Sciences are politically suspicious. The article advocated that the Government should have a "greater insight" into the HAS's work. In a similar vein and an attempt at sarcastic humour Figyelő presented a quiz where readers had to guess, based on the title of scientific publications on topics of gender, sexual minorities, and migration, if the publications were from "Soros-henchmen", CEU researchers, or from researchers from the Hungarian Academy of Sciences (Takács, 2019).

Critics though argued that despite the assertion of the minister Palkovics that the autonomy of institutes in the HAS would not be violated and the freedom of research would be guaranteed, it was undermined by his statement that certain topics must be selected for research as state subsidies should not be used freely (HVG, 2018). Palkovics has in the past criticised the HAS for venturing into politics. "Their job is to give scientific advice and recommendations," he said in an interview with a pro-government web portal. Palkovics proceeded to say, "In some cases, the academy has moved towards being politically active and this is not their task" (Walker, 2019b). Critics of the reforms have expressed fears that research that offends the ideological agenda of the Orbán government will not be funded. Emese Szilágyi, Scientific Secretary of the Institute for Legal Studies at the HAS, informed Human Rights Watch that researchers in the HAS feared they would not be free to choose research topics and would instead be compelled to conduct research in fields the Government wants and be expected to provide findings that support their preconceived ideas (Gall, 2019). In one interview an anonymous source stated:

> There is now great pressure in the HAS with the Government taking greater control of resource allocation which carries within it an element of threat. Research areas the Government favours such as the family get prioritised and funded and research areas not favoured are marginalised. At the moment there are few cases of individual academic rights being overtly violated but there is now a culture where managers warn their team members that a certain research topic may make problems and ultimately the proposal is dropped. You could say there is an element of self-censorship where a fear for future funding allocation or career advancement makes some fall into line or become more careful and cautious.

Indeed, there is a fear that the social sciences, often targeted in attacks by pro-government media like Figyelő (discussed earlier) will be marginalised. Such attacks by government figures and pro-government media and indeed the culture war that the Government has zealously stoked, it could be said, has created an intimidating atmosphere for Hungarian intellectual life, increasing the chance of self-censorship. Such censorship was evident in October 2018 when the Hungarian Academy of Sciences banned a conference presentation related to gender (Baird, 2020). Another presentation on the media was also dropped, Beáta Mária Barnabás, the Deputy Secretary General of the Hungarian Academy of Sciences, reasoned the presentation could not proceed due to the "political angles" of the subject matter. It was claimed by some observers that this move was an attempt by the HAS to save its financing by appeasing the Government through self-censorship (Adam, 2018).

Palkovics, the minister who spearheaded the reform of the HAS, was also to incur the distrust of some in the wider research community with the decision in 2020 by the Ministry for Innovation and Technology to alter the list of funded grants from the National Scientific Research Committee. Two researchers who openly supported the science policy of the Orbán government were identified by the ministry as deserving of financial support in their research and were included by the ministry in the list framed by independent scientific evaluators of those to be funded. One of those involved in the evaluation, the academic László Acsády stated that he did not consider the unprecedented intervention to be compatible with the principles of scientific evaluation he represented, therefore he resigned from his position (Spirk, 2020). Such actions have cast further doubt as to the Government's commitment to the integrity and autonomy of science.

Trust in the integrity of the Government's HAS reform and the ELKH board was further eroded by the Government's choice of president of the board, namely, Miklós Maróth, an Arabist and classical philologist and ally of Orbán. An interesting insight into Maróth's view on higher education is revealed in an interview in 1994 when he said the Eötvös Loránd University is too democratic, and systems with strong hierarchy are more effective. He has been described as the "rational face" of the government's anti-migrant campaign (Kolozsi, 2019). Maróth is reported to have said Europe's problem with reference to migrants is its excessive tolerance (Kolozsi, 2019). Bayrakali and Hafez (2016) report that Maróth warned against the Islamisation of Europe and a loss of Christian culture. According to Halmai (2019b) Maróth is said to have predicted a clash between the Islamic and Christian cultures, claiming Muslim migrants are incapable of integration into European culture because of religious attachments. His comments on Muslim migrants have reverberated across the Hungarian press (Kolozsi, 2019). According to Said (1978) 'orientalism' exaggerates and distorts the differences of Eastern peoples and cultures as compared to those of Europe. It perceives the East as uncivilized, and dangerous. Some commentators argue such thoughts are rife in Fidesz political rhetoric and thought.

In his first comments as president of the ELKH Maróth requested a performance-oriented salary system and for a system of professional employee evaluation to be established. Maróth complained that researchers in the Czech Republic produced significantly more scientific papers a year than in Hungary. Critics responded by saying this was a gross oversimplification, and Maróth was being selective in his use of data as although the Czech Republic produces more outputs, Hungarian papers are cited more. In addition, it was noted Hungary spends only 1.3% of its GDP on research compared to the Czech Republic's 2% (Index, 2019). Maróth's comments could be viewed as reflecting a longstanding trope in criticism of academics, in that they are deemed to be unproductive, a theme and mindset that formed part of the Government's rationale for the HAS reforms.

Resistance

Part of the HAS response to the reforms involved a legal challenge through the Constitutional Court regarding the HAS's right to hold property. Under the reforms, the HAS was obliged to provide usage rights over all of their assets to the new Eötvös Loránd Research Network. The HAS argued that although it was still the owner of these assets on paper, they had no effective control. In the opinion of the HAS, this was a form of expropriation, that legally can only be undertaken if done in the service of public interest, and with immediate and unconditional compensation (Index, 2019). To date, the legal challenge has gained little traction.

The General Assembly of the HAS voted twice with an overwhelming majority against the intentions of the Government. For example, at the extraordinary session on June 15th, the HAS demanded that the proposed amendment of the Law on the Hungarian Academy of Sciences and the Law on the 2019 state budget be withdrawn from voting in Parliament since these amendments were prepared without prior consultation with the Academy (Szigeti, 2018). Academics also staged demonstrations against the reform, one in February 2019 involved scientists holding books above their heads and forming a human chain around the HAS building (Gardner, 2019). The challenge to the reforms also drew international support. The European Federation of Academies of Sciences and Humanities expressed concerns about the law, which it saw as a government attack on academic freedom and a threat to the autonomy of science (Zubașcu, 2019). Many researchers in the HAS felt the Government reforms would impact negatively on the freedom of science and could lead to self-censorship. An assembly of academic employees held on 24th January 2019 drafted a statement on the autonomy of science and this led to the formation of the Hungarian Academy Staff Forum (HASF). The HASF is a legal entity with fifty active members but has a wider support base of approximately 500 people. Trade unionists are in the association, but the two main unions focus on negotiating working conditions and contract changes whilst the Hungarian Academy Staff Forum focuses on political interference and the threat to autonomy and academic freedom and has been prominent in organising protests, discussions, and disseminating information about the HAS reforms (HASF et al, 2019).

Palkovics was interviewed in the pro-Orbán business magazine Figyelő. According to him, an unprecedented situation had arisen. "The Hungarian Academy of Sciences has shifted to direct politicisation on certain issues and against the Government's negotiating and professional intentions" (cited in Nolan, 2018, 46). Clearly, trust between the HAS and the Government had become fractured. Tamás Czárán, a member of the Hungarian Academy of Sciences and professor of theoretical biology, was quoted as saying with reference to the HAS reforms

> any compromise is capitulation in this case. The autonomy of the academy either remains intact or will be lost altogether. Once the Government decides it will take control over an institution, it does so without asking questions or listening to expert advice. In my personal opinion, under such circumstances, it is only rigid resistance that may have some, at least symbolic, effect (Nolan, 2018, 46).

The next section through interview and discussion probes more deeply the nature of the resistance to the reforms and determines whether resistance was meaningful in the sense that Czárán wished to see.

Voices of Dissent

In this section of the chapter a former researcher in the HAS and researcher in the ELKH research network that was once administered by the HAS provide testimony.

Ziegler Dezső Tamás

In the following extract, Ziegler Dezső Tamás a former researcher at the HAS provides insights as to why he resigned.

I started work in an international (American) law firm and then became a research fellow at the Hungarian Academy of Sciences (HAS). The HAS was an inspiring place to be back in 2007 when I joined, it was generally a free-thinking, friendly community. There were many inspiring colleagues and older academics with great knowledge about their academic fields who you could learn much from. On the other hand, there were also some 'old school' type academics who were less productive and to some degree, most of us knew that there was a need for moderate reform.

After 2010 things started to change: an appraisal system (points/credit system) was introduced. This reform was fully in line with similar government initiatives, but it was prompted from inside HAS by a new leadership. Initially, I supported it as I thought it might help the HAS develop but eventually became an opponent of the whole system as I could see it created a toxic environment. People became afraid if they did not publish. Within the system there was a minimum set of points and a higher one, eventually, the minimum target was dropped, and then an average of points achieved was calculated and this seemed to push the bar higher and higher. As far as I was concerned this goes against the traditions of the academy, because this system mostly appraises highly ranked international publications, but not Hungarian ones, so we had to abandon our role in explaining changes to the laypeople outside the academic world. Furthermore, many of my colleagues had to leave the academy, because they also taught at universities and as a result of low points, they were banned from doing so, and most of these people chose university teaching over the HAS. While this limitation sounds rational, it had a horrible effect on the institution, we lost many important colleagues. Sometimes I was involved in important works, but points were not given to such work. For example, I worked with the Swiss Institute of Comparative Law on an EU funded research project looking at child abduction, but this did not receive points in the HAS system until it got published, neither did work I did for the OSCE or visiting professorships I held at foreign universities. It felt like a new form of barbarism where only publications mattered, it was a dumb interpretation of science that seemed to only count traditional academic outputs like book chapters and journal articles. I also feel there is a bias against East European topics and more original ideas in western journals unless you use the clichés and forms of Western science. In my opinion, this is a kind of East European academic self-colonisation trying to adhere to requirements that are criticised even in the west quite harshly. So Hungarian academics find themselves between western academic elitism and eastern authoritarianism, and the mixture has a horrible effect.

Later, HAS was stripped of its institutes, they created a new research institution called Loránd Eötvös Research Network (ELKH). I resigned because I did not want to work under a leader like Miklós Maróth, who was appointed president of the Managing Body of ELKH. Maróth has made controversial statements about Muslims. Maróth once made what he considered to be a humorous comment about dressing Muslim immigrants in pigskins and has argued integrating immigrants coming from Muslim countries is impossible. In addition, he believes Europe's problem is one of excessive tolerance.[1] In the past, he had different positions and was once open to the notion of an open society. His appointment was part of a power grab by the Government of the HAS.

During these reforms, the whole environment at ELKH changed – people started to talk less to each other in the corridor, and the welcoming and open community became a group of fearful, individualistic individuals trying to survive. I had seen such developments before. I had worked at the Corvinus, the part that eventually was separated from the Corvinus by the Government to form the University of Public Service (NKE). It was there I saw how toxic it is when politics directly enter academia. Government figures were regularly invited to speak at the university. I have to say there were also 'old school' types there reminiscent of academia under communism who were well disposed towards authoritarianism. Stories circulated that some staff who were publicly critical of the Government would not be promoted and indications that this would be the case had been signalled to them by line managers. In 2012 it was reported that the sociologist Ferenc Krémer was dismissed from NKE without explanation after 20 years in the job. Ferenc Krémer claimed that Fidesz is not a political party from the perspective of social science, but it stands closer to mafia-like structures. His professional competence was never questioned, and he believes he was dismissed for political reasons. In fact, he won a number of legal cases that found he had been sacked without proper legal reasons (See chapter 8).

I was disillusioned with the reaction to the new points system in the HAS, as many accepted the rationale and need for this reform and even later, when we saw how it works, they did not protest against it. When the HAS was stripped of its institutes, some within the HAS organised protests but it did not feel there would be proper resistance at the leadership level. The President of the HAS László Lovász did make some critical comments in interviews about the changes but I did not feel there would be a proper resistance. His deputies said nothing. When the major changes of 2018 came there were votes against it in the General Assembly of the HAS.

---

1 For a fuller description of Maróth see this report: https://index.hu/english/2019/08/14/miklos_maroth_eotvos_lorand_research_network_hungarian_academy_of_sciences_takeover/.

I think it does not work when people do not robustly protest, the cautious diplomacy of Lovász is not useful in such cases. People need to organise in an open way, attempts to have behind-the-scenes negotiations, and to make backroom deals that do not have satisfactory endings is not the best strategy. At the CEU the protests were more robust. Yes, they were forced out, but their cause attracted global attention, I do not think the same happened to the HAS, apart from the support of certain scientific institutions abroad. As someone teaching EU law, I was especially sad that the EU remained silent in the case of HAS.

There were only around four of us that resigned from ELKH, as we could not accept the new situation. Financially, my resignation had a severe financial effect, I lost half of my income. Emotionally I was very attached to the HAS but feel the integrity of the institution had been compromised even before the more recent changes, as I noted earlier through the points system. I felt pity for those who remained. I have good connections to several of my former colleagues, they tell me many stories about changes at the institution.

Today, it is not difficult to see what the Government rationale is behind the new higher education policies. They want to change the system and it has been a step-by-step occupation by stealth. There have always been tensions between social sciences, humanities, and science and indeed competition. I think in the Government there is a bigger agenda to break social sciences. They have a master plan and some might accuse me of being paranoid but I feel they wanted to break institutions like the HAS, and they are succeeding.

I believe this should not be described as a populist process but something more akin to fascism: not neo-fascism, but a form of post-fascism, to be more precise. It is drawing inspiration from historical Hungarian authoritarianism with its anti-Enlightenment values and social Darwinism. It is a mindset and outlook which puts an aggressive nationalist myth into the centre. This is why they hate academia: it is scientific, rational, maintains some minimum standards regarding rule of law and human rights (tolerance and humanism), and it is a threat to the dumbed-down nationalism peddled by Orbán. Traditionally, historical populism in the US tried to support the interests and involvement of laypeople in governance (it was not as anti-democratic as it is regularly portrayed) and introduced forms of direct democracy. However, Orbán wants to push a part of the society out of the country: in a Schmittian way he is always searching for enemies, is breaking democracy and rule of law, and manipulates electoral laws, institutions, and power to win elections. He does not attack "the elites" in Hungary, as he was always part of them. This is not populism, in my opinion, but something far more complex and dangerous. It is an enemy of an independent academia.

The actions against the HAS did not generate huge public protests and this may be a product of the elitism of the HAS and its failure to communicate its work and value to the wider public. It has to be said some really valuable work was done at the institution, though. However, this is partly the nature of science: there will always be an element of the 'ivory tower' and detachment but of course much can be done to reduce these tendencies. Such perceptions of elitism of an institution like the HAS can be found in other countries and, in part is a product of the fact that many of our academic outputs are not accessible to the public only being available in journals or university libraries and, in many cases, written in English making the outputs even less accessible. In summary, elitism is a problem of science worldwide. However, our scientific institutions are not attacked because of it, but because of the inherent nature of science itself, as it serves as a mirror to the society and authoritarian politicians.

Zsolt Körtvélyesi

Zsolt Körtvélyesi is an assistant professor, international, European, human rights and constitutional law at Eötvös Loránd University and research fellow in the Eötvös Loránd Research Network.

I am a regular member of the Hungarian Academy of Sciences (HAS) not an academician as such (the HAS has a corporate membership which everyone with a PhD can join and there are the self-elected academicians, full and corresponding members, who enjoy a number of benefits and a lifelong salary). I am a research fellow in a research centre that was once part of the HAS but now finds itself in the ELKH network (Eötvös Loránd Research Network). I have been in this position for about seven years.

The stories I was hearing about HAS from the time I started working there described an almost Byzantine organisation. In the past, some dissident researchers were able to work there because they did not have contact with students and thus people who had fallen out of favour with say the communists found some form of exile there but on the same corridor might be the judge who had sentenced them for some political crime.

While HAS is a leading academic institution in Hungary, it has not always lived up to its image of 'best of the best' standards, one keeps hearing stories of people not sufficiently qualified gathering positions and resources whilst on small technical points others are denied progression – one distinguished researcher was denied progression because they had never published a monograph in Hungarian. I heard this described as a case of monkeys climbing to the top of the tree and pulling the ladder up.

It is important for the HAS and its intellectual role to be shielded, this might sometimes lead to charges of elitism and being an 'ivory tower' although attempts are being made to popularise the work of the HAS through podcasts, blogs and bringing it to the attention of high schools by encouraging HAS members to visit them. In terms of popularising our work, it is something we should continue to strive to do. Social science that deals with topics like migration and vulnerable groups is more politicised and might thus arouse more controversy.

Tamás Freund (President of the HAS) complained about some social scientists only making progress because they criticised the Government, but some researchers contend 'illiberalism' is a major societal problem and they have a duty to highlight and challenge this. Hostility towards liberal viewpoints leads to forms of self-censorship, there are many such cases and presents a tip of an iceberg. One academic recently wrote an article dealing with the constitutional court and EU related judgements. The obvious conclusion is you cannot explain the differences of opinion between these bodies unless you reach the decision that the constitutional court is reflecting positions it knows the Government favours. This demonstrates that this court has lost its autonomy. However, the author failed to reach this conclusion, he said he did not want to be drawn into 'politics' and through various intellectual acrobatics failed to give a clear judgement. One former constitutional judge led a project funded by the judiciary that wanted some analysis on government referenda, the final paragraph of the report praised how the frame for good judicial practice is present, despite the well-documented arguments to the contrary. The field of litigating referendum initiatives is probably the most illustrative case of constitutional demise.

Voicing criticism of the Government usually is an invitation to retaliation, creating a culture of silence. This atmosphere, unsurprisingly, also weighs heavily on academic speech. Speech in academic settings is a peculiar beast where filtering speech, as opposed to uninhibited speech, is central to the endeavour. However, where both the pursuit of truth and free speech suffer under government pressure, one can know for sure that academic freedom is violated.

There have been cases of direct censorship. A documented case of censorship at the largest countryside university, in Debrecen (the institution that granted an honorary title to Russian premier Vladimir Putin) did not trigger any institutional or personal response from the academic or the wider community in the country. Ágnes Kovács, a colleague active in research on judicial independence, had a paper accepted in Pro Futuro, the journal of the Debrecen law school. Confronted with threatening messages relayed through the university leadership, the editors decided not to publish the article that documented the dangers the appointment procedure poses to judicial independence (the text was made available as a working paper, noting the rejection of the publication on non-academic grounds). The blatant violation of academic ethics was carried out by the institution, leaving no hope for remedies in the form of an ethics procedure. The journal is still recognised as an academic journal by the Academy of Sciences, as being in the highest tier. Some are punished for speaking out. Debrecen is not the only place where such things happen, but let me mention another case from that university. One academic working there was told that he would not be promoted because he made critical comments about the Government position on the CEU in a televised interview. There are others who have been denied promotion because of their views. Some are sacked. In 2019 Andrea Kozáry, a long-standing academic at the National University of Public Service who taught police students was dismissed after she criticised the cancellation, for political reasons, of an international conference that the National University of Public Service had earlier accepted to host. The topic was hate crimes, including anti-LGBTQI and anti-immigrant crimes (Körtvélyesi, 2020).

The HAS could have been more active by responding to cases of censorship and other violations of academic freedom not only by issuing more and stronger statements but by fulfilling its role as the leading authority in matters of the Hungarian academia. This could have included ethics inquiries (as most of the problematic moves should be regarded as violations of academic ethics) and denying recognition e. g. delisting academic journals if they blatantly violate ethical norms by politically motivated censorship. On the second question, I don't have a strong opinion on how far the Academy itself should have gone. Delisting a journal seems like a 'no-brainer' but delegating other actions to other entities could have been a legitimate strategic choice. There is really no recipe for successful resistance after 2010, given a weak opposition and a cause that is not likely to resonate with the wider public.

Lovász László when he became the HAS president was not elected on a platform of being a 'freedom fighter', that is not his style or how he saw his role. However, he did slowly realise that he had to increasingly speak out and challenge the Government. In a way, though he did become the ideal figure for the struggle, it was hard to attack him or portray him as a leftist or lazy, unproductive academic. A Hungarian Academy Staff Forum was formed to monitor and challenge the changes to the HAS and did mobilise a number of people and raise the profile of the issue in the international media. but more radical action would not have worked. However, it is clear the HAS has been affected by recent reforms.

The research institutes operating within the HAS, comprising the leading research body in Hungary, were put under the control of a new entity with increased government control. Few are convinced that the elimination of normative funding for ex-Academy research institutes does not raise the threat of ideolog-

ical filtering, even if the pill is sweetened with the promise of more funding overall. The autonomy of the National Scientific Research Fund had been curtailed by
a 2014 law, but it was only recently that direct political control was put into effect, a first in the 35-year history of the Fund. The Ministry of Innovation and
Technology overruled the decision of the life sciences expert jury on the 2020
grantees, which triggered the resignation of László Acsády, the president of the
life sciences college, in protest. As a result of the ministry's interference, a proposal evaluated by the jury as the weakest is now listed among the applications
selected for funding. The president of the Academy of Sciences objected in a letter publicised in the media, and research project leaders (many of them ERC
grantees) including those winning in this round, signed public letters of protest.
The minister responded that he is also an academic and he represents the welcome introduction of third-party remedies against jury decisions and fought back
by attacking people who leaked the changed list. A researcher, supported by the
Hungarian Academy Staff Forum, filed a complaint and asked for the annulment
of the grant round, that was rejected.

Politics, Business, and Science

The discussion and testimony in this chapter regarding the reforms at the HAS
provide important insights as to debates around the role of the state in knowledge production and what the relationship should be between science, the economy, and the public. The voices of dissent profiled in this chapter feel that the
Hungarian state's intervention in the HAS was an affront to academic freedom
and autonomy. Concerns are also raised in the testimony as to the nature and
role of appraisal in the academic world, criticism of an audit culture is a common theme and point of concern in the book. Was the academic diplomacy
and search for consensus by the HAS misplaced? An anonymous source expressed some concerns:

> László Lovász, President of the Hungarian Academy of Sciences sought to defend the au-
> tonomy and integrity of the HAS. However, this was high politics and as a professional sci-
> entist, he was at some disadvantage as he simply did not understand the political game
> and the politicised environment he had to operate in. He was perhaps too much of the gen-
> tleman scholar who disdained from the bitter struggles of politics and tried to rise above
> this, sadly we live in times when such nobility is not always effective or respected. A failure
> to fully connect with the public and galvanise public opinion against the HAS reforms was
> symptomatic of how this institution was an 'ivory tower', aloof and disconnected from the
> wider public. I am certainly not saying the HAS does not do valuable work, but the public
> often fails to appreciate or understand it because of poor communication and outreach

strategies by scientists as well as the demonisation of so-called scientific elites by the political class.

The quote raises a number of points worth exploring on the degree to which academia can popularise its outputs and dispel and undermine charges of elitism and being a distant and privileged ivory tower. Here some balance and caution may be required. Science should be open and its results communicated to the public in ways in which they can digest the essence of scientific outputs and make some response but there will need to be limits and safeguards as to the nature of such involvement to ensure that populist forces do not dictate what is good or bad science on the basis of dogma and emotion. The HAS is probably not alone in being charged as a national institution for culture and science with elitism and it is such perceptions that may have facilitated governmental attacks on the autonomy of institutions like the HAS in Hungary and elsewhere because despite their important work, they were not able to mobilise or arouse the kind of public concern that might have persuaded the Government to step back.

Of course, in efforts to popularise science safeguards should regulate not only the public's involvement in science but also that of politicians. Democracies should promote the objectivity of scientists so they can seek and communicate the best approximation of truth, using their training and resources. Opel (2013) calls for an approximation as we will never know reality but can get close with scientific evidence and logical thinking. Political choices and decisions are made after the evidence is presented but should not happen in the reverse order. If politicians reject the evidence because of partisan viewpoints they should be challenged by scientists. In a world of growing political instability and partisanship, scientists are increasingly being challenged and buffeted by hostile voices. The consequences of these tensions are such though that scientists face serious moral dilemmas if they refrain from speaking out, there are also dilemmas as to how scientists can and should operate in the world of politics. Concerns as to the ability and manner in which scientists can participate in the world of politics are evident in this chapter.

It could be argued though that some criticism of the HAS and Hungarian intellectuals may be valid. Throughout the history of the Hungarian state since the eighteenth century, sections of the intelligentsia have aligned themselves to nationalist and authoritarian agendas, be it the dual monarchy, the Horthy regime, or communism (Zarycki et al, 2017). Furthermore, traditional and elitist conceptions of science often rooted in scientism have derided alternative forms of knowledge production outside of the academy and failed to build bridges and dialogue between academic institutions and communities. It may be the case that such failure has stoked negative perceptions of the intelligentsia and created fertile soil for the irrationalism and anti-intellectualism of the Orbán administration and explains the relative ease with which they were able to seize and reform the Hungarian Academy of Sciences.

The ideological bias of the Orbán government is evident in its attempts to counter what it perceives as left-liberal influences by establishing new organisations to promote their conservative agendas. This has included establishing 'think tanks' and research institutes to celebrate conservative conceptions of Hungarian history, with strong criticism of Hungary's socialist past and the liberal age of transition society after 1989. This cultural conservatism has included attempts to rehabilitate the reputation of the authoritarian leader Miklós Horthy (Hann, 2020). Educational and cultural reforms by such an ideological and nationalist government were bound therefore to stoke controversy and division.

The actions of the Orbán government are also steered by a deep mistrust of the intellectual class. This anti-intellectualism is shaped by the authoritarian populism that Orbán and the Fidesz Party are aligned to. As is typical of populists, Orbán strives to speak in the language of everyday people and appeal to popular concerns and tropes, no matter how base they might be (Scheiring, 2020). Populism has been described as a 'thin' ideology with limited intellectual refinement (Mudde, 2017b). Hence, Orbán has appealed directly to reactionary sentiments and has not hesitated to deride and attack what he deems to be liberal elites, including academia. Such thinking includes the elevation of what can be termed 'common sense' thinking above that of intellectual. Hence, the Orbán government has been assiduous in framing its anti-migrant campaigns as being formulated through listening to public opinion.

To give credence to perceptions of the Government being directed by 'popular will' and 'common sense' thinking, it has organised national consultations on topics like migration, the Covid pandemic, and its clampdown on LGBTQ images in the media (see chapter three) and claimed that the data collected has played a pivotal role in shaping the Government agenda. It should be noted with reference to migration that a highly distorted questionnaire was sent to Hungarian households on the topic of migration with numerous leading questions designed to solicit hostile responses to migrants. Examples of leading questions included the following: "There are some who think that mismanagement of the immigration question by Brussels may have something to do with increased terrorism. Do you agree with this view?" Another asks: "Do you agree with the Hungarian government that support should be focused more on Hungarian families and the children they can have, rather than on immigration?" (cited in Miles, 2015) The UN derided the survey on migration as "extremely biased" and "absolutely shocking" (Miles, 2015). The 2021 consultation that touches on the Child Protection Law contained the following preamble to one question: "Organizations funded by George Soros have launched a wide-ranging international attack on Hungary over the Child Protection Law. This law prohibits sexual propaganda directed at children in kindergartens, schools and in media accessible to children" (Hungary Today, 2021). The slanted and leading questions in these consultations illustrate the dangers of government manipulating research for propaganda purposes.

The idolisation of supposed common sense thinking by populism rests on the notion that it is authentic because it is grounded in everyday experience, the real world (Saurette and Gunster, 2011). This is to be contrasted with the paternalistic science of established knowledge elites (Priester, 2011). Such academic elites are depicted as being ensconced in 'ivory towers' and are viewed as a subset of a general elite. Populists often portray themselves as being the converse of the academic elite, who are it is claimed juxtaposed to the interests of the people through their desire to maintain their undeserved privileged position as the arbiters of what is right or wrong. It is claimed that through pseudo-scientific agendas these academics seek to give their politically driven discourse and reasoning a scientific veneer (Mede and Schafer, 2020). For Orbán and his supporters at its worst, this elite is part of a communist deep state, in which a crypto communist elite has sought to maintain its influence in institutions like universities, in which some, like the Fidesz supporting rector of the Corvinus University András Lánczi, claim the university sector did not experience 'regime change' after 1989 (Halkó and Megadja, 2021). The dangers of the trajectory of such thinking should not be forgotten, for the foundation of totalitarianism is anti-intellectualism, which encompasses the veneration of practicality and a stifling desire for uniformity.

Dominant cultural and political discourses are negotiated in what Bourdieu called a 'field of power', a social arena of struggle, where elites can propound, frame, and legitimise their conceptions of the world (doxa). In this social area, doxa is forged through the contestation and interplay of economic and cultural capital and the agendas of an economic and political elite and intelligentsia (Bourdieu, 1983, Bourdieu, and Wacquant, 1992). It is in this context that we must assess Orbán's efforts to establish and bolster cultural and intellectual hegemony in the field of power as evidenced by its reform of the HAS and more generally a culture war in Hungary premised on the politics of backlash. Backlash movements contain a deep nostalgia and desire to return to an imagined past but also profound challenges to dominant scripts. This often entails attempts to revise and transform established principles, goals, procedures, and practices (Alter and Zürn, 2020). It is such thinking that has emboldened Orbán to challenge migration, globalisation, the merits of the European Union, and now the functionality and purpose of science, culture, and higher education. Such notions have fuelled the Hungarian government's challenge to academic freedom, and autonomy as evidenced by its interference in the operation of the HAS.

As presented in the chapter, lead Fidesz voices have framed academics as prone to meddling in politics, 'loopy' in the words of Orbán, lacking common sense. They have also been denounced by figures such as Maróth for being unproductive, hence the reasoning goes there is a pressing need to align business and scientific development more closely together and incentivise academic outputs and measure them through quantitative metrics redolent of the business world rather than the academic.

It is interesting to note that the Orbán government's desire to prioritise and privilege applied science and harness it to the needs of the economy mirrors the thoughts of thinkers like the communist Bukharin who believed science must be subservient to the comprehensive planning of the Soviet economy, whereas the Hungarian thinker Polányi advocated a society where free intellectuals search for truth for its own sake, free from political, ideological, and economical influences (See chapter one for a broader discussion). For Polányi, an important prerequisite for such conditions was academic autonomy and freedom and was fearful as to how these might be affected if the state became too influential in the world of science. Such a position it could also be said conflicts with Aristotle's conception of scientific spirit as 'philosophizing to escape from ignorance' and 'pursuing science in order to know, and not for any utilitarian end' (Barnes, 1985).

A serious danger of trying to align academia closely to the world of business is the fear profit and motive considerations will override scientific judgement. Another concern is that such an intense symbiosis between business and science might diminish the chance to explore broader and more philosophical universal research questions that do not always have a direct or clear economic impact. Will such research be funded? An important debate is how far modern technology is dependent on science. The empirical evidence indicates few links between basic scientific research and the great mass of technical developments. Citation analysis indicates science seems to accumulate mainly on the basis of past science, and technology primarily based on past technology. Furthermore, it is worth noting that where science has made a significant contribution to practical action, this contribution can become greatly exaggerated, thereby providing spurious support for common sense assumptions (Stehr and Meja, 2005).

Science can be said to contain certain fundamental principles of (self-)organising that it does not share with other institutional spheres of society, which have their similar fundamental principles of (self-)organizing. The economy upholds a balance between supply and demand by the price mechanism and stimulates innovation and renewal through profit accumulation. Politics distributes power through persuasion and negotiation and is legitimised by the popular vote and majority rule. Science though is shaped by functional descriptions and manipulations of the physical and social world where ideas and intellectual outputs can accrue status and recognition (Hallonsten, 2021). These three spheres are not identical and it could be dangerous to transfer principles from politics and business to the world of science. However, such merging and colonisation have happened increasingly with the advent of neoliberalism that has spawned a form of academic capitalism. Critics complain this has undermined professional autonomy, judgment, and expertise (Brown, 2015) and runs the risk of higher education institutions veering into Foucauldian surveillance regimes via audit culture (Foucault, 1977). As indicated in the testimony in this chapter, it also might be misleading and inaccurate to assume that the quality of a scientific finding correlates completely with the number of citations of publication or the prestige of the journal within which it is located (Hallonsten, 2021). Measuring intellectual potency in such a crude form misses the reality of knowledge production that cannot be fully or accurately measured with quantitative metrics.

The Hungarian government's intervention in higher education defies more market fundamentalist principles of laissez-faire non-intervention and through its centralisation of institutions like the HAS could be described as being more ordoliberal, a form of neoliberalism that sanctions intervention for the sake of market stability. However, in this case, centralisation is being invoked in the name of business and economic efficiency to bolster a cultural and economic agenda. Despite the link between scientific innovation and economic development being exaggerated (see earlier discussion) the results of science can of course have some impact on innovation, wealth, and improved living conditions. It was this assertion that led to the institutionalisation of academic freedom and autonomy (Merton, 1970). Thus, interference in academic freedom could have economic implications but also consequences for political rights as academic freedom is a cornerstone of free and open societies.

Ethical codes in research have become an increasingly important concern but have tended to focus on legalistic contracts between the researcher and the researched centred on informed consent and anonymity. Little consideration has been given to the ethical duty of researchers to challenge interference in academic freedom and the autonomy of universities despite a reference to such values in a number of national and international conventions. It may be time to initiate such ethical discussions and codify concerns about overt statist and business interventions in the affairs of academia, giving academics a clearer steer as to the positions that should be taken when there are encroachments and giving greater clarity to the triadic relationship between academia, the state, and business.

The Public and the Popularisation of Science and Culture

As was noted in the historical section of this chapter that the HAS for a large part of its early history, especially in the nineteenth century had close connections with the aristocracy being major patrons of science, arts, and culture but also being prominent as scientific and cultural innovators. Later the HAS was closely aligned with political elites in the inter-war and post-war periods. As has been noted in the chapter the HAS has to varying degrees been disconnected from the wider public, in part this is an inevitable consequence of the increasing complexity of science and the nature of scientific innovation that is often reliant on detachment and autonomy. Indeed, such autonomy has been a major catalyst for scientific innovation and national socioeconomic development. However, as hinted at in the testimony some of the detachment may be attributable to academic elitism and aloofness and a failure to popularise science.

The popularisation of science is conceived as a process whereby science is made understandable and accessible to the wider public, to some extent it is shaped by a deficit model that sees the public as suffering from forms of scientific illiteracy (Vidal, 2018). Such an assertion has some credibility given the rise of pseudoscience that has manifested itself in climate change denial and hostility towards vaccines. Such scientific misunderstanding is a reflection of the weakness of public education but also a public sphere that according to Habermas (1989) has been refeudalised through its propensity to trivialise, overtly simplify and distort. Of course, public mistrust of science also stems from the mistakes, folly and some would argue arrogance of science and progress that has reaped numerous environmental crises that now confront the planet. In part though, as noted earlier, this gulf between the public and science and culture is also accountable to elitism.

Traditional approaches to popularisation have been framed as top-down efforts to inform and educate a passive audience (Tang, 2019). In popularising science and culture it is though not just a case of scientists becoming adept at parcelling their outputs into blogs, videos, and even memes in order to better communicate their findings, as important as such communication methods are. The popularisation of culture and science it could be argued should also have a democratising element, whereby the public might be engaged in forms of co-production with cultural and scientific leaders. Of course, this democratising process would need to be handled with care to prevent unscientific and even irrational public conceptions steering science and the arts and avoid the trivialising of scientific and cultural outputs (Daum, 2009). However, it should be noted that such activities have been strengthened through participatory research approaches and involvement where appropriate in research design, data collection, and interpretation. Such approaches are especially suited to the social sciences but there could be scope for some application of such approaches to other branches of science and culture. This is something the HAS may need to give greater consideration to, in order to dismantle public conceptions of ivory tower elitism. In democratising science and culture though the public should not be categorised as a homogeneous mass, tailored and nuanced outreach strategies will be needed to connect with a range of groups in Hungarian society.

The concept of academic freedom could be interpreted as creating a science and arts culture that gives the public greater access and propensity to understand science but also involvement. This would not be an easy operation as the integrity of scientific principles would need to be protected and inevitably there would be conflicts and tensions. However, the alternative of an increasingly alienated public may be more dangerous leading to pseudoscientific moral panics and a state of affairs as evidenced in Hungary where an authoritarian populist government can undermine the autonomy of an institution like the HAS without arousing a great deal of public indignation. The HAS needs to remember the safeguards for scientific and cultural independence are free inquiry, free thought, free speech, tolerance and the willingness to arbitrate disputes and formulate positions based on evidence but to also communicate to the public the importance and value of its work.

HAS and National Identity

As was noted in the historical section of this chapter the conception of the HAS at its foundation in 1825 by elite figures such as is Széchenyi was part of an effort to protect and preserve the Hungarian language and consequently also national identity. At the time there were fears both were in decline and the German language was becoming dominant, at least in elite circles. It may be the case that the HAS could have an important role in helping to facilitate and help guide a national conversation as to what being Hungarian means. Such a mission forms a standard role for institutions charged with the national guardianship of culture, science, and learning. The need for a national conversation in Hungary, as in many modern nation-states is pressing, as evidenced by the culture war and polarisation that is becoming increasingly evident in Hungary.

There are competing conceptions of how national identity is formed. Identity in a nationalist sense can be related to space but may also consist of a series of shared symbols and codes utilising myth, history, tradition, and language which can create a sense of solidarity and answer the questions: Who am I? Who and what are we? (Smith 1991). For some (primordialists) national identity derives directly from a priori ethnic group and is based on kinship ties and ancient heritage (Bellamy, 2003). Others (constructionists) perceive national identity as something that is imagined, being constructed through the interpretation of history and culture, and indeed for some (instrumentalists) is perceived as a phenomenon that can be manipulated and orchestrated by political elites (Ryder, 2020). Some such as Gellner (1983) have argued that nations are essentially a modern phenomenon, facilitated since the eighteenth century by modernisation and industrialisation, bound and nurtured through state institutions and apparatus, education, and mass communication.

If we take the view that national identity can be reshaped is it possible that identity can be refashioned through a more democratic and deliberative approach than say elite manipulation? How could this be done in Hungary and what direction should such a process take? Hungarian nationalists have drawn heavily from episodes in Hungarian history in framing their vision of national identity, often centred upon heroic struggles to repel invaders or shake off the yoke of occupation. Hungary has indeed had a tragic and difficult history, but the framing of such events has in some cases created something of a siege mentality that nationalists have been able to manipulate to some effect. Traditionalist conceptions of history have nurtured insular and even nativist conceptions of identity. There are though alternative seams of history and tradition centred on diversity that a modern Hungary could tap.

Hungary linguistically and culturally can be described as something of an outsider in Europe because of its Eurasian origins as reflected in its unique language, unrelated to the main language families of Europe. Historically Hungary was also a very diverse nation, once it had large Jewish and German minorities and although now greatly reduced in numbers their presence is still felt alongside large ethnic groups like the Roma. Roma arts and culture has a unique place, forming a central part of the country's culture, comparable perhaps to flamenco and the Gitano in Spain. Other minorities can be found in Hungary such as the Serbs, the Ruthenians, etc. These waves of migration have played an important and valuable role in the development of Hungary, the acknowledgement of such an argument should be part of the foundation for more inclusive conceptions of national identity in Hungary.

Although Hungary's reputation has been tarnished in recent years through acts of well-publicised intolerance and nativism it should not be forgotten that in the 1990s Hungary was considered to be a lead nation among those that were to be granted EU accession in 2004 and 2008. Hungary not only had a stronger economy than other accession members, but also it appeared at the time of accession to have a strong commitment to democracy and European integration. Such traits though now seem long forgotten but indicate the cultural and political pendulum that impacts on most nations' fortunes can shift. In other words, reorientation can happen.

As was noted in the introduction the neoliberal consensus that EU membership heralded in Hungary with rising poverty and a growing gap between the rich and poor may have been key factors that soured Hungary's attraction to the EU. A major revision in the scope and direction of the EU might be the much-needed foundation for political and cultural reorientation in Hungary. In tandem with this socioeconomic regeneration, the HAS might have a role to play. Of course, cultural institutions like the HAS should tread carefully in such cultural debates and avoid becoming the puppets of central government in identity-building projects. Nevertheless, academics and scientists by helping to steer debate and dialogue in accordance with basic principles such as truth and objectivity could assist in national debates on identity. Well formulated projects could also enable new interpretations and assessments of history and culture that can help a nation reenvisage itself.

Such cultural reorientation if coupled with a new socioeconomic agenda could give rise to a more civic form of nationalism. Civic nationalism is inclusive and welcoming of diversity and based on the guarantee of rights (Seidler, 2018). It is a vision of nationalism based on 'inclusive citizenship' where citizens from a diverse range of backgrounds can feel part of a nation centred on rights and residence, blending an aspiration for self-determination (political nationalism) with forms of social (equality and rights) and soft cultural nationalism (Moskal, 2016). It is a form of national identity that allows people to become part of the nation as long as they conform to its core values. It is a form of social contract where alignment to institutions and values has more importance than ethnicity. In other words, civic nationalism is a form of patriotism that avoids stridency and nativism. It is a vision of a nation that allows for more fluid conceptions of identity that allow for innovation and adaptation, but which strives to nurture soft and inclusive expressions of national pride. Present-day Scotland may with some justification be viewed as the best embodiment of such ideals and has been fuelled and conceived through the work by the Scottish Government but also the public sphere of the arts and media including cultural bodies without too much overt manipulation by political elites. The Hungarian government in alliance with a body like the HAS could seek to replicate such work. However, the HAS and its propensity to carry out such a role may have been compromised by the reforms outlined in this chapter that have undermined its autonomy and neutrality. Reforms that have been shaped by an ethnic and insular nationalism that emphasises ethnic or cultural features such as one's language or religion, common descent, a shared history, or shared territory. It is considered an exclusive type of nationalism.

Identity is a performative act, as Goffman (1959) notes a form of dramaturgy in which people use certain codes, symbols, and cultural narratives in formulaic and routine scripts to assert who and what they are. Relations with Europe, migrants, and culture war have acted like a screen to which ethnic and exclusionary nationalists in Hungary have articulated and projected their core values. In this task, the Hungarian government under Orbán is seeking to harness the institutional power of the HAS and Hungarian research and cultural and scientific activities. This chapter in its discussion of the HAS has concluded by defining and discussing what can be described as Manichean views of Hungarian national identity, although the exclusionary conception is at present in the ascendancy the power and potential of civic conceptions in Hungary should not be underestimated. Time will tell what role the HAS and scientific community will play in reimaging Hungary.

Chapter Six
The Corvinus: Privatisation and Audit Culture

In 2019 Clare Ariel, an American student who had studied communications studies at the Corvinus gave, on behalf of the student body, a keynote speech at the graduation ceremony that bemoaned the fact that due to the privatisation of the Corvinus it would be coupled to an oil company and potentially become an elitist institution. In a key passage in the speech, she stated:

> This ceremony is the end of more than just our personal stay at Corvinus, it is also the end of an era for this historic university. As of next year, Corvinus will be transformed from a public school serving the population of Hungary into a private institution.... I know I'm not supposed to put this so bluntly but I'm honestly terrified about the future of my alma mater and our planet in general. The Ministry of Innovation and Technology which now controls this university has already compromised the integrity of the Hungarian Academy of Sciences by stripping it of its research network, taking over its buildings, and diverting its funding. Who knows what is in store for our troubled but resilient university? It survived socialism but how will it fare under neoliberalism? Already the administration has cut merit-based tuition reimbursement and promised to replace almost a third of the Hungarian students with internationals, whom they hope will help them turn a profit for their foundation. I know this game. I am an economic migrant from the American university system. I came here to avoid the shackles of debt and now I am watching my university implement the same policies that are drowning my friends back home. Is this what Corvinus 2030 will look like? Is this what we represent as alumni? A broken system, an oil company? My dearest hope is that this university will flourish and stay true to its mission to provide education for all Hungarians, that it will fill the gap that the CEU's exile leaves in this country's academic landscape. Only time will tell (Ariel, 2019).

The powerful speech by Ariel referred to the Hungarian government's announcement in 2018 that the Corvinus University Budapest was to become a foundation that, it was claimed by the supporters of this model change, would increase the autonomy of the university. Critics denounced the plans as having the opposite effect and would impair the independence of thought that had characterised this institution and had helped establish it as one of the lead universities in Hungary. This chapter outlines the nature of the foundation reforms which are to be extended to other universities in the country and the implications for academic freedom.

As noted in chapter two, the Corvinus was originally established in 1934. Under communism, it was known for producing the country's Marxist intellectual elite, but in the latter stages of the socialist era became a hub for anti-communist dissent. In the transition period, it sought to establish itself as a liberal arts and economics institution but had floundered from 2010 because of budgetary

https://doi.org/10.1515/9783110749816-008

problems and the alleged animosity of Orbán towards the institution, described by one observer as the bête noire of Orbán (Hungarian Spectrum, 2018). Rumours had even circulated as to whether the Corvinus would be allowed to continue to operate as an institution (Brückner, 2017). Such fears seemed to be reinforced by the decision to enable a number of faculties to break away from the Corvinus. In 2012, the Faculty of Public Administration was attached to the newly established University of Public Service. In 2016 the Faculty of Agriculture and Landscape Architecture was also separated from the Corvinus (Somfai, 2020). However, now the fortunes of the Corvinus seem to have been transformed and the university is no longer a pariah but instead an elite university that will set the template for wider educational reforms in Hungary.

The Model Change

In September 2018, the Rector and the Chancellor of Corvinus announced an agreement with the Ministry of Innovation and Technology that the university would be taken out from the Law on Higher Education and would continue to operate as a private institution established on a governmental foundation (Maecenas Universitatis Corvini). In other words, the university would be privatised. The foundation was to hold a 10 % stake in Hungarian blue chip companies MOL (an oil and gas company) and Richter (pharmaceutical and biotechnology) that would fund Corvinus University through dividends (BBJ, 2019).

The model change was to be led by a team that included the conservative philosopher and Rector, Lánczi András, who had held his position since 2016. At the time this appointment had seemed an ominous one to staff at the Corvinus given the ideological and political connections Lánczi had to the political circle of Fidesz. In 2019 a new position was created of president that was filled by another political insider with close connections to Orbán, namely Anthony Radev. Radev, a Bulgarian businessman who held senior positions in McKinsey and Company, a lead business consultancy, and had established political and economic ties in Hungary (Brückner, 2017). Under the model change arrangement, all important decisions would be made by a presidential body, in which the rector (Lánczi) and the chancellor (Lívia Pavik) were to be responsible for continuity, while the president, Radev, focused on strategy (with specific responsibility for Human Resources, Corporate, and International Relations and Student Services). Within this triumvirate, Radev was deemed by some insiders to be the driving and leading figure behind the model change (Teczár, 2021). Radev has been described as the 'strongman' of the university leadership (Somfai, 2020). Some feel that Radev's authority has undermined the power of the university senate and that his business background does not qualify him to lead a university. The rector Lánczi, despite his strong support for the model change, in an interview seemed to acknowledge the tensions that might arise by trying to fuse business and academic principles of governance. He reflected on whether business morality can be reconciled with university morality. He noted the differences could cause tensions. Furthermore, he noted a university is as hierarchical an institution as, say, the church or the military. However, in the corporate world, there is only a boss and a subordinate, with completely different conditions of authority and advancement (Halko and Megadja, 2021). These reflections are pertinent.

Behind Radev and the model change, is the new management Board of Trustees responsible for the (Maecenas Universitatis Corvini) foundation that was appointed by the Government and presided over by MOL Chief Executive Zsolt Hernádi. The appointment of Hernádi, another political insider, caused some disquiet as he was indicted in Croatia for allegedly bribing former Croatian Prime Minister Ivo Sanader to enable MOL to become the key decision maker in the Croatian energy company INA. An international arrest warrant was issued through Interpol for Hernádi (Reuters, 2018b). In 2021, Croatia's supreme court affirmed a Zagreb court's prison sentence for Hernádi. It was reported that because of alleged "serious injustices" experienced in the course of Croatian legal procedures, Hernádi will appeal to Croatia's Constitutional Court (Hungary Today, 2021). Critics were concerned because the majority of the foundation trustees were closely aligned with the Fidesz government and it was feared the model change would have the opposite effect of the avowed aim of extending the Corvinus's autonomy. The centralisation of decision making and marginalisation of traditional power structures like the senate was confirmed by the fact the Corvinus Board of Trustees now make all major decisions before the senate (Teczár, 2020). In fact, it was reported that faculty councils were to be abolished and the powers of the university senate would be reduced, as they no longer would have powers in institutional maintenance and budget matters. The Board of Trustees now had such powers (Kósa, 2019). As part of the new top-down governance, academic staff and students were informed of the decisions to merge a number of institutes into new entities.

Opposition to the model change was muted. One notable resignation letter was from Professor Robert Braun (2019) a professor of business ethics and corporate social responsibility. He asserted that figures like Hernádi and Radev ran counter to the principles he tried to instil in his students. Many were appeased though by the strength of the companies forming the Government's endowment and reassured themselves the university would be in a good financial situation (Somfai, 2020). The university trade unions criticised the model change because they were not sufficiently consulted and in their view the proposed changes restricted the autonomy of the university (Sárosi, 2020). According to Deák (2019) in the decision to privatise the Corvinus no impact evaluation studies were published and there was no consultation with stakeholders.

Hernádi outlined key objectives for the new foundation: "It will be different; we will create a performance-based value system and increase our competitiveness. We need to change and be better than anyone else…. We are determined to provide the best business, economic and social science training in Central Europe" (Corvinus, 2018). The central aims were therefore focused on getting the Corvinus listed within the top 200 global universities, making it responsible for its income generation, creating a new career and evaluation and remuneration structure, and forging new links with industry. This was sometimes referred to as the '2030 vision', as the plan was to achieve these goals in the space of a decade. In the opinion of one expert observer the decision to privatise the Corvinus was forged in a narrow political circle, there was no detailed blueprint for reform. It seemed much more like a social, educational experiment than a well-thought-out and prepared action (Somfai, 2020). Concerns and alarm about the model change were to become more apparent as the nature and scope of the reforms became evident. In the two years following the announcement on model change there were only a handful of resignations, including my own, but these became more pronounced as the nature and reality of the model change became more apparent.

A major theme emphasised for the model change at the Corvinus was a call for more practical teaching and meeting the needs of the economy by producing graduates with the skills required by the economy. Radev (2020) stated in support of such aims that he hoped one day to see a Corvinus degree have the same prestige and economic value as an Oxford or Harvard degree. Radev (2020) noted the slower pace of development in the Hungarian economy had caused backlogs in domestic universities. Consequently, Hungarian graduates did not have the skills needed to hold a position in a world leading company today. As far as he was concerned skills such as problem-solving, managing performance pressure, and managing top-down communications were becoming increasingly important for companies. Sadly, though, in the opinion of Radev, Hungarian graduates lacked these skills but the new Corvinus would address these problems. It was also hoped that with the privatisation of the university there might be a chance to attract new private resources through a more flexible regulatory environment that would facilitate links and partnerships with business and external agencies (Berbas, 2020). A fear of some critics is this aspect of the model change reflects a wider trend in the commodification of higher education that forces university curricula and institutional ethos into a narrow job-training mission. Critics deride such narrow objectives for moving away from the academic mission of preparing citizens for critical participation in democracy and society (Cole and Heinecke, 2020).

As part of the model change, academic staff would participate in a new career model that allowed for specialisation in teaching or research. Staff were also promised a significant wage increase to deter teaching staff from having to take two jobs to support their families and to attract world-leading scholars to enable the university to join the ranks of the top 200 global universities. It was envisaged that in future 20 percent of teaching staff would be foreign with 50 percent of the teaching programmes in English, as opposed to the current 20 percent. The new remuneration policy involved a differentiated base wage and a performance-based bonus. Parallel with the new wage structure, in January 2020, Corvinus employees were claimed to have received a differentiated, on average, 25% increase in total wages (Radev, 2020). The teaching union within the Corvinus surveyed teaching staff on the pay ranking/evaluation system: based on nearly 300 responses received, more than 90 percent of staff did not support this procedure, with some claiming it undermined trust and cooperation (Teczár, 2020). Some of the academic staff felt this company-like performance appraisal system did not correspond to the nature of education, and especially not to research. The Corvinus trade union leader Gábor Toronyai argued such appraisal regimes would lead to academics adapting their research to the will of leaders "Freedom of research and education becomes illusory". In his opinion in such a regime, teachers cannot fulfil their mission to serve the common good (Ballai, 2021). Some staff feared that the audit of publications might lead to researchers choosing more mainstream topics and journals and focus on quantity rather than quality to secure favourable evaluations.

A major change to work practices came with the loss of civil service status. The trade unions complained that the loss of legal protections encompassed within civil service status would lead to redundancies. It should be noted that a common feature of model change and restructuring is redundancy. Such trends have been evident in higher education restructuring and the neoliberalisation of universities in countries like the USA that has led to reduced job security, lack of tenure, and the casualisation of teaching staff employed on temporary, and casual contracts (Karter et al, 2019).

The model change also included a desire to increase the number of foreign students from an estimated 15 percent to 45 percent of the student body. These students would be tuition-paying students. Some feared that tuition fees could rise steeply. Radev (2020) contemplated a tuition fee of approximately 600,000 HUF/1700 euro per semester, which Radev considered to be an average tuition fee among internationally competitive universities. For Hungarian students, there would be some scholarships for highly talented students but the chance to secure such funding would be reduced. It has been reported that the Corvinus aims to increase the number of students who pay tuition to at least 60%, the current situation is exactly the opposite: 60% are state-sponsored students, and 40% of the students pay for studying (Béni, 2018). This could change the character and ethos of the university into an elite institution. Students raised concerns about the impact of increased tuition fees on social mobility and inclusivity with the rector Lánczi allegedly asking the students whether they wanted the Corvinus for the "talented poor" (Záborszky, 2019).

Although at an early stage of development a number of concerns regarding the model change are apparent, these proposals may have had an impact already with reports of parents and schools being hesitant about tuition fee changes and the nature of the model change (Somfai, 2020). As part of the model change, the Corvinus leadership hopes to attract foreign staff who may have the requisite language skills. However, even with the proposed wage increases, which might be relatively good in terms of academic wages in Hungary, it compares poorly with remuneration levels in the Hungarian private sector and indeed academia in the West. It should also be noted that some, possibly many, academics outside of Hungary, will be hesitant to align themselves with a university that in all probability will be viewed as the elite and favoured university of the Fidesz government. Concerns about academic freedom in Hungary are increasingly being voiced in the European Union and this will only add to the hesitancy of foreign academics to be connected with the Corvinus.

Another point of concern is the financing of the Corvinus from the 10 percent shares and dividends of the companies MOL and Richter. Hernádi had indicated that the overall sum of money derived from these dividends would be more predictable and higher than the former state-funded budget of the university. However, the negative impact of coronavirus on the oil industry that led to a drop in oil prices led to MOL announcing in the spring of 2020 that the company would not pay any dividends that year (Berbas, 2020). Richter announced a 30 percent reduction in its dividends. It should also be noted that as well as being susceptible to economic fluctuations, the Corvinus is vulnerable because of its narrow portfolio. By only holding dividends in two companies means risks cannot be spread. The actual shares cannot be sold and there is always the risk that the university might have to sell assets such as property or make staff redundant during periods when the dividend yield might be low (Mátyás and Bőgel, 2021). In its first year of operation under the new funding regime, the Corvinus received 13.6 billion HUF, of which 11.7 billion came from MOL and 1.9 billion from Richter. It would appear that given the shortfall expected in 2021 that the university will need to use its reserves, which are estimated to be sufficient to cover its operation to make up the shortfall. However, future economic difficulties could place Corvinus in a very precarious situation (Fabók, 2020). Péter Bihari, an academic commentator who has taken a close interest in the model change, believes the university would need a quarter of the state's shares in MOL but this would still fail to generate a stable income. He sees the solution in government bonds, that are predictable and would not burden public debt either, as the foundation could be formally part of public finances (Záborszky, 2019).

The financial precarity of the Corvinus and the future need to generate external finance could lead to the university, as with other private universities, relaxing the academic requirements of student admission. Such action would impact negatively on the academic performance of the university and the chance to join the ranks of elite global institutions (Hungarian Spectrum, 2018). The Hungarian government has also undermined any market advantages the Corvinus may have by supporting an initiative to allow the Chinese Fudan University to establish a university campus in Budapest. The Fudan University is an established and elite university in China with extensive experience in providing high quality education in English. Such a university will probably lead to potential Hungarian and more likely international students, especially those from China, choosing the Fudan rather than the Corvinus (Bodnár, 2021).[1] Following large protests inflamed by the fact Hungarian taxpayers are expected to finance the project, the Government changed its stance, saying it would offer a referendum on the university – but only after the general election in 2022.

The Hungarian academic Gábor Halmai (2019a) described the model change at the Corvinus as an oligarchic privatisation with implications for freedom of speech. The power now enjoyed by the Corvinus president and Board of Trustees can be seen as being indicative of a process of total administration. Structures like university senates are products of a rich history of academic development and founding principles rooted in autonomy, which was supposed to create internal democracy, but these have been increasingly subverted and debased, not just in Hungary but beyond (McCann et al, 2020). The vignette presented below provides some insights into the expected decline of the authority of university senates in the higher education foundation reforms in Hungary.

Following the Hungarian government's foundation change to the University of Theatre and Film Arts (SZFE) that was considered by some to be confronta-

---

[1] The Hungarian government announced it would spend 1.5 billion euros on the project and construction of a campus, including a 1.25 billion euro loan from China, this is a greater sum than what the Hungarian government spent on higher education in 2019 (Vaski, 2021).

tional (see discussion in chapter seven), the Corvinus trade union leader Gábor Toronyai, proposed a motion to the Corvinus University senate. Toronyai proposed an extraordinary meeting of the senate to be convened to stand by the SZFE in a statement of solidarity. The proposal had the support of 9 senate members, a number sufficient under the senate's procedural rules for such a proposal to be discussed. However, the rector Lánczi over-ruled the proposal arguing that the senate did not have the competence to discuss such matters. Toronyai disputed Lánczi's interpretation of the rules and argued that the senate has the right to form an opinion on any issue that senate members deem appropriate to put on the agenda. According to a number of students a petition of solidarity with the SZFE had been organised at the start of the 'Free SZFE' campaign in September 2020 but neither the HÖK (Students' Association) nor the university leadership was willing to address and acknowledge this initiative (Windisch and Nagy, 2020). The passivity of the HÖK might confirm fears expressed by a number of students in Hungarian universities in interviews I conducted for this book that formal student associations are dominated by careerist student politicians. In the opinion of some, the rector's act of censorship presents ominous consequences in Hungary for freedom of speech and the propensity to challenge and speak out when confronted with injustice, a point that is elaborated on in the next section.

Voices of Dissent

In this section of the chapter Corvinus academics provide testimony on their perceptions of the changes at the Corvinus.

Zoltan

Before becoming a professor, I had studied at several long-established universities outside of Budapest, in Miskolc and Pécs. I worked for a while in the business sector and then decided to study for a PhD in Holland. I returned to Hungary and then took up a part-time teaching post at the Corvinus and continued my market research interests alongside the teaching.

I think a turning point in the development of the university and a change in attitude occurred in 2016 when Lánczi András became rector. Lánczi was close to the prime minister and was the founder of a think tank connected to the Fidesz Party, he could not be viewed as a neutral and non-partisan figurehead. Around this time the National Bank got a department at Corvinus, others close to the

Government gained positions. A key flashpoint occurred in 2017, around the time of the Central European University (CEU) closure furore, the Corvinus rector issued a statement informing teaching staff they should not make political statements in the media. This was interpreted as an attempt to stop staff from speaking out in support of the CEU. With the model change staff are worried about their future; for example, they have lost their civil service status that gave them some job security and wonder what the future may hold. Some critical thinkers though seem to shy away from discussing the dangers of the model change, it's the 'elephant in the room'.

The Government is reorganising public universities as private property and distributing these resources to political and business loyalists (who are overrepresented in basically every foundation board). As I noted, even critical thinkers shy away from mentioning this political aspect, which ultimately plays into the hands of the Government. If we only raise minor technical issues and concerns, it is not difficult to actually satisfy several of these demands but then we will not have real ground for more serious systemic change. Although I do understand why the trade union does this to a great extent, it is kind of their job to fight for the best conditions the workers can get. But it is disappointing that the wider university community was not able to stop or even to slightly challenge this process, and I think there is not much to do about it three years later after the initial change, so now (and in the future) criticising the technicalities/minor issues is what is left for us. The SZFE (the art and film university) protest is the exception to the rule (and that protest is also basically over). I do not expect anything similar to happen anywhere else.

I think the issue of academic freedom, just as other types of freedoms in the Hungarian authoritarian state, is tricky. In theory, we have a high degree of academic freedom, so long as you are not criticising the crucial decisions made by the political leadership (model change, banning Gender Studies, etc.) or the university leadership, you are free to express your opinion, you can even criticise migration policy or educational segregation or other similar issues. And you are free to research and teach whatever you want to, at least I have never experienced or heard about any sort of such interference. I think most practical limitations to academic freedom result from self-censorship which is partly based on realistic fears of losing one's job, but mostly are the result of the lack of solidarity and collective action. At an institutional level, the business model (work contracts instead of public servant contracts) and the priority of business and political aspects over academic ones increase the vulnerability of the teaching staff. If you mean academic freedom at the institutional level (self-organizing academic institutions driven by academic/scientific perspectives and priorities) then these new institutions are clearly not free.

Honestly, I do not really think that fighting for academic freedom should be the task of the students. I think workers at these universities should stand up for themselves instead of expecting it from everyone else (students, the political opposition, even from the Government or certain members/ministers, etc.). On the other hand, in the case of Corvinus, I do not see what can be done now as more than two years have passed since the start of the model change, it is strange to thematise the political aspect now (and people shy away from this aspect anyway), so technocratic debates remain, which actually do legitimise the new model and leadership in my opinion. The expressions of solidarity the Corvinus trade union and some workers express with other universities is a bit strange as well, as it has the underlying message that we are basically happy with what we got (since we are not protesting) and we just wish it went that 'well' with other model changing universities as well.

I was concerned about how the model change occurred and the Corvinus was privatised. However, some aspects of the bureaucracy have been improved. It seems though that the model change has made the university feel like a multinational company with middle manager heads of department/institutes no longer acting as academic leaders did in the past who had some autonomy but now merely telling us in meetings what the senior management, people like Radev and Lánczi, want. A business model may be good for a company but not for universities. Universities like the Corvinus are becoming a mirror of the situation of the wider society, dominated by an authoritarian leader. However, it is authoritarianism with a streak of incompetence.

Deák Dániel

Deák Dániel is a research professor at the Institute of Economic and Public Policy/ Comparative and Institutional Department of Economics at the Corvinus University, below he provides his views on the changes at the Corvinus.

I started to work at the Corvinus in 1998, before that I was a lawyer. I was attracted to the Corvinus because of its unique role in economics, for many years it was the only institution where it was possible to study economic science in the real sense. Today other universities teach this subject but the Corvinus remains the leader in theoretical economic science. I fear though that with the market demands that the Corvinus is now being exposed to, where we subordinate ourselves to market forces, there will be pressure to streamline our curriculum and tailor it to customer demand rather than pursuing what are considered worthwhile intellectual pursuits. This development can be viewed as a threat to academic freedom and a serious danger to the scholarly profile of the Corvinus.

We are under a double pressure; the market and new leaders of the university expect us to be a business school but some of us want to preserve ourselves as a university of economics. Theoretical economics educates the competencies of professional intelligence and a critical mind. The subject of business administration delivers knowledge that can be applied to practice, the student in this subject is not supported, however, to become independent-minded. The second pressure is politics, we have a government that is autocratic, is not democratic, and does not respect the rule of law. It is increasingly prone to interfere in higher education. With the loss of our civil service status, I can imagine purges eventually taking place against those staff with a different worldview to the ruling regime in Hungary, such action is within their autocratic nature. However, the nature of the political regime will ultimately undermine efforts to make the Corvinus into an elite university. The new leadership say they want to attract international staff, but they will not come because of Hungary's deteriorating political reputation, these academics will not want their reputations to be tainted.

My views and those of other critical voices may be at the periphery of the university. Increasingly the academic staff at the university seem to be separated and isolated from each other. Middle managers in the university are increasingly loyal to the goals of the university, as determined by senior management. There have been huge changes in the character and ethos of the university. Let's consider the microclimate, ten years ago it was normal to go into the corridor and by chance meet colleagues and spend some time chatting, sharing information, and having a joke. This happy atmosphere has now totally disappeared. People at the Corvinus are now full of fear and uncertainty, unsure of what will happen. We are no longer involved in decision-making. We are delivered 'ready-made decisions' within the guise and framework of formal regulations. In the past, there was mutual trust and some chance to shape and influence decisions. Now things are regulated like in the army with clear hierarchies, to have any chance of restraint or influence you now have to operate like a lawyer in the university. By this I mean, the management of academic matters has become very bureaucratic, informal agreements have disappeared, and the expected behaviour is that associates have to adjust themselves to formal regulations accurately.

Under this new regime, we are like 'piece rate' workers in a factory[2]. It is important to measure academic performance but in academia, measurement cannot be the same as many other branches of life. If you are committed as an aca-

---

2 Piece rate pay occurs when workers are paid by the unit performed (e.g., the number of tee shirts or bricks produced) instead of being paid on the basis of time spent on the job. Critics claim such systems undermine production quality and a sense of team spirit.

demic you will gain prestige and this is the most important indicator of achievement. A committed academic makes little distinction between work and leisure, they are excited about their research and teaching, it seems unnecessary to meticulously measure this. If you lack this enthusiasm and commitment it will be clearly evident. Now with a micro audit culture of staff appraisal, it is psychologically dehumanising. Academic productivity cannot be measured on a year-by-year cycle, it depends on the project cycle, really all that can be done is to make an estimation of productivity. Under this total management system of appraisal, I recently had to ask a colleague to provide me with a certificate to verify that I had participated as a tutor in an international project involving several international universities and many foreign students. At a normal university, such evidence is not needed, but now we are 'piece rate' workers and this inhibits our academic freedom. There is little sign of staff getting more publicly concerned, in most cases, they live without hope or expectation, the main aspiration is to survive.

Why am I speaking out? I have been active for over a decade in the civil movement. The catalyst for this activism was the higher education Act in 2012 (see chapter one for more detail), it had many restrictions that I found difficult to accept and included a dramatic cut in resources, it also spawned a students' movement that used student occupation as a strategy. I feel I have a responsibility to show civil courage, this cannot be measured in monetary terms. Only a small group share my stance, we are small in comparison with state power, but in my life, a central value is to be loyal to my inner values and to live like a scholar and uphold academic freedom. I am not interested in conventional success but in defending values, that are valuable assets, this struggle gives me some hope and optimism.

Another academic (untenured) who resigned from the Corvinus explains the rationale for their departure.

One reason I resigned was because I had bad feelings about the changes in the university. We did not have much information but in the context of Fidesz politics, the signs were not good. The way the process was managed within the university deepened my bad feelings, there was no transparency. I could sense a growing tension as what senior management planned started to appear within the faculties and departments. There seemed to be no platform where we could share our views or express our thoughts. Divisions emerged within the staff between those who supported the changes and those who were against them, many were anxious as to what the future held.

The transformation of the university was the 'last drop', the changes were made with no real dialogue. At a faculty event they elaborated on the reforms and managers said it would make the university more financially sustainable and raise the academic standards, we would also increase the number of foreign students. It was difficult for me to believe this could happen especially as it relied on a process of privatisation. I think for a while I put my 'head in the sand'. I did not feel integrated enough to take a stand, I was connected to my students and courses but not really to the institution. If I am honest, I did not want to risk my future. If I raised my voice, there might be repercussions. People with the power to make important decisions on my academic career might take offence if I spoke out. I was not brave enough to speak out, but if I had a tenured job there and been there for longer, I would have fought more. It's sad, but I remember in 2018 asking some of the students if they had participated in a protest event about academic freedom and privatisation. I felt it was my responsibility to help raise awareness on this matter. The students' reaction though was disappointing, they were apathetic and had a lack of interest. Their focus was their diploma and nothing beyond that.

A clear milestone and confirmation of my fears and concerns took place in 2018, the rector Lánczi András outlined the model change at the Corvinus, hundreds of colleagues attended the event. The Corvinus trade union leader Gábor Toronyai made a speech from the floor of the hall raising a number of concerns. The reaction of the rector was shocking and arrogant, he responded like an old-style authoritarian schoolteacher, he was very rude and shut down and dismissed the intervention by Toronyai. This meeting though was merely symbolic, they had to go through the pretence of staging what appeared as a consultation, but everything had already been decided.

A trade union activist in the Corvinus expresses their views on the changes taking place within the university.

Regarding the model change, autonomy does not exist. There was talk and promises that there would be equality and shared decision making between the senate and foundation board, but in reality, it is the opposite. The university leadership did everything from a one-sided approach. The Government, two years later, through legislation passed a law that retroactively endorsed these actions. Little time was afforded in the parliamentary debate to raise concerns and objections about the nature of the reforms. In none of the privatised universities will there be autonomy, this is clear now in 2021.

Many teaching staff have concerns about the appraisal system. The appraisal system that audits in a detailed manner the outputs of teaching staff could lead to academics losing their autonomy and is the cause of great stress. Academics conscious of the appraisal system may become more careful and less challenging both in their research and, in expressing their opinions in public affairs, and a small circle of department and institute leaders, who lead the appraisal, will see their power increased. These leaders will be influenced and directed by the senior leadership of the university, in this way the university could change greatly.

The teaching staff have also lost their civil service status, this could increase the chance of redundancy. Many of the teaching staff have not spoken openly about the problems within the university, they fear for their positions. After the election in 2022, if the Fidesz Party is re-elected, some fear a process of redundancy and purging could emerge.

Sometimes the passivity of the teaching staff is frustrating but that is the situation everywhere and at every time. It is always a small minority that speaks out and is willing to take action. However, there have been some important signs of resistance. In September the union tried to take a motion to the senate expressing solidarity with the SZFE, but the rector would not allow this to be voted on. However, what is significant is that nine senate members supported the motion being debated and voted upon. 600 of one thousand staff signed a petition expressing concerns about the nature of new employment contracts. Furthermore, when a new works council was formed 600 colleagues voted for trade union delegates to be elected and all were elected. This was a great victory. The university leadership tried to promote its own candidates, but none were elected.

The students have been fairly passive. For thirty years a system has been in place, where the university leadership can grant patronage and privileges to the leaders of the students' association. At one point there was a more challenging faction within the students' association but these days another group, more pro model change and coming more from the business side of the university, appear to be dominant.

The Neoliberal University

The fears expressed in the statements may not be without foundation given the university leadership's avowed intention to make the Corvinus into an elite university, reliant on corporate finance and potentially high tuition fees and directed through the audit and surveillance culture of 'new managerialism'. These are the classic traits of the neoliberal university.

Cole and Heinecke, (2020) note that the neoliberal university has a propensity to hierarchical leadership and an audit culture with an increased focus on outputs, especially publications. At the core of the neoliberal university is the belief that universities should effortlessly transition students to the needs of the economy and be harnessed in terms of knowledge production to the interests of business. Such a view disparages more liberal and deliberative educational environments that nurture freedom of speech and challenge these as 'ivory tower' utopianism. With the introduction of new staff appraisal systems dominated by performance indicators, Corvinus academic staff were being conditioned to a culture of audit, surveillance, and performance management. In this sense, Corvinus was increasingly resembling the practices of higher education in countries like the UK by replicating a regime of indicator and market fetishism, where mistrust permeates the institution and senior academics are defined by managerial functions. Audit culture can be seen as a kind of administrative and power control, that changes the way academics conceptualise themselves (Mackay, 2021).

The rise and strategic value of this technocratic stratum of academic managers has been noted for some time, the perception of some observers is that the least intelligent professors are very often the most powerful by virtue of the managerial positions held (Wilson, 1995). It is though a system of surveillance that can be likened to Foucault's panoptic vision of governmentality that was discussed at the start of the chapter, where technology is used to observe and control human behaviour (Foucault, 1977). Audit culture creates a perception that teaching staff can no longer be trusted to regulate themselves or be assumed to be acting in the interests of students, the 'customers' but need to be closely monitored to ensure that they offer value for money and conform to a series of performance-based targets (Macfarlane, 2017).

The notion of academic appraisal rests on several fallacies that fail to appreciate there is no completely objective basis for judging the qualitative achievement of an academic. Though the quantity of his output is of some importance, its qualitative significance also needs to be considered and this can be a somewhat subjective assessment. Administrators struggling to audit their academic associates turn to personal estimates and perceptions and involve so many intangibles as to render them incapable of any purely quantitative or statistical summation (Wilson, 1995).

In the neoliberal university, some feel pressure to comply, new submissive norms of behaviour appear that tame and pacify teaching approaches and academic outputs (Cheng, 2010). The notion of universities having a role as political and social institutions aligned with social justice and social transformation has been replaced with aspirations of elitism and the students' (clientele) contentment (Sparkes, 2013). In the culture of audits and competitivity staff feel under continuous pressure, promotion and remuneration is dependent on publications, giving meaning to the maxim 'publish or perish' (Mok, 2000). The level of toxicity created by such a culture in many universities has prompted some to describe them as 'anxiety machines' (Hall and Bowles, 2016).

The model change at the Corvinus demonstrated another trait of the neoliberal university, namely an obsession with corporate branding (Webb, 2018). As part of the model change, the Corvinus leadership unveiled a new logo of a raven with a gold ring in its beak. According to legend, the fifteenth century King Matthias' mother had summoned him to Hungary to take the throne by sending a raven with a ring in its beak. The raven supposedly flew non-stop from Transylvania to Prague and thus Mathias was crowned. The raven-with-ring motif became part of the family crest, as well as the family name: Corvinus (Latin for "raven"). The logo appeared on the university webpage and products and was even portrayed on black banners draping the main entrance. Critics of the model change felt the new logo of the raven, an opportunistic and predatory bird with gold in its beak, was an apt symbol for the "hijacking" of the university.

The model change was marketed as an attempt to increase the autonomy of the university. Autonomy can be defined as policy-making autonomy and an institution's capability to avoid external controls (Kohtamäki and Balbachevsky, 2019). The nature and composition of the Corvinus leadership and its alliance with the values and aims of the Fidesz government undermined any pretence of trying to increase autonomy. The degree of control and direction coming from the Hungarian government and the introduction of foundation-managed universities with strong audit cultures mean that the changes could be better termed as ordoliberal rather than neoliberal. Foucault (1988) recognised that neoliberalism when applied to institutions did not reflect classical liberalism and encourage laissez-faire and 'self-regulating' free market practices but instead had an inclination to centralisation, surveillance, and forms of state interference through what he termed 'governmentality', but which others might term 'ordoliberalism'. In ordoliberal academic institutions, self-governance and the notion of autonomous institutional spheres are replaced by 'top-down' managerial models, directed from the centre. The idealistic vision of the university as part of a so-called fifth estate, a safeguard for democracy, and humanism, in the ordoliberal university is superfluous (Raaper and Olssen, 2016). Some would argue that the autocracy of new managerialism and the ordoliberal regime upon which it depends makes foundation universities like the Corvinus in Hungary more reminiscent of the university of the neo-Stalinist Kádár period in Hungarian history. Audits, mission statements, and development plans take on something of the nature of five-year plans (in the case of Corvinus a '2030 vision'), where staff and students feel disempowered and monitored. Neoliberalism/ordoliberalism as with Soviet Communism relies on what can be described as 'total administration', forms of bureaucratic or managerial ideology premised on supposed rationality and productivity (Marcuse, 1986).

However, there are features of the model change and more generally audit that contradict the neoliberal approach. The university as with the Hungarian economy is subject to political interference as reflected in favouritism towards those closely aligned with the Orbán administration. Hence, lucrative contracts are given to pro-Fidesz businessmen and in the case of the Corvinus leadership positions in terms of management are given to those closely aligned with the Government or who will do its bidding without offering a challenge. Thus, free competition and meritocracy are stifled.

The overview of the Corvinus University model change does not convey a sense of optimism for the future. At the time of writing the Hungarian government planned an ambitious programme of extending the foundation model to a large number of Hungarian centres of higher education, unlike at the SZFE criticism and opposition to these changes has been non-existent or muted. There has been a sense of tired inevitability towards foundation status on the part of these new or soon-to-be foundation universities. Reluctant universities, it is said, have accepted what seems to be a fait accompli believing that those outside of the reform programme will lose resources. If true such a threat undermines the initial government pledge that participation should be free and not coerced (Vass, 2021).[3] This chapter suggests that if other foundation universities follow the model and trajectory of Corvinus University there could be serious implications for institutional autonomy and academic freedom.

In 2021 the Law on Public Interest Asset Management Foundations was passed which lists 32 foundations, 21 of which were related to higher education. The initiative was denounced as the creation of a state within a state, as these foundations would be free of government oversight and managed by Boards of Trustees composed of government loyalists. Some denounced the initiative as part of an insurance measure by Orbán in the event of him possibly losing power in the 2022 election to retain a huge amount of influence and resources even when out of power. The weekly *HVG*, an important Hungarian magazine, compared the foundation scheme with 'feudal goods' that feudal rulers give to their vassals. The opposition denounced it as robbery. Professor Kim Lane Scheppele of Princeton University has noted that the reform removes all trans-

---

3 Following on from the designation of the Corvinus as a so-called foundation university in 2020 the University of Miskolc, Moholy-Nagy University of Art and Design, the University of Sopron, Neumann János University, Széchenyi University, and the University of Veterinary Medicine Budapest and University of Theatre and Film Arts (SZFE) were made into foundations. In 2021 Semmelweis in Budapest and the universities of Debrecen, Szeged and Pecs were among others identified as foundation universities. These other universities unlike the Corvinus were not granted an endowment and will probably continue to rely heavily on state funding.

parency from how E.U. funds are spent, and any assets that go into these foundations go off the public books, in other words out of the purview of the state audit office, out of the reach of freedom of information requests, and out of all public accountability (Novak, 2021). Orbán though was bellicose in his defence of the foundation scheme, in a weekly radio interview he argued that attacks on this proposal came from the Left and were politically motivated and driven by their internationalism. In his mind universities were national institutions and he did not want them to be globalised and lose their national character (Vass, 2021). The statement affirmed what many already knew, that higher education in Hungary was the locus of a culture war that could have profound implications for Hungary's future direction and notions of national identity.

Chapter Seven
'Free SZFE': Resistance at the University of Theatre and Film Arts

Social movements and periods of political upheaval and contestation are invariably subject to foregrounding by historians, journalists and social scientists. Those events and periods become known by their metonymic title – e.g. '1968', 'Tiananmen Square', 'Occupy Wall Street'. These are events that epitomise a movement and time of rupture. Although there is a risk of reductivism, where too narrow a focus on a single event or episode can exclude wider consideration of the structural and historical factors that made them possible, such events have the power to trigger social change (Hensby, 2019). As part of the metonymic process, these events take on a mythical status and occupy a central part of the framing that steers and directs a movement. At the time of writing, the occupation of the University of Theatre and Film Arts in Budapest (*Színház-és Filmmű-vészeti Egyetem* – SZFE) is a recent event, and although the student occupation of the campus has ended, the dispute remains very much part of an ongoing struggle between the Hungarian government and students/academics that is centred on the notion of academic freedom. The occupation, as is typical of metonymic events, was a 'scene-stealing' moment of agency and resistance that prompted a wide audience to take note of the students' grievance. For some who had grown cynical and despaired of the capacity of Hungarian youth to offer a serious challenge to the Government, this event was in fact a huge surprise and source of inspiration. This clash has already assumed an iconic status that will certainly be remembered for many years to come and has the potential to become a pivotal turning point that shapes the tactics and imagination of future protests in Hungary. This chapter narrates the factors that prompted a student occupation, the nature and framing of that resistance, and seeks to locate this event in the context of the literature on radical and innovative social movements and the cultural politics of 'eventing'. Before embarking on such a discussion, the chapter details the history and mission of the SZFE.

The SZFE was founded in 1865, making it one of the oldest academic institutions in Hungary. Past alumni include several Oscar winners, including "Casablanca" director Michael Curtiz. Recent graduates include Geza Rohrig, the lead actor in "Son of Saul", a film that won the 2016 Academy Award for best foreign-language film, and the filmmaker Ildiko Enyedi, who is known internationally for her award-winning 2017 film, "On Body and Soul." (Novak, 2020). With approximately 450 students, the SZFE is the smallest arts-focussed higher education es-

https://doi.org/10.1515/9783110749816-009

tablishment in Hungary. A variety of professions are taught at the university: acting, musical and puppet theatre, film and theatre direction, choreography, film editing, cinematography, set design, and television production.

In 2020 the Hungarian government announced its plan to include the SZFE into its privatisation programme of higher education that was being applied to seven other centres of learning. The reforms were ostensibly designed to allow these centres of learning to become free and autonomous of the state, but critics say that in reality, the changes made these institutions subservient to the diktats of the state by appointing boards to manage them that are packed with government supporters. At these other institutions the reforms were met with protest that was generally muted and on a small scale, and the changes proceeded as planned. This was not to be the case at the SZFE.

Takeover

A feeling that the Hungarian government was growing increasingly hostile to the SZFE was evident as early as 2018. According to some observers, the Government started to instigate a culture war that attacked the lead figures associated with the SZFE for their liberalism. This campaign of denigrating the liberal arts was assisted by disturbing 'Me Too' revelations of the sexism, emotional abuse, sexual abuse, and discrimination allegedly perpetrated by two academics who taught at the university (Sárosi, 2020). It should be noted that the allegations referred to incidents that actually took place outside of the university; nevertheless, both staff members were suspended by the SZFE.

One figure fuelling the animosity towards the SZFE for over a decade was the now-deceased Imre Kerényi, a cultural adviser to Hungarian Prime Minister Orbán and a theatre director. Among his many controversial statements, Kerényi claimed that the Fidesz party, led by Orbán was a gift from God. Also, according to him, 80% of all Hungarian plays are sacred works inspired by Christianity, and therefore it is important that the director of such plays be a Christian. In the opinion of Kerényi, Hungary needed a "Christian theatre". Kerényi also declared that the theatrical world should be liberated from the "lobby of the fags", called for the establishment of an "anti-college of the performing arts", and said the present one, the SZFE, should rot (Hungarian Spectrum, 2014). Such thinking at the very centre of government perhaps explains the animosity of the Government towards the SZFE and the aggressive position it took in seeking a change to the institution's model of organisation.

In February 2020, the SZFE was informed of the Government's privatisation plans that were to be finalised by January 2021. The then-SZFE leadership entered into negotiations to stop/suspend/postpone the process. In April they learnt the plans would proceed. Then, about a month later, the SZFE learnt (from a TV interview, not from a direct announcement/letter) that the new deadline for the change to a foundation would in fact be even earlier, September 2020. The university decided this was insufficient time and applied for an extension; in addition, they recommended several candidates for the soon-to-be appointed board of trustees (*kuratórium*). A new board of trustees was appointed, with power over the heads of the university, and was led by the nationalist artist Attila Vidnyánszky, who could be viewed as the heir of Kerényi in terms of his views towards the SZFE (discussed above); there was no dialogue or consultation about his involvement (Szirtes, 2020). In addition, the SZFE Senate announced that their powers to decide on budgetary, organisational, and personnel issues had been taken away from them, as power had been transferred to the new board (Vaski, 2021). In effect, Vidnyánszky moved beyond what the role of a board chair should be and assumed a leadership role that included interference in academic matters.

Not only did the speed and manner of the changes cause offence, but so did the appointment of Vidnyánszky as chair of the new SZFE board of trustees. Vidnyánszky, an ethnic Hungarian who had been raised in the Ukraine, had operated a theatre in Transcarpathia, Ukraine, in the early 1990s. Vidnyánszky had run the theatre under extremely difficult conditions, given there was hostility in Ukraine towards the Hungarian minority and expressions of Hungarian culture. Vidnyánszky has been referred to as Hungary's 'culture pope', as he has been awarded several important cultural positions by the Fidesz administration. In 2013 he was made the director of the Hungarian National Theatre. Vidnyánszky is held in high esteem by Fidesz because he has frequently called for the arts to give greater focus to the national identity and Christian values of Hungary. He is seen as something of an outsider to the liberal arts establishment, having complained of being bullied and marginalised by the metropolitan liberal elite (Kafkadesk, 2020). Vidnyánszky's animosity to the SZFE was evident when, at the onset of his appointment in July 2020, he disparaged the institution as having a leftist bias in its curriculum, offering a "harmful, monotone, somewhat ideological training" (Kentish, 2020).

On 31 August 2020, the full leadership of the SZFE resigned in protest at what they declared was an affront to the autonomy of the university. Laszlo Upor, the former deputy rector of SZFE who was among those who resigned, derided the transition as "forced" and informed a meeting of MEPs attending the European Parliament's Culture and Education Committee that the new system is "private with a twist". He elaborated on this by stating that the university still lives on public money "but without public control, without checks and balances" (Zalan, 2020).

A poll conducted by the Student Union at SZFE found that 100% of their members opposed the institutional change (Spike, 2020). Students organised a street farewell party for the resigning staff at the main university and to mark a farewell to the 155 years of an autonomous SZFE. The event became a political demonstration. Thousands of supporters came to express support and this led to the occupation of the main university building, an occupation that was to last for 71 days in what became known as the 'Free SZFE' campaign. In conjunction with this, strike action was taken by the staff, although it should be noted that staff continued to teach and administer the needs of the students (Sárosi, 2020). The students had a number of demands that were expressed in a declaration, including the reinstatement of the independent institutions of the university, such as the Senate. In an act of defiance, they rejected the new private foundation and its board. The unity of teachers and students was an important component that bolstered the 'Free SZFE' campaign; staff support has been noted elsewhere to be a valuable factor in student protest (Dawson, 2011).

One student observer noted

> While I don't agree with it, operating a university via a private foundation isn't necessarily a bad thing. The issue here is not the actual 'remodelling', because the institution has needed reform. The issue is that in a country that calls itself democratic, those changes were instigated rapidly, without a nominal agreement, with complete disregard for the students and their Student Council. These reforms aren't serving a transparent, well-intended revamp (Komjathy, 2020).

The Hungarian establishment was surprised by the militant response from teachers and students at the SZFE. András Bencsik, the chief editor of the pro-Government weekly *Demokrata*, denounced the SZFE and its former leadership as a "stinking old sect" hiding in a "grungy nest." As far as he was concerned, the Government measures were "cleaning up universities one after another. We have to get past this post-communist period." Such sentiments reflected a popular frame in Hungarian nationalist thinking, namely, that there had not been regime change in Hungarian higher education after the collapse of communism (Nepszava, 2021). Ironically, Bencsik had, during the communist era, worked for pro-government publications including Népszabadság, the daily newspaper of the Hungarian Socialist Workers' Party.

The events and emotions that gave rise to the occupation of the SZFE give credence to Castells' notion (2012) that protest movements are, at their roots, emotional movements where, in a catalyst moment, there is the transformation of emotion into action. It is difficult to say whether the Hungarian government deliberately concocted this confrontation through its desire to stoke conflict as part of its relentless culture war campaign about national identity versus an alien and cosmopolitan liberalism, or whether it was the product of arrogance and the assumption that opposition would be minimal. Perhaps it was a combination of the two. The next part of the chapter seeks to give some insights into the strategy and tactics of the SZFE student movement.

'Free SZFE': Strategy and Tactics

Student occupations have occurred before in Hungary; from 2012 to 2013 there was a series of protests and occupations at Eötvös Loránd University (ELTE) against the Government's higher education reforms, which had significantly reduced state scholarships. The Government announced in 2012 that it would only fund 10,480 student places that year, down from over 44,000 in 2011, and required those who received scholarships to stay in the country after graduation or incur a financial cost if they choose to leave the country. The only other country where such a rule applies is Belarus. Another source of concern was frustration with the revisions by the Fidesz government to the Fundamental Law (See Chapter One). At one point ELTE's largest lecture hall became a 'square of debate', a place where daily forums could be held and, through non-hierarchical means, allow the mass of protestors to participate in the protest decision making. A key group was *Hallgatói Hálózat* (student network) that became known as HaHa, a student movement formed in 2006 that expanded in 2012 following the Government's education reforms; a central slogan was 'a free country, a free university' (Fuzessi, 2013). HaHa had originated at Corvinus University, but an influx of ELTE students helped shift the centre of operation and action to the ELTE campus and to a 'collective action frame' reliant on more participatory, innovative protest strategies. As was typical of the wider Occupy movement, this reflected a counter-culture politics, being horizontal with pretensions to being leaderless, fluid, and unpredictable (Zontea, 2015). In 2018, the protest repertoire of HaHa was to flicker into life again with the *Szabad Egyetem* protests and the occupation of Kossuth Ter (See chapter three). As important as those protests were, they never achieved the scale, challenge, and audacity of the SZFE occupation. One student involved in the SZFE occupation correctly summed up the situation: "I believe that our university is at the centre of the cultural battle, it has become one of the most important front lines" (personal interview).

As part of the occupation, the protestors set up an 'Education Republic' that created learning spaces within the protest. Some of the teaching there followed standard academic conventions, other methods were said to provide a more open, transparent approach to teaching (Komjathy, 2020). The learning programmes had an element of interdisciplinarity, where students could attend classes other than those in which they were enrolled, and interdisciplinary projects were created; the occupation itself became the subject of certain projects and an active learning experience. Within the occupied university, new conventions were introduced, with decisions being made collectively by a forum of teachers and students (Kalan, 2020). The organic, bottom-up structure to the organisation of the SZFE occupation was redolent of the HaHa student protest principles discussed above, as well as the Occupy Movement of a decade earlier; this point will be revisited below.

Another striking feature of the SZFE occupation was the flair and professionalism of the protestors that, in many respects, drew upon the artistic, communicative, and creative skills of the students. The protests had a strong visual, theatrical dimension. One observer noted that the draping of the SZFE building with red and white police caution tape, the protest banners, and the teachers and students standing guard as if expecting an imminent invasion was reminiscent of an art installation.[1] It was an installation that conveyed the message at the heart of the protest, which was that this was an institution under attack. The facade of the building featured a counter marking how many days the blockade had been underway, and the image of an open hand was a prominent symbol of the protest (Gergely 2021). Yellow pandemic masks with the logo of the open hand and the inscription "FREE SzFE" were to become a common feature and fashion accessory among Hungarians on the streets of Budapest, going beyond the spatial confines of the actual protest site.

The SZFE protestors staged events with the energy of flash mob activism in terms of their performativity and ability for wide participation in them. On 6 September 2020, just days after the campus occupation started, the SZFE protestors organised a human chain from the SZFE university to the Parliament, where protestors handed over a charter declaring their commitment to the importance of academic autonomy and freedom in Hungary. Many thousands joined the human chain, giving them an active rather than passive role in the event. On 9 October 2020 a watchtower was constructed by the protestors in front of the Ministry of Innovation and Technology, where student protestors read aloud and proclaimed their demands every hour from 8 AM to 8 PM, hoping in particular that Minister László Palkovics, who was responsible for higher education re-

---

1 The then-Chancellor of the (SZFE) Lajos Vonderviszt was indirectly responsible for the caution tape. The students had suggested using wooden planks for their installation, but Vonderviszt opposed this, as he felt it was a fire risk. In response, the students used caution tape, and this became a common feature of the protest and campaign imagery.

forms, would hear their appeals (Sárosi, 2020). Another performative event was the delivery of a formal complaint to the Constitutional Court, carried by a student costumed as Iustitia (Goddess of Justice). The complaint noted that both the manner and the conduct of the change to the model of the organisation of the SZFE violated the Basic Law.[2] In November 2020 a student posing as the Goddess Minerva, with an owl, the mythological symbol of wisdom, delivered a document to the state education authority, the Office of Education, appealing for a legal audit regarding the situation at the SZFE and providing evidence that classes had been properly conducted, contrary to the assertions of the new government-appointed SZFE leadership. However, the Office of Education refused to accept the submission; a judgment by the Metropolitan Court in March 2021 ruled that the Office of Education had rejected the request without due reason, thus violating its duty to clarify facts and state reasons for its decisions.

Social media played a prominent role in the SZFE campaign. Facebook pages promoted and disseminated the staged events and core messages. The protest was propelled and built-up wider support through 'hashtag' activism where supporters liked and shared 'Free SZFE' posts and memes and made the 'Free SZFE open hand' part of their profile pictures. Short videos of staged events and student appeals also encouraged 'TikTok activism', the sharing of online videos. As is typical of innovative, participatory social movements, social media was thus able to foster bridging forms of social capital, creating solidarities beyond the SZFE student body and the wider community. Such methods created opportunities that could force their stories into the mainstream media by virtue of an action's novelty and the staged events, despite the conservatism of the mainstream media, particularly in Hungary where it is highly aligned with the Government. Furthermore, through the volume of social media support, the 'Free SZFE' campaign could match the outreach and connection of the mainstream media, an advantage to these innovative forms of activism that has been proven elsewhere in recent years (Tsatsou, 2018). The SZFE protestors also became adept at organising daily press conferences to cater to growing media interest.

The effectiveness and professionalism of the 'Free SZFE' campaign became evident not only in the support it was able to muster in Hungary, but also in

---

2 The complaint centred on the following principles: the principle of legal certainty had been violated because the law did not provide sufficient time for the university to carry out the tasks arising from the change of model; the prohibition of discrimination had been violated because the change discriminates against the University of Theatre and Film Arts on the basis of its presumed ideological approach; freedom of expression had been violated, which protects the right of university lecturers to express their views; and the freedom of education and autonomy had been violated, which is enshrined in Article 10 of the Basic Law.

the international attention and support it generated. The staged events drew the interest of several international news outlets. In a letter published by the *Financial Times*, world-renowned actors such as Dame Helen Mirren, Cate Blanchett, and Eddie Redmayne urged Prime Minister Orbán to stop the full-scale culture war aimed at robbing all cultural spheres and institutions of their autonomy (Khan et al, 2020). European Film Academy President Wim Wenders and the group's chairman, Mike Downey, issued a statement of support that declared "The art of cinema can only breathe in an atmosphere of openness, transparency, and democracy. In support and solidarity for a successful outcome of the occupation" (European Film Academy, 2020). In contrast, Vidnyanszky accused the protestors of being manipulated and accepting aid from international organisations. In a presentation to a hearing of the European Parliament's Committee of Culture and Education, he stated in a rather histrionic manner that the students had been used as "a tool" by left-wing politicians, as they had allegedly been "trained by well-known left-wing movers to take the university in the summer", a reference to the university's summer school. (Kalan, 2020). Others accused Soros of being behind the protests. The pro-Government *Magyar Hírlap* news outlet condemned the protestors for supposedly being the successors of the Lenin Boys, the Red terrorist brigades who committed violent crimes during the revolution in 1919 (Sárosi, 2020). The conservative journalist László Szentesi Zöldi, writing in *Magyar Demokrata* denounced the protest as a "liberal, communist, anarchist, feminist and homosexual" campaign to preserve the hold of an elite over the arts (Kentish, 2020).

On 29 September 2020, the Government appointed a former military colonel, Gábor Szarka, as the new chancellor of the university. Szarka had no previous expertise in the arts and was twice denied entry to the university building by students. He sent an open letter to the professors participating in the strike action calling for an end to their activities. The strike action was also legally challenged. However, after a series of court cases, it was eventually affirmed that the strike action was legal, a decision that can be said to uphold workers' rights to strike not only against low pay or poor working conditions, but also when the autonomy of a higher education institution is compromised (Mohos, 2021). Szarka did manage to close the university's Neptune platform, an essential online educational tool, and the locks were changed on the SZFE auditorium where the protestors had staged meetings. Szarka also sought to cancel the university's autumn semester on 6 November, 27 November, and then on 21 December.[3]

---

3 Despite the strike action the teachers and the students protesting did go on with the education but with severe limitations. The decrees and attempts from Szaka and Vidnyanszky and others

The student body challenged the cancellation's legality and took the matter to court. The court ruled that the board's actions in November 2020 had been unlawful (Vaski, 2021). Lajos Aáry-Tamás, the Commissioner for Educational Rights, confirmed that the suspension of teaching activities had violated the constitutional rights of the students. On 25 November 2020, a government decree was issued stipulating that for public health or public safety reasons, or in case of a natural disaster or an unavoidable situation directly jeopardizing the order of the academic year, it was permissible to cease academic activities. There was a perception that the decree was designed to assist the new government-appointed leadership of the SZFE. Critics argued the decree violated basic constitutional principles and was in breach of the Fundamental Law, which stipulates that emergency measures should only be taken to protect citizens' life, health, property and rights and to maintain the stability of the national economy (Fleck et al, 2021). As noted above, prior to this decree, at the end of October 2020, Chancellor Gábor Szarka and Deputy Rector Emil Novák had suspended the autumn semester of SZFE, claiming they could not see through the course of education due to the blockade because they could not control the operation of the building and perform their duties. The aforementioned decree allowed the Constitutional Court in October 2021 to reject an appeal against the suspension of education at the SZFE and rule that the act did not violate the autonomy of higher education (Horváth, 2021).

The blockade ended after 71 days of occupation, due to a desire to comply with new restrictions against the coronavirus epidemic that had closed all higher education establishments and switched them to online learning (Frei, 2020). Although the occupation came to an end, important legal battles continued to be conducted. Following a number of court cases and legal proceedings in 2021, the Metropolitan Court requested the Constitutional Court to declare the 2019 amendment to the SZFE Act and the Higher Education Act unconstitutional. The court would need to decide on the constitutionality of the change to the model of organisation of the University of Theatre and Film Arts. The final legal outcome could affect the entire system of private foundation-managed universities in Hungary. The court found it troubling that the SZFE Act was promulgated on 8 July 2020 and entered into force partly on the very next day and partly on 1 September, leaving limited scope for a legal challenge (Domány, 2021). In June 2021 the Constitutional Court announced that it did not support the legal challenge to

---

apparently made it very difficult and near impossible to work. So, while the new SZFE leadership declared teachers were not doing their job, they in fact made it almost impossible through their various measures (László Upor testimony).

the adoption of the law, and an appeal will probably be made to the European Court of Human Rights in Strasbourg. In February 2021, 26 staff members of the SZFE, including Laszlo Upor, resigned from their teaching posts. A new 'Freeszfe Society' was formed that, in partnership with a number of universities abroad, offers educational courses and organises cultural activities.

Dissenting Voices

László Upor

László Upor is a dramaturg, literary translator, and author; he was the Vice-Rector of the SZFE and from the spring of 2019 was the Acting Rector/Rector Elect. The Government never confirmed the latter appointment, nor did it ever explain why it failed to do so.[4] *In November 2019 he was nominated as Rector by the university's Senate, but his official appointment was never confirmed as part of the Government's so-called 'change of model' of the organisation of the SZFE. He resigned from his managerial position in the fall of 2020 and then left the university in early 2021.*

On reflection, I feel the Government acted in a provocative way with regard to making the SZFE (University of Theatre and Film Arts) into a foundation. In the late spring of 2020, we were given a date of January 2021 by which to complete the process and expressed concern at the short time accorded. In response, the Government moved the deadline to September 2020. Every time we had an objection, the Government would either respond with an even harsher proposal or wouldn't respond at all. I think the Government did not take kindly to being challenged and that is why they tightened the process. I am not sure if they pre-planned this confrontation, but they certainly made the process harsh.

Due to the nature of our discipline, students and teachers work together intensely; we thus already had intense relationships, and when the foundation process started, the community of the SZFE acted as a group, we shared information, we shared our viewpoints, and we reached something of a collective view; this was evident in our negotiations with the Government, something that again aroused their suspicion.

---

4 The former SZFE Rector's time in office had run out in March 2019 so Upor, the former second in command, became the legal, legitimate leader (normally that should be a temporary appointment) until the new Rector was appointed. Then in November Upor was elected by the Senate and became a Rector-elect until he resigned.

The SZFE had been under attack from government figures and their traditionalist friends in the art world for some time before the foundation process started, in what can be described as the culture war gripping Hungary. The list of board members selected for the new governing body indicated the Government wanted firm control of the institution and an obvious course change. None of the Government appointees were picked from among our recommendations, whereas a number of appointees were picked from among those who had attacked us fiercely. I had no real hope that we could see discussions lead to the evolution of any real change to the Government's plans.

The protest and resistance to the foundation process quickly escalated; our experiences with the heavy-handed approach of the Government gave us insights into where autocracy was taking us, and we wanted to show its dangers. Unfortunately, nobody really listened, it was all widely regarded as "our problem" and part of the culture war. In April 2021 Hungary's Parliament voted to transfer state assets into foundations that will control many of the country's public universities and cultural assets.

The strong protest that started in the spring and reached its most spectacular and unprecedented form/stage with the occupation of the SZFE building in September was, in part, a product of the learning environment nurtured by the SZFE. Our work is about exploring the human condition, understanding motivations, relationships and the consequences of our actions. When we work and study, we investigate, so we can analyse whatever happens around us through our drama and arts-based activities. This helped forge our collective response to the foundation proposal. I would not say that we acted in unison, but that we acted collaboratively with exceptional unity.

We managed to prevent political movements from using or abusing our campaign. We found very creative ways of demonstrating what was wrong – in this, the students were leading us, their activities had a quality of lightness that highlighted and revealed the nature of the forces ranged against us. The images were powerful, appearing on social media and even on pandemic face masks. The protestors avoided the roles of either victim or hero.

A legal campaign was developed alongside the protests that generated statements, interviews, and demonstrations. If not for the Government's harsh, provocative position, nothing would have happened as it did. We have had quite a few legal victories, some minor losses, and we are still waiting for the outcome of several other cases. The most important ones, maybe Strasbourg, could still be to come. Even cases won will not make a big difference, though (or will they?). Look at the Central European University story. Will they move back to Budapest? No. This is all about the long-term victory of truth and justice – not the practical, present-day issues. This is also about precedent, an example for people who will find themselves in similar situations. This is also about the record in the future history books. We will not (could not) ever return to where we were before the destruction. What's broken is broken, very little can be mended (the consequences are still to be investigated and measured). However, this has all been recorded and shown.

The protests were a learning experience. We were shocked at the Government's approach; key questions were at the forefront of our mind: Is this really happening? Why are they doing this? We learnt, though, that we could be strong if we were united, and collectively we could offer a real challenge. We learnt that you can organise through non-hierarchical processes, we learnt that you do not have to submit to autocracy and that our fate can be changed.

The pandemic gave the protest another dimension. I was very concerned for the welfare of the students involved in the occupation, they formed an action group to work on pandemic safeguards that were actually stricter than the ones developed by the Government. Such collective work was a feature of our 'Education Republic' (learning spaces and experiences within the occupied building). As an applicant for the job of Rector, I had explored and promoted the possible transformation of the university, and students were interested in those ideas. When the Occupation started, the organising of the building and the protests took lots of energy and time; somehow it was decided to combine study and protest, we had the best of both worlds, and the learning experiences became more open, through protest, we learnt about sociology, social movements and honed our communication skills through the theatrical nature of our protest. Again, the students' innovative ideas and intuition led, very often, in this way. We harmonised our teaching activity and activism. Teachers adjusted their classes to accommodate the changing situation; for example, in the film class students shot hundreds of hours of footage for a documentary they plan to produce.

I had concerns for student welfare, because the kind of activism they were involved in can be very demanding; they were not just being attacked by the Government and the media, but also attracting huge public support and sympathy, plus constant media attention. I told them to be cautious and aware of becoming 'rock star' activists and the dangers that involves. The protest has had a long-term effect on everyone. People were living and working in the SZFE building, after sleeping in a corridor or classroom they were planning, organising, and learning, it was very intensive, there were 'ups' and 'downs', and it was exhausting. There were high expectations, people were expressing support and urging us on, it was uplifting, but sometimes frustrating, others wanted us to fight their fights, and it is frustrating to see some people who, although they were concerned, chose to be passive and/or to ignore what is happening in Hungary and the freedoms being lost. I have a strong memory of speaking to the Hungarian Rectors' conference in June 2020, where I informed the other universities that the experience of the SZFE should be a warning to them as to where foundation status could take them. This warning was met with complete silence and the chair, perhaps out of nervousness, called for the meeting to move to the next point on the agenda. However, during the break many university officials came up to me and expressed concern about the SZFE case and their concern for their own futures. A key thing we need to be alert to is fear, it is fear that holds many back, and in the process such passivity bolsters and emboldens this Government. We must overcome fear!

This "culture war" (with an unfortunate, painfully long history) has now gone way too far. Our case is the last straw – however, it is a very important one. The fight became so fierce that the whole art world is deeply divided, no return to "normal" seems likely soon. Since "high politics" interfered with us with such arrogance, representatives of the art community were forced, provoked, and blackmailed into "taking part" individually and as groups/institutions. Eventually, people, colleagues and fellow artists who until recently had worked together in peace, regardless of their different tastes and political views, found themselves in no-negotiation, no-collaboration, no-communication situations. It will take generations to mend, I fear. In fuelling and igniting this, the ruling party committed a horrible crime, damaging society severely.

The polarisation, though, could get even worse with the foundation plan for universities and museums, described by some as an attempt to create a 'parallel state' (See chapter six). This is just too obvious, and what I don't understand is why and how it was NOT so obvious to so many and for such a long time. We were blowing the whistle on this a year ago already. Culture war or not, the point of this exercise has been and still is to secure the present ruling party's (and their financial circles') exclusive control over and access to this huge national asset, no matter who holds political power in the coming decades. The whole of higher education (including intellectual/spiritual and material property) and whatever it is related to has now been sold out to a group that is privileged, small, and watertight. University autonomy is not just an inherent value, but also an important aspect of the nation's political immune system.

The whole experience of the SZFE campaign was very intense and demanding. The six months preceding the leaders' resignation (on 31 August) and the occupation of the building (which were not planned to happen in succession, by the way) were already very intense and depressing (the "foundation issue" had been put on the table as early as in February and fights began immediately on various levels). Then there were the 70-odd days of occupation and constant actions, and then the withdrawal from the building due to the pandemic. Then there was the "goodbye and grief" period, and then the silent building/construction of something new. This was an incredible rollercoaster experience – all the while under heavy "incoming fire". Of course, people dropped out – some for a few days, others for weeks or months. The good news is: that we have too many warriors to collapse as a community, even when some people took a step back. There were always others who stepped in.

A new and major priority is the "Freeszfe Society". We found wonderful partners in Europe to complete our mission and usher our young people to their degrees. Then, independently and in collaboration with these partners, we are offering new courses, some that are similar to our old, traditional ones, and others that have no precedents. In other words, we are trying to turn the emergency exit into a new start and a winning situation. We dream about eventually building a very open, very flexible institution with a free, creative spirit with a maximum level of personal involvement from everyone in the community, and a minimum level of hierarchy in running the operations.

Tamás Cseke – Romanian Erasmus Student

I am an ethnic Hungarian from outside Hungary, I came to the SZFE as part of the Erasmus programme. I was accepted for a place in March 2020 but could not be certain I would come due to the pandemic. The summer saw the spread of the pandemic decrease, so I grew more hopeful of coming. I heard about what was happening with the SZFE during the summer via Facebook and what some friends living in Budapest told me. Some Erasmus classmates decided not to come after they found out about what was happening, but I still felt that it could be worth it, and I had also wanted to live in Budapest for a long time. I arrived in late August 2020.

I arrived as the tensions between the SZFE and the Government were rising and the protest was growing. I remember the night of 31 August 2020, everyone was inside the SZFE building and someone yelled "should we occupy the building?" There were no questions about that. Everyone was like "Yes, this is our university, we won't let them take it away from us", that was how it started. At first, I did not know if I should take part, I did not have much to lose, being a visiting student, and I had a university back home to which I could have returned at any time. I wondered if it was my fight and whether I should get involved. As the occupation of the SZFE building started, I spent more and more time there. By early October 2020 I was heavily into what was happening because I wanted to stand up for my friends.

We were somewhat separate from the Education Republic, as the Erasmus students had separate classes in English and the SZFE kept to the requirements of the course as set out in the Erasmus contract. Through the occupation I learnt a lot – in fact, I learnt more in 70 days than I had in the previous three years of higher education. I learnt how to speak up for values I believe in and how not to judge people for their opinions. Everyone had their highs and lows, but we learnt to stick together, there were more than 400 people there with very different political views. What I loved was having one common goal. A core principle of the campaign was the fight for academic freedom, which is a basic right, like that the university should be free to choose its own rector. Many agreed with us and joined us. It felt like our rights and freedoms were being clamped down, we were being stamped on. When something happens directly to you and those around you, it makes a bigger impression than seeing it happen to others.

Even I, who was a visitor as an Erasmus student, seemed to have value and a place in the SZFE forum where students and teachers discussed what to do. The forums could be just informational updates on what was happening, but there were also wide-ranging debates with the students and teachers. The rules were simple, with moderators who organised the discussions and votes. To speak you had to raise your hand and speak through a microphone. The meetings would last for hours until a consensus emerged. Sometimes four different strategies would be identified and the forum would be divided into four groups, and each group had to assess the pros and cons of a given strategy, and a spokesperson from the group would present the discussion to the forum, and then we would vote to decide on the most-favoured option. I remember how, the night before the SZFE Chancellor was to come to the university, the forum met and decided to offer passive resistance – the forum debated this into the night and we did not get much sleep. The forum ended at 5 AM and we were outside waiting for the Chancellor between 6 and 9 AM.

My emotions were mixed. It was exciting and stressful. Courses ran as usual, so there was academic work to do. We felt a huge sense of responsibility in this struggle. Within the group, there was great kindness and patience. Everyone, even if they did not know someone well, showed support and kindness to each other, there was a huge sense of fraternity. If you made a coffee, you would make it for others, if you saw someone mopping the floor, you would help them. Sometimes there was a sense of 'burnout' and despondency, but it would be enough for one person to say 'let's carry on and try and break through this wall', or at least feel that we had tried to dispel any demoralisation.

There was some fear that the courses would not be accredited, and the new leadership tried to stop the courses from being validated We brought evidence that the courses were being properly organised to the authority that regulates education, but they would not accept the submission from us. We went to court, and the court said we could not be denied on this matter. We had an amazing legal team, and we had complete trust in them. Eventually, when they enrolled in the new SZFE run by government appointees in the second semester, students were told they would get credit for the first semester. The question of credit was stressful for me, as we Erasmus students needed it – otherwise we would have had to pay back the Erasmus grant. Our situation was complicated by the fact that we were only scheduled to be at the SZFE for one semester and would not be there for the second. We wrote to the Chancellor, but we never got a reply and waited for weeks, but we did get our credits in early February after all.

In September 2020 I had little fear about the pandemic; the numbers were low, but the occupied SZFE had a strict policy, temperatures were taken as you entered the building and you had to wear a mask. Social distancing was enforced and there was a working group who would identify whom sick people had spoken to and met in the previous days, and they would ask people to self-isolate. It was surprisingly effective. There was a fear we would be thrown out because of the pandemic, so we had to be very strict. I actually became sick with Covid in late November 2020, weeks after the occupation ended. In November 2020 the Government introduced a second lockdown, and we left the building to conform with the health and safety rules.

Ending the occupation was stressful and sad. It was like building a house and then having to dismantle it brick by brick. It was devastating, some people had not just studied there, but also slept there. We knew it would not be the same, we would not be together anymore, the sense of togetherness had been the most energising thing about the experience. The last few days were like an ant farm. Everyone was doing something. Dismantling shelves, packing the food, mopping the floor, taking down the banners. It was the day after the press conference at which we had stated that we were going to leave the building and take the protest with us. It took two days to move out. There was a lot of work and crying. A video was produced at that time, featuring a girl playing the piano in the main hall. She plays, then she suddenly stops, closes the lid of the piano, and says: "There is nothing to cry about."

I think the most significant thing about the protest was that the border between teachers and students was broken through, it was beautiful to be in a group with a professor of 70 where the teacher and the students were on the same level and everyone was heard. We learnt a lot from the teachers, and they learnt a lot from us. We all somehow got a kind of diploma from this experience. Many in Hungary and beyond were inspired by our protest. When had anything like this happened in Hungary in recent years?

To some extent, this experience changed me. I understood that I have rights and I learnt how to stand up for them. I learnt more about my thoughts and outlooks and how to interact with people.

Insights into 'Free SZFE'

The testimony from those involved in the 'Free SZFE' protest powerfully conveys the power and importance of solidarity and deep bonds in forging an effective social movement. The protest was also historic in its scale and level of challenge to Fidesz's authoritarianism, and it is likely to form a deep imprint in the narrative of the counter-authoritarian movement in Hungary. It is an inspiring story of courage and dignity, one that in part prompted me to write this book.

'Free SZFE' felt like a critical moment in Hungarian society, the tension and drama of the moment were heightened by the strains created by the Covid-19 pandemic and the increasing conflict between Hungary and the European Union. Added to this was the impending election in Hungary, scheduled for 2022, which started to focus pro- and anti-Fidesz minds on the prospects and political fortunes of Orbán. Some contemplated whether the SZFE protest might be a turning point. For Laszlo Upor, the former Rector-elect at SZFE, the student occupation was a defining event for a whole generation. "For the first time, they [the students] have experienced naked, almost totalitarian methods of exercising power that impose their will and leave no space for negotiations. Also, they have learned how to unite and how to capture the interest of the rest of society" (Kalan, 2020). The radical Methodist priest and social worker Gabor Ivanyi, a prominent critic of Orbán, seemed to gauge the magnitude and transformational potential of the protest when he told the students at a demonstration "You are our future – you are our hope, I know this is a terribly big burden, an unbearable burden, but I would like to thank you all for thinking this through and taking it on."[5]

Student academic freedom can be thought of in social and political activist terms. Students protesting what they perceive to be injustices have become

---

5 Iványi's Hungarian Evangelical Fellowship (MET) supports a number of schools and social institutions and is, at the time of writing, appealing to the Supreme Court after the Tax Authority has debited their tax account due to owed payments. MET says they haven't received the state subsidies they are entitled to, hence they could not pay their taxes and bills. In the opinion of some, political motivation is behind the authorities' actions, as Iványi is a prominent critic of Orbán. In 2020 Ivanyi and his church were awarded the European Parliament European Citizen Prize, in 2021 the Freeszfe Society was an awardee too.

something of a truism, rooted historically in 1960s' student radicalism, a period of considerable social upheaval. Following this tradition, universities ought to be important centres of critical conscience, and students should be important actors in challenging the status quo and campaigning for a more just and equal society (Macfarlane, 2017). In this sense, the example and resistance of the SZFE students adds another interesting dimension to debates on academic freedom.

As noted above, the ease with which Orbán has been able to dismantle democratic safeguards, checks and balances meant that some had become cynical about Hungary's ability to rise up. It should also be noted, though, that this was not just a protest of Hungarian youth, but a protest where academics worked in unison with their students. Academics, not just in Hungary but globally, have been timid in the face of the new managerialism, corporatism, reforms and change being imposed in general that tame and erode academic freedom, autonomy, and critical thinking by imposing audit culture and surveillance (Halffman and Radder. 2015, Jemielniak and Greenwood. 2015). The 'Free SZFE' protest was profoundly different, though. The fact that an educational building was occupied and managed by the students, who together with the staff established a new organisational culture and learning regime, was unprecedented, not just in terms of the philosophical principles that guided the occupation, but also in terms of its 71-day duration. The protest was redolent of the 2011 Occupy Wall Street movement that was a response to the 2008 financial crisis and austerity, an anarchic moment of rupture, democratic participation, clear focus, solidarity, and theatre (Ewalt, 2013).

The SZFE occupation was a rupture, in terms of its audacity, that took many by surprise. The 'Education Republic' established by the SZFE students and staff was in some cases project- and student-centred, based upon the actual protest and, together with collective campaign decision-making, was a radical move away from formalised 'banking education' and hierarchical political campaigning. Such approaches are more akin to Freire's (1972) radical, critical pedagogy that seeks to nurture awareness of oppression, critical thinking, and to envision and strategize radical alternatives through deliberation and collective action. The 'Education Republic' can also be said to have been shaped by principles of student-centredness, a core, mainstreamed principle in higher education, although the extent to which it is applied is debatable. In the opinion of some, student-centred learning as a concept has been too narrowly interpreted and has failed to see higher education as a process of emancipation, rather than as one of constraint and control that is imposed by a panoptic culture of student performativity. To be truly student-centred requires understanding what it means to be a learner and respect for the ideas of freedom and democracy. Radical conceptions envisage an emphasis on the importance of independent learning, allowing students to make more choices about their curriculum and how they engage at university (Rogers, 1969). Rather than being viewed as customers or passive repositories to be filled with facts and numbers, students should be seen as 'co-learners' (Macfarlane, 2017). The 'Education Republic' at the SZFE could be viewed as an important experiment in student-centred, experiential learning.

The fusion of learning and activism also brings to mind bell hooks' (2014) view that engaged pedagogy is an expression of political activism. Creating and remaking a learning community, imagining a new society, stems from an assumption that existing institutions and learning conventions are flawed and in need of change. Such a discourse, as is the case with the SZFE campaign, is invariably grounded in the language of democracy, democratic processes and participation (Cole and Heinecke, 2020).

The clear focus and solidarity of the Free SZFE campaign perhaps stemmed from their unity as art students in an exceptionally small institution that had created strong bonds between students and teachers even before the protest. The blatant, audacious power grab by the Hungarian state regarding SZFE autonomy and the imposition of a new leadership also no doubt strengthened the resolve and unity of the protestors. This sense of strong group identity must have been intense, as such deep, emotional solidarity is a prerequisite for the type of high-risk activism in which the SZFE students were engaged (Nepstad, 2004). It should also be noted that senior academic staff shared information and discussed strategies with the "citizens" of the university from the outset. When the first lockdown began (that coincided with the beginning of the transformation in mid-March) it was decided to take the unusual step of having a senate-meeting evey week), and these senate meetings were open for all employees, students and teachers. The average attendance was between 50 and 150 people. This was in contrast to the secrecy and lack of transparency concerning the privatisation of other universities in Hungary.

The 'Free SZFE' campaign had the carnivalesque qualities of the Occupy Movement, the protests and direct action, and the deployment of what has been described as the 'public screen' was evident (DeLuca and Peeples, 2002). This is a stratagem that, through audacity, creativity and visuality, can force its message into the mainstream media or through TikTok activism (discussed above) propel the activists' message via social media. The framing and communication of the 'Free SZFE' campaign was also effective because the core message and goals were kept simple, namely academic freedom and autonomy. These goals were not, at least in the communication strategy, embellished with any deeper philosophical or political pledges. In an interview, Mihaly Csernai, a SZFE student and leader of the SZFE student government, stated "We don't want to get into politics at all ...Our goal is to stay independent. We would have protested if the other side of the political spectrum had tried to do the same." (Kalan, 2020). These tactics in the short term may have been astute and made the protest more typical of 'new social movement' activism. Some would question, though, the validity of such a stratagem in the long term, given the fusion of populism and authoritarianism with neoliberalism in Hungary and the need to frame new political messages that could appeal to and unite alienated intellectuals and working-class communities in Hungary.

The 'Free SZFE' protest was also unique in the sense that it managed to create an insurgent space within the academy. Despite the corporatisation of the academy, it remains one of the few components of the public sphere with the ability to present what has been termed 'militant utopianism', a space where critical consciousness and transformative action might emerge through radical teaching and learning Giroux, 2014). Militant utopianism in the academy can create an 'insurgent space' that spawns challenges and resistance to hegemony and nurtures experimentation (Coté et al, 2007). Occupation as protest and insurgent space presents a form of direct action and anarchist thinking that is highly participatory, fluid, and non-hierarchical, where a vision of a new society might be sketched out. For some, the 'Free SZFE' campaign presented such traits. Ultimately the aim of such episodes of activism is to reach beyond the campus and provoke a rupture, an insurrectionary moment (Webb, 2018). The 'Free SZFE' campaign certainly caught the public imagination, crystalising and utilising campaign methods pioneered by previous radical student movements in Hungary more effectively than ever before. It is too soon, at the time of writing, to fully assess the impact of this radical rupture and the potential chain of events that it might set in motion. It will certainly be a metonymic, iconic moment in Hungarian radicalism for many years to come. It may be the case, though, that the 'Free SZFE' campaign was just a fleeting moment of radicalism.

The SZFE students might be an exception in terms of the risk and commitment they displayed. The same point can be made regarding the teachers. Would other academics and students be prepared to sacrifice their careers and studies for principles and a commitment to academic freedom? Some would argue that academic staff have a responsibility to fight with and for students in challenging injustice in the sphere of education (Smeltzer and Hearn 2015). If one accepts that universities have a role to promote "civic values," including political awareness and critical thinking, then when governments undermine civic values, it might be especially incumbent upon academic staff to offer dissent (Dahlum and Wig, 2021).

After the Hungarian state managed to reclaim the SZFE building, the 'Free SZFE' campaign seemed to lose some of its momentum. The occupation's end meant the campaign had lost its locus and propensity for artistic and political installation and spectacle. The students were offered new classes by the newly-appointed SZFE institutional leadership; some of the new teachers were said to have close ties with the Government. However, great energy has been poured into the Freeszfe Society. As part of the 'Emergency Exit' programme, as it was termed, partner universities adopted former SZFE students who, officially, became their students. The Freeszfe Society signed a contract with these universities that they teach "their" students the courses, and these universities "give" the due credits (and, eventually, the diploma). About 140 students in all took this option. In October 2021 students trained through the Freeszfe Society received their diplomas at partner universities in Ludwigsburg, Germany and Salzburg, Austria. The Emergency Exit programme, devised by the Freeszfe Society as a solution for those students who decided to leave the University of Theatre and Film Arts Budapest following the forced takeover, was one of the awardees of the 2021 European Citizens' Prize, launched by the European Parliament. The story and struggle of the 'Free SZFE' is far from over.

Generally, social movements operate in cycles with highs and lows of activity. It should not, therefore, be assumed that the SZFE campaign has been quelled. It should also be borne in mind that during periods of normality, students are under supreme pressure, challenged in some cases by poverty, but in general by the demands and rigour of academic life (Karter, et al 2019). Activism, especially in the case of something like the SZFE occupation that can place young people literally on the frontline against an authoritarian regime, certainly brought them added pressures. It should be noted that these pressures were accentuated by the challenges of operating amid a pandemic. Exhaustion was evident in Mihály Csernai's letter of resignation as the student leader at the SZFE: "I strived by all means to serve the interests of students, even by putting my own opinion or university studies in the background. I feel like at this point my job has reached a limit. Not only do I think I'm tired, but I also feel like I've reached my realistic limits" (Csernai, 2021). Time was needed by SZFE students like Csernai, not just to recharge, but also to regroup. During lulls in protest and social movement activity, instrumental work continues with organisational development and the framing of new stratagems, waiting for the next moment or crisis that might act as the catalyst to the next episode and showcase for a counter-narrative (Donovan, 2018). The metonymic memory of the SZFE campaign will be an important factor in shaping the next steps. The question of how the campaign for academic freedom and autonomy in Hungary and beyond should be framed is the theme of the concluding chapter of this book

Chapter Eight
Critical Reflections on the Past, Present and Future

This book has sought to provide a great deal of historic context to the issue of academic freedom in Hungary; in this short chapter three critical thinkers, Peter Futo, Ferenc Krémer, and Miklos Hadas present personal insights pertinent to the limits of freedom under Communism, the move towards liberalism in transition and the drift to authoritarianism post-transition. Futo is a retired academic who reminisces about higher education under Communism. Krémer was dismissed from his academic post a decade ago and some feel was one of the first victims of the decline of academic freedom in Hungary. Hadas is a prominent critical thinker in Hungary and was a vociferous critic of the model change at the Corvinus. In the text below, Futo reflects on coming to Corvinus University in the 1960s, Krémer narrates the story of his dismissal and Hadas articulates his aspirations for critical sociology in Hungary.

Experiences of education in Communist Hungary

Peter Futo

Peter Futo is a statistician and economist who was course leader of the MA in local development at Corvinus University. He is a Cîmzetes Egyetemi Tanár (Affiliated Professor) at the Corvinus University.

I came to Corvinus, or the Karl Marx University as it was called then, in September 1966 as a student, immediately after finishing high school. The choice of the course, Mathematical Economics (called at that time "Terv-Matematika" Plan-Mathematics), was a compromise on my side. Initially, while still at the high school, I decided to study maths and philosophy, which at that time was taught only in the framework of teacher education. However, the director of the high school refused to issue a letter of recommendation on my behalf, stating that I was not eligible to become a teacher, due to my "bad behaviour". Indeed, previously I had a minor verbal conflict with one of the teachers, who had slapped me, and subsequently, I refused to participate in his lessons. This behaviour was then evaluated as rebellious and served as a pretext of not recommending me for the course I wanted to study. I chose my second option then at the Cor-

https://doi.org/10.1515/9783110749816-010

vinus, but I was only there for one year before I eventually managed to fulfil my dream and transfer to maths and later to the philosophy faculty of ELTE.

This was an age when all facets of freedom – freedom of travel, media, entrepreneurship, academic freedom, etc. – were limited. There was strict country-wide censorship. I remember going to the state library as I wanted to study yoga and asked the librarian if there were any useful books on this subject. I discovered that such books were only accessible for people having "special permits": yoga was classified as an 'idealistic philosophy'. From this time, I recall that in 1966 the streets were full of policemen as it was the tenth anniversary of the 1956 uprising. Such an oppressive environment also led to self-censorship, you had to be careful about what you said.

In the mid-60s the Corvinus was a lively place with ambitious students and some very good professors. Economics, history and even geography could only be taught in Marxian terms, yet nevertheless, I found the lectures interesting. Our maths professor set a strong and demanding pace and I am still grateful for this to him. At the time there was a deeper divide between teaching and research. Bolder academics were often confined to so-called research institutions, and not allowed to spread their "heretical" views to the students.

Later there came some signs of change, a relative thaw. This was the time of Kádár and the advent of what became known as 'goulash socialism', which to some extent started to liberalise some aspects of the communist state.

An example: Liska Tibor, a great man, and economist whom I knew through my schoolteacher who was married to him, was permitted to teach at Corvinus in the second half of the 1960s. He could be described as a reform communist who felt that Stalinist economics did not work and wanted to save communism from its own stupidity by developing an economic approach that was socialist but allowed entrepreneurialism and freedom. At the time such views were heresy. He was ahead of his time and a real pioneer. However, because of his revolutionary past in 1956 and due to his reformist views, he was marginalised for a decade and had to work as a travelling salesman. He was barred from working as an economist or publishing. After a decade of punishment and being at the periphery he was allowed to teach at the Corvinus.

Let me mention a parallel, non-state urban institution, which flourished in those times: our parties given for each other, for friends and for friends of friends. This was the so-called "házibuli", a weekly event held at different flats. These were not only parties in the classic sense with music, drink, socialising and partner search, but they were also opportunities to exchange news, obtain practical information, and develop useful professional contacts. In these times you could of course learn nothing from the media which was heavily censored and controlled. Some of these parties became 'radical learning spaces', social institutions in their own right with a vibrant intellectual atmosphere.

Liberalisation was gradual and very slow; it lasted for almost four decades. The epoch of Kádár started in 1956 with state terror killing hundreds, incarcerating thousands, firing tens of thousands from their working places, spying on hundreds of thousands, limiting free travel of millions, and intimidating practically everybody. However, from the 1960s onward, with each year we enjoyed a little bit more freedom: one year a slight relaxation of censorship or travel, or the next year a decree allowing some tiny-tiny freedom in culture or in the academic world. I remember, what an incredible feeling it was when in 1987 some apparatchik in Parliament stood up and said that having a passport and being able to travel was a human right. It was a turning point!

Today we are going backwards, we have our personal freedoms, we can travel and publish but we are losing important political rights.

Life in Hungary as a Critical Thinker

Ferenc Krémer

Ferenc Krémer is an academic expert on policing.

I was born and grew up in the outskirts of Budapest, Csepel, where at that time blue-collar workers lived; it was then a major industrial centre. My father was a shoemaker, my mother was a semi-skilled worker. (She is now 102 years old). Both branches of my family had a close connection to the labour movement. One of my grandfathers was a member of the trade union of woodworkers, the other a left activist who was deported to Dachau in 1944 as a Schuldgefangenen (political prisoner) and died in Buchenwald. My father, a Hungarian German, was deported to Crimea for "a bit of work" (malenkij robot) in 1945. During this time of Russian occupation, Hungarians were being rounded up to work as manual labourers in the USSR. An estimated 130.000 Hungarians became 'Malenkij robot' (forced labourers). My father came back in 1947 but he became ill in 1960 and my mother was the only one who had work; in brief, we were quite poor.

The elementary school in the outskirt of Budapest that I attended wasn't an elite one, so if you hadn't got any special talent, it was almost impossible to rise from the underclass of society. Fortunately, I had one! I wasn't an eminent student, but I loved the fine arts and drawing, so I wanted to be an artist. I was admitted into the art school in Budapest as a decorative painter. In the art classes, we learnt not only aesthetics and surface techniques but philosophy and the history of philosophical visions of the world. That's why we began to debate about avant-garde painting and sculptures, and the role of arts in society. That was one of the educational experiences that deeply impacted upon me, which oriented me to the social sciences.

The other major point of influence was political. We started in middle school in 1968, the year of the Czechoslovak 'Prague Spring', a failed attempt to liberalise the socialist regime, leading to the invasion of the Czechoslovak Republic by the troops of the Warsaw Pact. The second important event was the Paris student protests of the same year. Because my family background was Left, and the possible choice of social science publications was limited, I started to study Marx's works. I felt the nineteenth century radical thinking to be very attractive, and it was for me a starting point of the criticism of social conditions. I wanted to be a philosopher, so applied to Eötvös Loránd University (ELTE), but I didn't begin studying philosophy. I had to choose another subject besides history and I selected scientific socialism. Fortunately, this department was open-minded, and my thesis, which was on the personality cult in Hungary (1949–1956), was unique in 1979.

So, I became a left critical thinker, which wasn't so simple in the 1980s. Being a historian too, I turned to ancient Greek history and got a doctor's degree writing a study about Homeric epos (1992). I studied sociology at Eötvös Loránd University (ELTE) and designed surveys nationwide on poverty for local authorities. I began dealing with police matters during a visiting scholarship at George Washington University, Washington in 1996. At Washington University I came across for the first time a large body of theoretical literature on policing, which was almost unknown in Hungary and which was the basis of my later works and research in this field. Coming home, I made the first surveys in Hungary about police occupational culture and police corruption, and I participated in an international survey organised by the University of Delaware.[1] My empirical and theoretical results were summarised in my second Ph.D, which was published in the following year.[2] So, I became a social scientist with expertise in law enforcement.

My broad goal as a social scientist was and is to change the living conditions of people, regarding political, economic, and environmental conditions. In this work I professed from the beginning, the belief that democracy is not only for the elite or just for intellectuals but for the poor and vulnerable people as well.

---

1 Kockars–Ivkovic–Haberfeld (eds.): The Contours of Police Integrity, Sage Publication, 2004.
2 A rendőri hatalom természete. Társadalmi szerep és foglalkozási kultúra, Napvilág, 2003 (The Nature of Police Power. Social Role and Occupational Culture).

I taught for twenty years at the police academy (later absorbed into the National University of Public Service, Faculty of Law Enforcement), that job coming to an end in 2012. From 2010 I wrote every week at least one political essay on current political questions for the news outlet Galamus, a website featuring news and opinion pieces that gained a reputation as an honest media outlet that cared about Hungarian democracy. As was reflected in my articles I considered from the beginning that the Orbán regime was a new kind of dictatorship. I accept that Orbán was elected with a two-thirds parliamentary majority in 2010 but many dictatorships in the twentieth century were formed by first occupying the overwhelming majority of the parliamentary seats and then striving for monopoly in the economy, in culture, in the education system, and other parts of the public sphere by putting their loyal men in leading positions. This is exactly what Fidesz has done. They took away the independence of the Constitutional Court and the media and stole all the money from private pension funds. In the modern interpretation, Fidesz can't even be called a political party. Since Fidesz is mostly the private property of Viktor Orbán, it's more similar to a great landed estate from the middle ages. Orbán himself decides the direction of Fidesz and who can be a lead member just like in fiefdoms back then.

I hoped that I could influence in a certain sense the thinking of people and alert them to the dangers facing the country. I believed too, that it was absurd that Hungary could find itself in a new dictatorship, given the terrible experiences the country has historically suffered under such leaders. Sadly, Intellectuals from across the political spectrum are unable to find a solution to many of the problems Hungary faces, since the change of regime. Their words are rarely backed up with actions. The idea that Hungary should face its past is repeated over and over again, but so far nobody has presented any ideas on how it should be executed. Liberals and socialists are constantly debating about whether or not hate speech laws should be implemented, some arguing that they would limit freedom of speech. They cannot decide on the issue, even though one of the fundamental rules of democracy is that an individual is free to do anything as long as it isn't harmful to others. They did nothing to prevent the increase in racism. The reason why the current government could deconstruct the constitution is that there hasn't been a strong dividing line between democracy and dictatorship ever since the change of regime. If intellectuals can't come up with something to control the chaos, Fidesz will be in power for decades

Concerning my dismissal, the dean of the National University of Public Service, where I worked, called me on a Friday at 8 p.m. asking me to visit him the next day in his office for a talk. I asked him what it was about, and he said: the termination of my work contract – this is how I learnt my fate in June 2012. It seemed to me that they couldn't suffer anyone from the opposition to teach at their so-called national and public university. I was also excluded from two research projects and since then, it has been difficult to conduct research in my specialist areas in Hungary. Anyone doing research on the police must apply for permission which is issued by the national police headquarters; there is little chance of me receiving such permission. In the United States and the United Kingdom, such work is not subject to special authorisation and, researchers are encouraged to investigate the police.[3] Another problem is that in Hungary people are increasingly becoming too scared to give interviews and testimony on law enforcement; there is a growing culture of fear that inhibits academic investigation.

I have to say my dismissal from the police academy was not my first experience of being ostracised at work because of my views. In the later stages of communism, during the 80s I was pushed out of a college where I taught but at least they gave me time to find another job, meaning the emotional impact was not as hard as in 2012. So, I have challenged communism as well as Orbánism; I cannot abide authoritarianism and oppression. It should be noted too that, before I was fired, the 'Tettrekész Magyar Rendőrség Szakszervezete', a police association with right-wing leanings, complained to the rector of the police academy because I called 'Jobbik' (a radical right party in Hungary) and the police association, "neo-Nazis" (at one point the police association had a cooperation agreement with Jobbik). After some months the rector rejected this complaint, but I was becoming a target and upsetting some people on the political right and, after a year, a new rector fired me without any justification. I believe I was fired by the academy leadership because of my beliefs. My public views on Orbán being an autocrat together with my connections with the police academy I think made me a target. I saw the dark nature of the Orbán dictatorship first-hand. After being fired, I made a legal challenge. I went through two cases where it was found the university did not have the justification to fire me and they had to pay me compensation.

The department I worked in at the police academy was divided in a certain sense. My line manager and many staff agreed with me, they were critical of the Fidesz policy, but some of them wouldn't publicly speak about it. The day of my firing was the last day of June 2012, which meant the semester had come to an end, limiting the opportunities for any protests. The timing was typical of the political calculation of Fidesz. My line manager and one of my colleagues helped me to get over what happened, and they also helped me to get some work

---

3 See Policy Solutions (2017) Political Discrimination in Hungary: Case Studies from the Hungarian Justice System, Local Government, Media, Agriculture, Education, and Civil Sector.

when I had financial problems. My friends at other universities also helped me. Alas, the trade union was of no use; the unions are now very weak.

Critical thinking was and is not common in police training. The Hungarian police work according to commands and most of the lecturers in police-related teaching consider such a regime normal. So, some colleagues did not raise concerns when I was fired. I think a social science department was a foreign body in police education in a certain sense. The surveys which we designed on police corruption, prejudices, and other police deviances, and what police officers think about the social role of police, caused antipathy against our department. The leadership of the police college thought our mission is to follow what the police leadership wants to know. My conception was the contrary: our mission should be to find how the police can serve citizens in the best way.

After being fired my first reaction was a feeling of being free; no one could now tell me what to write and how to think. For some months this feeling of freedom remained but, as I had no job and no money coming in, things became harder. The financial situation was tough, my income decreased by 80%. Luckily, I had some savings and some work to make money but had to limit my expenses for years. You know, the unemployment benefit only lasts for three months, after that, I had only 36.000 Ft (approx. 100 euro) monthly income. Fortunately, my children were grown up and had left home and my partner was supportive. After four years I found a job in a company and remained academically active by continuing to publish; I published two books and a number of studies and did some teaching at Eötvös Loránd University (ELTE). I have no regrets about the positions I took, I am a critical thinker, I cannot be anything else.

The leadership at the police academy and the University of Public Service, that it was absorbed into, were more political than others; these leaders had close connections to Fidesz and the Government. Our social science department at the police academy was reorganised and lecturers were put into other departments. Some academics protested and dissented, but some staff were passive, while others behaved like soldiers and followed orders. It's very much like the behaviour of Hungarian society in general but of course, there is another group, as with the rest of society, who like this regime. Everyone has a price, and this government will reward those who follow its line and are subservient. With the strategies of passivity and compliance, few stop to think about the consequences for the country.

If you look at protests like the one at the Színház- és Filmművészeti Egyetem (SZFE) and students in general today, they are very critical of Orbán, which is very different from how things were a decade ago. In this culture war the Government loses the support of the intellectuals, on not only the left but the right. Of course, anti-intellectualism does attract support in the countryside, and this is where most Orbán supporters are to be found. The 2019 local elections clearly showed the cities and large towns are anti Orbán but in the countryside, there is solid support for him. Some though support Orbán because they are tied to jobs such as working for a Fidesz Mayor. It seems feudal

The attack on academic freedom started in 2012 with the creation of chancellor posts and more recently we have seen a campaign to privatise many universities. I do not think I would have been fired in any other EU member state as the autonomy of universities is working properly. In Hungary, it has almost completely disappeared since Orbán's party began forcing its will upon the institutions of higher education via the selection of faithful financial specialists, namely the chancellors. They want everyone in the universities to be loyal to the governing party, which is completely absurd and unconstitutional. The Hungarian version of liberal democracy wasn't popular with the people as demonstrated at the 2010 election and elections since then. It has created a society where workers are easily exploited by their employers. In 2022 we have to change the system; this is the only way we can save academic freedom and the autonomy of universities.

Post-script – In October 2019, Andrea Kozáry, a renowned expert on hate crimes was scheduled to give a lecture on that topic, including anti-LGBTQ+ and anti-immigrant crimes, to police students at a conference at the National University of Public Service. Three weeks before the lecture, the university cancelled the event, reportedly because of its subject matter. According to the Scholars at Risk Network when Professor Kozáry confronted the university leadership about the cancellation, she was fired (Scholars at Risk Network, 2021).

The Challenge for Sociology and Critical Thinking in Hungary in the Twenty-First Century

Miklos Hadas

Miklos Hadas is a former professor of Sociology at the Corvinus University. He left in 2020, after 35 years of teaching. His recent book, "Outlines of a Theory of Plural Habitus: Bourdieu Revisited" was published by Routledge in 2021.

In framing my thoughts on what I think are the challenges for sociology and critical thinking in the coming years in Hungary I want to go back into the past, to the development of sociology in Hungary.

I started to teach at Corvinus University (then named the Karl Marx University of Economic Sciences) in the mid-1980s; I had been a PhD student of Bourdieu in Paris prior to this and he supported me in my decision to start my teaching career in Hungary. I also had the support of the head of sociology at the Corvinus, Rudolf Andorka (1931–1997), who later became the rector. Andorka was a close friend of the first transition prime minister Antall József. During the Second World War, his father was Hungary's ambassador to Madrid and maintained excellent relations with British politicians. He was one of the first to be arrested by the Gestapo in 1944 for his well-known anti-Nazi views. He was deported to Mauthausen. In communist Hungary, Andorka found for many years his path to university blocked; he was considered politically undesirable no doubt. However, after working in the state statistical office in the 1970s he was allowed to find a way into academia. Andorka was a leading Lutheran and a morally engaged Christian. In the mid-80s, he attained the position of head of sociology at the Corvinus, reflecting the increasing relaxation of the grip of communism in the 1980s. I knew Andorka well because he was my doctoral thesis director.

The late 80s and the final part of the twentieth century was a good period for sociology in Hungary, including Karl Marx University. People like Janos Kiss, a founder of the liberal Alliance of Free Democrats (SZDSZ) and a lead critical voice under late communism, came to speak to the department about 'regime change'. Andorka attended this meeting and supported such events. At this time, it seemed practically everyone at the Corvinus was critical of the communist regime in Hungary. Andorka though can be described as a cautious reformist who avoided confrontation, but the general mood was that change was needed. Bertalan László was another who was an expert on Weber and who helped establish rational choice theory within the department. Lengyel György was also prominent as an economic sociologist. All these voices helped make the department and the sociology taught strong and vibrant, able to play a role in fashioning a new Hungary as the country emerged from communism. When Andorka became rector after the fall of Communism, the position of the university was further bolstered as his links with prime minister Antall helped give the institution standing and political embeddedness in transition society.

Somehow, I would like to see sociology at the Corvinus return to the heady days of Andorka, where there was a range of views and philosophies within the department and intellectual figures not afraid to speak out. However, the sociology department of the Corvinus began to change rapidly from about 2010, reflecting processes at work both in political life and in many departments and universities. Academic leaders of institutes and departments emerged who in effect stopped being academics but became instead managers who supported and aligned themselves with the increasing commodification of higher education and the audit culture of assessment and appraisal, designed and introduced to control and pacify intellectual thinkers.

This system saw the promotion of mediocre thinkers to leadership positions because they revelled in technical detail and were prepared to administer the tyranny of audit culture, but also because they were loyal to a regime, namely Fidesz, that has sought to tame and intimidate academia. The bright young intellectuals, many of whom were powerful critical thinkers coming out of the sociology doctoral programme who should have been the future of the sociology department, were overlooked, they drifted away, many went abroad.

Of course, during the 90s things were not always perfect for sociology and critical thinking in the Corvinus; there was rivalry and tension between social sciences, economics, and business studies. Some within the university contended that social sciences were less prestigious than economics and sought to limits its influence. It would appear though that the Business Studies dimension of the Corvinus has become dominant as reflected by the leadership of the new president Anthony Radev, who owes his appointment to being a card playing partner of Viktor Orbán, and who has intensified the commodification of the university and who is seeking to promote applied studies that will constrain further the scope for critical thinking. Most worryingly, it presents a form of thinking that seeks alliance and intellectual support for the authoritarianism of the Hungarian government, it is an intellectual regression to a darker time in Hungarian history. Within such a university the position of sociology and critical thinking is greatly endangered; sociology has now become an alien body in an institution that exalts conformity above and beyond academic freedom and critical thought. We are in a similar period to the 1980s, Hungary is not a free country. We need sociology as we did in the 90s to help generate new discussions especially on social inequalities and gender issues. We, Hungarian sociologists, bear a huge responsibility, as critical thinkers; it is important we challenge the authoritarianism of present-day Hungary and nurture and present alternative visions.

In the culture war that currently grips Hungary and many other countries, critical thinkers are sometimes seen as the converse yet also a reflection of their nationalist opponents, gripped by rigid ideological mantras that polarise debate and argument. Such binarism needs to be challenged through reflexivity. Bourdieu understood the importance of being self-critical and controlling and assessing our dispositions. Critical thinkers need to take care in the search for something better, a quest for purity can hold the danger of generating hate and inflexibilities that fragment progressive alliances and which can play into the hands of authoritarian populists allowing them to frame themselves as the defenders of national identity and tradition against an unreasoning and strident left. As social scientists, we must strive to understand the perspectives of others. I agree with Donna Haraway (1988) who emphasises the privilege of partial perspective and the situatedness of knowledge-claims. Thus, I cannot accept the standpoint of some feminists who think that all men are enemies and are in power positions. We have to understand the predicament of subaltern men and there is a need to view social relations through an intersectional frame, that gives recognition to the influence of race, class, age (etc.) as well as gender.

We need a sociology and critical thinking for the twenty-first century, which is reflexive, complex and relevant providing 'thick descriptions' of the lifeworld. Burawoy (2004) describes different approaches to sociology: Professional sociology defends the conditions of science, policy sociology proposes policy interventions, public sociology understands politics as democratic dialogue whereas critical sociology is committed to opening up debates within our discipline. My preference is for critical sociology, a moral sociology that seeks transformations.

An exemplary and model sociologist should aim to achieve high academic prestige, public influence, and activity rate. Perhaps the most important task of every sociologist and social scientist, in general, is to create works that may elevate them to the level of a public scientist. Of course, only a few of the hundreds of thousand social scientists in the world have the chance of becoming public scientists. But even without achieving this status, the ambition itself has a lot of gain for the sociologist and sociology alike. A sociologist should not seek universal subjects but construct the subject relationally and discern whom the oppressor and the oppressed are in a given historical/cultural power relation. When that is defined, it is safe to formulate the value postulation: notably, one that tries to represent the oppressed or underprivileged as against injustice and suppression. In this regard, the first step is to choose as research topics inequalities fuelling social problems. In addition, we should also do our best to transmit the exposed injustice to as wide a public as possible in an intelligible manner.

In principle, there can be no objection to the active role of a sociologist in exposing social injustices and supporting social movements. The main question is how far (s)he can go in the action chain without risking his/her own and the discipline's legitimacy. As a person of thoughts, (s)he may go to great lengths in promoting the favourable development of a public cause: write background studies, sign petitions, participate in public disputes (in which, needless to say, (s)he must adduce scientifically well-grounded arguments). I think it is desirable that the sociologist try to reshape the professional field so that the change is beneficial to the cause (s)he deems important. For example, it is in his/her right to initiate the training of more experts (e. g. social workers) for the handling of certain social problems; I also accept that as an activist, the social scientist may lie down at the entrance of a military base or tie her, or himself to a tree selected for felling. Only, if (s)he does so, (s)he must do it as a private person and not as the lecturer of such and such university. I believe that a social scientist participating in public affairs and assuming an active role in the action chain must strive, however difficult it may be, create a clear separation between his/her self as a citizen and as a public sociologist. Otherwise (s)he might risk the impeccable legitimacy not only of him- or herself but also of his or her profession (Hadas, 2007). The critical sociologist needs academic freedom to express and develop their interests; if given the requisite freedom and autonomy, the contributions that they can make to debates in the public sphere might be profound leading to socioeconomic and cultural transformations. The stifling of academic freedom is one reason why I have profound fears for the future of sociology in Hungary.

I hope and work for change in Hungary, but we face incredible challenges. The forces that constitute Orbánism in Hungary, or whatever you want to call it, are deeply ingrained and structurally embedded within Hungarian society. There is a tension between urban and rural; much of the support for Orbán comes from the countryside steeped in tradition and fear that views the urban, especially Budapest, as foreign and dangerous. We have to remember that Budapest was viewed as a city of foreigners, Jews, and Germans, and that mindset is still strong. Orbán in his attacks on Soros taps into the latent antisemitism of Hungary and given liberalism is often connotated with Jewish intellectuals his revelling of Hungary as an 'illiberal' state has sinister implications.

I remember around the time of the migration crisis in 2015 being in a small rural Hungarian village and seeing an old woman cry because of the fear people like Orbán had aroused regarding migrants fleeing the war in Syria, she was thankful that Orbán was there to protect us from the "hordes of migrants flooding into the country". It is shameful that the local priest spoke against migrants to the old lady and his congregation, helping to stoke this fear. Such behaviour is common and deeply embedded in our society.

Hungary is a country where authoritarianism is venerated. Yes, we need a new government and constitutional reforms, but the deep and fundamental changes needed to our national psyche – the legacy in part of previous regimes that side-lined important national debates –will take generations. Under Horthy there was no debate in the universities as to why Hungary had allowed itself to be pulled in the Great War of 1914 – 18, under communism there was no debate as to how the Treaty of Trianon destabilised Hungary (the country was left as a landlocked state, losing two thirds of the territory that had constituted the pre-war Kingdom of Hungary), or how and why Hungarians were complicit in the Holocaust. This lack of a national inquest in which universities should have played a central role has left us with the horror that present-day Hungary constitutes. We Hungarians failed to learn the lessons of history, we failed to be reflexive. Hungary has not been alone in Central Eastern Europe in making such mistakes, Poland is perhaps the stand-out case alongside Hungary. Open and autonomous universities that act as catalysts for the debates and discussions about the new Hungary are needed and in this goal, I believe critical sociology will have a profound role to play.

Conclusion

The testimony presented in this chapter provides personal insights into the nature of oppression and challenges to academic freedom in the past and present. Futo draws upon his memories of Communism to reflect on the present and how the country is going backwards in terms of losing political rights, the degree to which such perceptions are shared and take root will be of critical importance in determining the future of Hungary. Krémer's testimony reflects the fears a growing number of critical thinkers now hold in Hungary, that there are negative consequences for speaking 'truth to power'. Hadas's testimony provides insights into the deep historical and cultural roots of authoritarianism in Hungary, implying the need for thorough cultural reflection and reinterpretation.

The testimony though reflects hope, that change could be possible and not all are cowed by such authoritarianism. Resistance is possible, as reflected through the radical learning spaces of the "házibuli" parties and the practice of being a critical scholar in academia seeking to speak truth to power. Of course, such a practice can incur risk but critical challenges to authoritarianism continue despite this risk and hopefully set an example and inspire the wider academic community.

In the concluding chapter of the book I develop these themes and discuss the role of critical scholarship in protecting social, political and academic freedom.

Chapter Nine
Conclusion: Speaking Truth to Power

The book has provided an overview of a series of major reforms that have taken place in higher education in Hungary in recent years. The analysis presented provides insights into the nature of the political regime under Orbán and the health of democracy in Hungary. The evidence and testimony presented in the book demonstrate that there are grounds for concern. Academic autonomy and universities' roles in knowledge production and as centres of debate and dialogue have an important part to play as an intellectual check and balance that along with legal and political safeguards can help democracies function. Universities should be able to 'speak truth to power' (Brühwiler and Goktepe, 2021). However, a programme of privatisation and marketisation as well as a culture of intimidation, as part of a culture war that has demonised liberal and critical thinkers, is undermining the role of higher education in the political, social, and cultural life of Hungary. These are serious points of concern not just to the stability and development of Hungary but also to the European Union. Can the EU tolerate such developments that have clear implications for core European conventions and values? Will other countries try and emulate the direction Hungary has taken? How can academic freedom be protected? A key aim of this final section is to identify how legal, cultural and societal change might come about, that could protect and enhance academic freedom.

Protecting Academic Freedom

As has been noted a lack of definition as to what academic freedom is but also inertia on the part of those charged with the guardianship of laws to protect academic freedom has assisted and emboldened those who have sought to undermine academic autonomy.

The book described how the European Commission took legal action against Hungary for infringing academic freedom with reference to the measures that impacted upon the Central European University's ability to operate in Hungary, eventually leading to the university relocating most of its teaching operations to Vienna. The Hungarian government asserted that the EU had no legal jurisdiction, as there was it claimed, no European definition of academic freedom. To make its point and to protect academic freedom the EU had to rely on a legal argument connected to the freedom to deliver commercial services under World Trade Organization rules (Liviu, 2021). It would have been better if the case

https://doi.org/10.1515/9783110749816-011

could have been presented as a clear and direct infringement of academic freedom and freedom of speech rather than infringement of commercial activity. However, it should be noted that Article 13 of the EU Charter of Fundamental Rights, which seeks to protect academic freedom, was also invoked in the case. The EU Court of Justice judgment in 2020 on Hungary and restrictions on academic freedom related to the Central European University (C-66/18, Commission v Hungary), discussed in chapter three, can be seen as an effort to make Article 13 of the EU Charter of Fundamental Rights more developed and recognised in the European legal space. This process needs to continue, and the aforementioned case creates an important legal foundation for this. Another option would be for EU citizens, if the injured party in a dispute over academic freedom, to invoke their rights under Article 2 of the Treaty on European Union (TEU). Article 2 contains commitments to the protection of human dignity, democracy, and the rule of law (Ziegler, 2021b).

Scheppele (2016) has noted that the EU is experiencing a crisis of values because some Member States are faltering in their commitments to the basic principles that were supposed to be secured by EU membership. The strongest sanction the EU has is Article 7 TEU that permits the EU to remove a Member State's vote in the European Council, to allow for the rogue member state's eventual rehabilitation. Scheppele advocates creating the notion of a systemic breach of fundamental Treaty obligations by a member state. This would entail bundling alleged violations together and presenting a case to the Court of Justice of the European Union that the infringement of EU law is not minor but is systemic and persistent. The classification of a dispute as systemic would make it harder for a member state to resist the legal and moral prompts of the EU for corrective behaviour through minor and tokenistic adjustments.

At present EU infringement actions that focus on narrow points of law are slow and cumbersome and rarely galvanise public opinion or attract meaningful media attention, factors that rather embolden member states in continued non-compliance or merely introduce half measures to appease the European Commission. A charge of a systemic breach might be harder for a member state to ignore, especially if connected to EU funding. Indeed, the EU has been moving towards linking funding to compliance with the rule of law.[1] Legal disputes prompted by

---

1 One powerful instrument that could be utilised to punish an EU Member State that undermines the values and rules of the European Union is what is termed the horizontal enabling condition with reference to Cohesion Policy, it stipulates that the effective implementation of the EU Charter of Fundamental Rights must be applied to cohesion funds. The EU cohesion policy is the largest source of EU funding in less developed Member States, including Hungary, and focuses on the promotion of economic, social and territorial convergence, through sustainable compet-

perceived systemic and persistent breaches of the rule of law would presumably also necessitate a systemic and fundamental change in a state drifting towards authoritarianism. For any successful club or association to work there need to be clear rules and penalties for those who transgress. Backroom negotiation and soft diplomacy have worked to some degree for the EU in the past, but it may need to rely increasingly on harder law to protect EU values and stem democratic backsliding. A principal case in support of applying stronger sanctions for the contravention of EU law and values is evidenced by the fact that the accession process for admitting countries into the EU at the start of the twenty-first century was fairly effective in transforming these new member states into liberal democracies through a combination of sticks and carrots. Once within the EU, it was clear that there were few tools to ensure these new member states continued on the trajectory of democratisation and hence democratic backsliding became increasingly pronounced (Bohle and Greskovits, 2019).

As noted in the introduction of the book the UNESCO statement on higher education and academic freedom (UNESCO, 1997) is an important soft law instrument. Reversing the decline of academic freedom in Hungary and other countries that are drifting into authoritarianism will require serious efforts by NGOs, academics, universities, and other public voices to devise and promote campaigns that bolster the ideals enshrined in the UNESCO statement. UNESCO itself needs to implement a more thorough process of monitoring and evaluation to raise the alert when principles of academic freedom are being challenged. Academic freedom cannot just rely on hard law provisions but needs to be popularised in terms of the general public understanding and supporting the need for academic freedom, and for commitments to this principle to be ingrained into the ethos and conventions operating in a range of institutions. Academic freedom needs to be perceived as a kind of covenant with the public to protect the university's mission of serving the public good. Academic freedom needs to be appreciated alongside other fundamental freedoms and taught in subjects like civics and history at school. Something like a European Association of University Professors within the European Union could play an instrumental role in promoting institutional and cultural respect, and support for academic freedom. Hopefully, academic trade unions would also play an active role in such a campaign (Karran, 2009). Academic freedom needs to be seen as a principle and value at the core of European identity.

---

itiveness, research and innovation, digital transition, and the European Green Deal. The direct relevance of the horizontal enabling condition is that academic freedom (Article 13) is among the fundamental rights (EU Regulation 2021/1060 Annex III).

In terms of academic freedom, it should be noted that such freedoms and rights also entail responsibilities: a duty of truthfulness but also commitment to disseminate that truth as widely as possible, including to those subaltern groups traditionally excluded from intellectual discourse. In recent years ethical codes centred on contractual agreements over informed consent have become increasingly important, but these codes make scant reference to academic freedom and the responsibilities of researchers. The time may be appropriate for wider-ranging ethical codes to help researchers consider their moral obligations under the concept of academic freedom. Something like a Hippocratic Oath for academia that would preclude narrow prescription and merely prompt researchers to consider their moral and ethical duties. In creating a new conceptual framework of academic freedom greater consideration needs to be given to students who too often have been neglected in debates., they have a right to express dissent but also learn in open educational environments. Such rights would elevate students above the status of a customer where they are performatively expected to conform to regimented and audited learning cultures that are too often static and hierarchical.

Some caution is needed concerning attempts to enshrine academic freedom into legal and institutional conventions. There have been cases of conservative students who have complained about having their opinions in class derided by liberal professors, and even of academics creating a tyranny of political correctness in the classroom, stifling proper debate. Conservative activists like David Horowitz have been prominent in championing this cause through his organisation 'Students for Academic Freedom'. At the core of Horowitz's campaign is an effort to see US state legislatures adopt an 'Academic Bill of Rights' to protect students from biased academics (Eberhardt, 2006). Horowitz focuses on concerns with the alleged indoctrination of students as a violation of their freedoms and the chance of unfair assessment, which might affect a student who expresses opinions contrary to those held by their professor. However, there is a fear that Horowitz's campaign could intimidate academic staff and stifle academic freedom.

In the UK, a white paper (draft proposal for a future law) 'Higher education: free speech and academic freedom' has been published by the Government headed by Boris Johnson. The proposal seeks to establish a 'Free Speech and Academic Freedom Champion' located within the ombudsman the 'Office for Students'. There is a danger that such a policing role could become highly politicised and partisan. Fines and penalties are proposed for those who transgress and there would be options for legal recourse for those who feel their rights to free speech have been violated. It is believed the measure is aimed at previous student opposition to controversial speakers visiting universities who are deemed to offend various mainstream and or liberal norms and values. A letter from the then Education Secretary Gavin Williamson to the Office of Students stated he was "deeply worried about the chilling effect on campuses of unacceptable silencing and censoring...That is why we must strengthen free speech in higher education, by bolstering the existing legal duties and ensuring strong, robust action is taken if these are breached" (Department for Education, 2021). The University and College Union general secretary Jo Grady in response stated:

> In reality, the biggest threats to academic freedom and free speech come not from staff and students, or from so-called cancel culture, but from ministers' own attempts to police what can and cannot be said on campus, and a failure to get to grips with the endemic job insecurity and managerialist approaches which mean academics are less able to speak truth to power (Bothwell, 2021).

Williamson may well be engaging in a British act of culture war, orchestrating a conflict with supposed 'left-wing students and academics' so that he can parade his libertarian credentials. As critics note though the measures themselves could present a significant curb to academic freedom, intimidating some from speaking out and even enabling far-right speakers to enter campuses. Balancing and resolving such disputes is far from easy especially when dogma bolsters partisanship. The danger is that such micro tussles add an Orwellian dimension to learning, where radical right students leap upon any comments or thoughts by teaching staff and report them to the authorities. In Hungary, in 2016 a pro-government website called on students to report the names of professors who espoused "unasked-for left-wing political opinions" (Foer, 2019). This mirrors the 'Professor Watch-list' in the USA, a radical right webpage set up in the wake of President Trump's 2016 electoral victory that allows students to report and complain about supposedly left-wing biased academics. The webpage has been denounced as a return to McCarthyism (Guterl, 2016). Indeed, such incidents give a sinister insight into the potential landscape of the academy in the midst of an accentuating culture war, not just in Hungary but beyond.

Culture War and the Academy

Culture war is a term that has been repeatedly referred to in the text, attempts to remodel universities and attacks on the supposed bias of teachers and academic subjects are connected to this concept and have profound implications for academic freedom. There is a fear that forms of censorship and ostracism within universities, stemming from social movements on the right and left might present serious challenges to academic freedom (Suissa and Sullivan, 2021).

Academic staff need to have the freedom to express their opinions and demonstrate how such views are supported by evidence but also refer to competing hypotheses and allow space for critique and discussion. I believe the vast majority of academics are professional and conform to such conventions. Sadly, though I have seen students on the left and the right become highly politicised in their thinking, and any deviation from their worldview is deemed as extremist, unscientific, and biased. To a degree, there is an element of the 'horseshoe' theory here, a view that contends that we should not view the political spectrum as a straight line from communism to fascism, but rather as a horseshoe. In this horseshoe, the far left and far-right are said to have more in common with each other than they do with the political centre (Choat, 2017). The theory that the radical left and right have a propensity to drift into authoritarianism can be too generalising, but there are elements of truth within it. Left and right populism do share some similar traits such as a conception that elites control and manipulate information in their favour, hence much of the information circulating in the public sphere is deemed to be untrustworthy. Furthermore, binarism and sharp and emotive invective characterise both strands of activism often centred on moral panics and furores that help galvanise and mobilise activists. On the left, such direct action-orientated moral panics might be directed at the need to remove a statue of a slave owner or 'no platforming' controversial speakers, or in terms of the right it might be attempts to ban Gender Studies. Such actions are sometimes referred to by critics as 'cancel culture', where activists set themselves up as the arbiters of right and wrong and use supporters, direct action, and the media to make their points. Cancel culture is seen as an affront to freedom of speech and it has implications for academic freedom. However, there can be valid reasons for the removal of statues, honours, and accolades and a need for the reinterpretation of history, especially where existing practices and traditions might bolster oppression in the present, but as will be discussed later such action might be more effective if coupled with dialogue and explanation.

In terms of cancel culture and forms of populism in the university most of my experiences in Hungary have been with right-wingers. I have had to patiently explain that news sources like Breitbart cannot be seen as legitimate news sources and form the central argument in academic essays. I have had to explain that tolerance and listening to others without getting emotional or angry is another facet of academic freedom. I have had to explain that racism and sexism contravene the etiquette of human rights and academic discussion. With reference to the Left, some complain about positional fundamentalism in which a person's place in the social structure is narrowly equated with conceptions of an individual's privilege and worldview, which in turn makes them personally responsible for various oppressions. Such microaggressions can lead to oversensitivity and even stridency that has the danger of polarising opinion and creating a backlash. Such a mindset is sometimes described as 'wokeism', these are the activists who have awoken, who understand the nature and workings of hegemony, patriarchy, and white supremacism.

Despite such criticism, we should not ignore the value of critical thinking. Critical thinking with its conception of hegemony within the Foucaultian notion that 'power is everywhere', is a worldview that provides nuance and rich insights into the complexity of the world we live in. It prompts thinkers to explore the interconnection between economic power, culture, history, and language in upholding a status quo that privileges some groups over others. Black Lives Matter (BLM) can be described as a social movement reflecting the frames of critical thinking with its conception of hegemonic power, intersectionality, and grassroots activism. Some of its actions may have been counter-productive and lapsed into what some would term militant 'wokeism'. However, BLM is a social movement that has managed to create what Freire (1994) described as a 'pedagogy of hope', a belief the system can be changed, on the part of highly marginalised individuals and communities. It's a movement that has been able to mobilise those at the margins, not just in protests but in highly effective voting campaigns. Would Trump have won the US presidency again in 2020 if groups like BLM had not been able to mobilise the Black vote?

Furthermore, BLM has empowered those at the margins, believing it is important to give voice and agency to the oppressed, and in academia has helped prompt participatory and collaborative forms of research, demystifying knowledge production, and opening up the academy (Matache and Trehan, 2021). However, not only have social movements like BLM managed to connect with those at the margins and young intellectuals but have also been able to capture the imagination of the mainstream. The popularisation of bending the knee at sports events is testimony to this but also reveals the fluidity and inclusivity of such social movements. This gives hope to my aspiration to see forms of rational thinking, deliberation, and dialogue incorporated in the work of critical activists and thinkers seeking transformative change and new truths. It is a vision of transformative change that does not rely upon inquisitions and stridency, and in that sense, can create distance between itself and the radical right.

Social movements like BLM have been criticised for narrow forms of identity politics that fail to adequately conceive the nature of modern-day capitalism and its role in fuelling multiple oppressions. However, the intersectionality of critical thinking social movements allows us to understand the complexity and interconnection of oppressions, an important frame of movements like BLM. Intersectionality can help to understand and challenge the role of capital in oppression and its interconnection with racism, sexism, disablism, etc. This though is a work in progress and care is needed to ensure that intersectionality is not tokenised or lost in a fog of postmodernist abstraction. In particular, care is needed to ensure the concept of intersectionality does not dilute an understanding of the core role of neoliberalism in shaping many of the ills of the contemporary world.

Forms of postmodernism reject notions of truth, believing that hegemony shapes and distorts truth and objectivity (Pluckrose and Lindsay, 2020). This interpretation of the lifeworld has some validity and is useful in terms of encouraging us to challenge perceived wisdom and establishment accounts but there can be dangers in such a mindset. A complete rejection of the notion of truth and objectivity can breed cynicism but also deny those who seek transformative change important persuasive tools. Such postmodernist thinking on truth has touched critical thought, but a growing number of critical thinkers believe we can get closer to the truth through deconstructing the ideological and cultural power of hegemony and in areas like the social sciences seek to value and harness lay knowledge. This especially applies to those traditionally disempowered in knowledge production by constructing truth from the ground up. These I believe are important components in the search for truth and are elaborated upon later in the discussion on the transformation of the academy.

Challenging Academic Capitalism

A recurring theme in the testimony and analysis of the book has been how an audit culture together with forms of micro-management and total administration in tandem with the marketisation of higher education has undermined academic freedom, especially when an authoritarian populist government is in power. These instruments of surveillance and audit have individualised knowledge production, fragmenting forms of collective identity and solidarity in the workplace. Some academics have profited by these processes, enabling some to compensate for their lack of academic prowess with managerial skills suited to forms of micro-management, allowing them to reach middle management positions as heads of departments and institutes. As noted in the book there is a perception that this culture will push academics into more mainstream and less controversial and practical teaching and research areas, and consequently blunt academic inquiry. Added to this, the marketing and branding of universities and academics can steer academic work into the mainstream and away from areas of research considered to be marginal and or unpopular. Such areas though can be at the cutting edge of knowledge production. Some areas of investigation might be considered at the margins and lack institutional support, until innovation reveals them to be of great importance, and thus they eventually enter the mainstream.

Furthermore, research into minorities like the Roma, although considered by some to be at the fringes of legitimate social sciences, provides an important litmus test as to the levels of tolerance and inclusivity in a given society.

Academic capitalism has also led to an increase in the precarity of university employment as more teaching staff work part time on temporary or fixed-term contracts (without tenure), reflecting broader trends in the neoliberal economy. The lack of tenure for some in Hungary and the dilution of employment rights, which has been a feature of the Government's foundation programme, is another factor curbing academic freedom. To be able to speak truth to power academics need to know that their chances of securing tenure or retaining their positions will not be dependent on their passivity and compliance to hegemonic world views. Many of the younger academics who provided testimony for this volume chose anonymity. Some are awaiting their award of a PhD and one day hope to secure tenure, which will be in part dependent on institutional goodwill.

As noted, in Hungary and other countries, the state is trying to more closely regulate research and increase the links between industry and academia to boost economic performance. A crude belief that measuring academic outputs might lead to increased productivity and economic benefits for Hungary partly explains the emergence of audit culture here. This issue is relevant to Polányi's argument, presented in chapter one, for intellectuals to be free to search for truth for its own sake. A prerequisite for such a state of affairs is for science to be free from political, ideological, and economic influences. There is a danger that liberal perceptions of higher education could be lost or undermined through tying higher education too closely to economic, state, and political interests.

Of course, links between universities and businesses should be encouraged. Audit cultures and challenges to academic freedom can though undermine the symbiotic relationship between the academy and business, and it was for that reason that academic freedom was conventionalised as an important academic norm in the nineteenth century. Engaged and bridging academics have played an important role in developing new synergies between universities, business, and government, but often there is limited institutional support or guidance (Benneworth and Fitjar 2019). Improved outreach programmes through innovations like science shops, where universities and businesses and community organisations come together to develop new innovations and more bottom-up, community-driven, measures, are examples of potential synergy. Such approaches will serve industry better than crude statist interventions and business-orientated audit cultures being inappropriately applied to knowledge production.

Countries like Britain have been at the forefront of the commodification and marketisation of higher education and there is now serious debate as to how to extend the marketising and financialising of universities through a process of 'unbundling' and outsourcing, leading to new forms of privatisation. Critics claim these proposals are ill-thought-out and dangerous to future development and are underpinned by ideology and self-interest (Lewis and Shore, 2019). Hungary is in danger of making a similar mistake. Efforts to extend the influence of market forces in higher education may be moving against an emergent current of new thinking that could offer a serious challenge to the Washington Consensus and notions of neoliberal fundamentalism that seeks to apply the logic of the market to all aspects of society. The increasing crisis of neoliberalism, evident since the financial crisis of 2008, has acted as a catalyst for new conceptions of the world we live in. The dysfunctionality of unrestrained market forces has become more apparent and the precarious economic situation that many are now experiencing in a neoliberal world order is increasingly fuelling anxiety and presenting a challenge to the neoliberal consensus. The Covid 19 pandemic might also increase the public mood for new changes in direction and a desire for less precarity in their lives. This could also prompt new challenges to the hegemony of market forces.

Transforming the Academy

A large proportion of the book has been devoted to what is wrong with Hungarian higher education and has offered some critique of similar trends elsewhere in the world, especially where shaped by forms of academic capitalism. What new directions should higher education take?

A key message is that whilst the state should refrain from overt intervention into the autonomy of higher education it does have an important role in terms of ensuring consistent funding and quality control. The Hungarian foundation programme that will see many Hungarian universities have to supplement state support with private sources of funding could create serious difficulties to an educational network that has been seriously under-funded for over a decade. Such underfunding is not just unique to Hungary. Investment in higher education should be seen as an investment in innovation and the success and stability of a nation that cannot be left to the vagaries of the market and the conditionalities of private benefaction. University decision-making bodies such as senates should remain sacrosanct institutional centres of power to retain academic autonomy and, correspondingly, academic freedom. However, there is great scope for such bodies to be more transparent and open to student involvement in decision-making processes. Marketisation has seen a greater focus on the student but this has been in the guise of a customer, and as is evidenced by some of the testimony in this book, it is even debatable whether their treatment could be classified as good practice customer care. Universities' poor performance in offering effective welfare support during the Covid 19 pandemic in Hungary and elsewhere indicates serious failings in customer care. What is more, the stresses and strains overloaded teachers experience in the prevailing culture of audit regimes and the increasing pressure to conform and 'play it safe' (self-censorship) in their work damages the quality of learning experiences offered to students.

Notions of academic freedom need to consider how students' ability to access open learning is being eroded by a performative culture that fails to respect their rights to engage and develop as autonomous adults. Students, as with their teachers, are being subjected to forms of surveillance and audit in which how they learn, when they learn, and what they learn is being increasingly narrowed and regimented through compulsory attendance registers, class contribution grading, and assessment. Some would say the rationale behind such measures is to nurture conformity. This new hidden university curriculum is intolerant of students who may prefer to learn informally or experientially (Macfarlane, 2017).

New approaches to higher education should entail a new culture of learning that is premised upon open learning and critical thinking. At the heart of this approach should be the view that the search for knowledge should be a dialogic process dedicated to seeking the truth. Here the German term of Bildung as conceived by Humboldt and discussed in chapter one has relevance. Higher education should contribute to the self-development of people who will become informed and responsible citizens (Matthews et al, 2021). Dialogic and open learning environments can be described as radical spaces of learning but here the university, as one among other spaces of learning, should not seek to dominate the intellectual debate. Public pedagogy also includes film, television, literature, sport, advertising, architecture, media, faith groups, and where we work (Webb, 2018). However, academics can popularise their work and even mobilise greater support for what they have to say by working through and within these spheres. The search for truth through dialogic practices in itself presents a serious challenge to the intellectual narrowness and stridency of authoritarian populism that in Hungary and elsewhere seems to place little value on the opinions of experts, dialogue, and open-mindedness. Instead, ideological fervour, emotion, and nationalist nostalgia and tropes seem to hold greater sway in shaping populist thinking. Such characteristics add weight to the charge that populism can be viewed as a 'thin ideology'.

Universities need to adopt and nurture inclusive educational approaches, this is especially pressing in Hungary and other such countries where an authoritarian and teacher-centred approach to learning continues to be common. It should be noted that increased class sizes, a product of commodification and desire to maximise profits, have pushed an increasing number of academics into more formal teaching approaches as more communicative and creative forms of teaching are constrained by large class sizes. Sometimes in Hungary, even seminars that are supposed to create opportunities for more innovative and dialogic learning approaches are restricted by the presence of as many as 40 students in one seminar. Commitments to inclusive learning should be at the centre of an appraisal system that is less aligned to forms of micro-management and audit and more supportive of skills development and innovation, and where staff work collectively to develop inclusive learning strategies rather than compete with each other in a scramble for points. A key consideration for the inclusive university is to try and challenge a culture of elitism that permeates many institutional practices. Change is needed to make the student intake more diverse and less privileged. An important action in increasing the socioeconomic and ethnic diversity of student intakes would be efforts to reduce student debt, the fear of which discourages low-income students from applying to university. In Hungary, increasing levels of student debt and a decreasing number of university places, the latter going against global trends, run the risk of bolstering elitism. Such academic elitism may be desired, dictators having realised in the past that an under-educated populace reduces the scope and scale of dissent.

A key component needed to achieve inclusive education is the decolonisation of knowledge, an attempt to challenge the western epistemologies inherent in the curriculum of many universities reflecting institutional sexism, racism, and elitism. The decolonisation of knowledge should be seen as part of the effort to raise academic freedom. Notions of academic freedom should entail the reframing of core questions about the world, challenging the doxa that universal truths and universally applicable theories are produced in the West and the masculinised hegemony of an academic, white male elite. Academic freedom is not only about the rights of individual academics, it is also about the rights of communities of knowers to be recognised and enabled to name and define their own world (Freire 1972, Lynch and Ivancheva, 2015).

Inclusive education should consequently involve greater outreach beyond the university and dialogue and partnership with a wide range of community stakeholders. This should especially involve working with 'silenced voices' groups such as ethnic minorities, low-income groups, and the disabled who too often have felt disconnected from the work of universities. This inclusivity would challenge forms of cultural and intellectual hegemony, creating space where alternative worldviews can be heard and acknowledged, enriching the dialogic scope of the university (Gibson, 2015). Such approaches should seek to defy the strictures of scientism, with its emphasis on detachment and objectivity, that can create unneeded divides between academia and wider society. Instead, there should be more scope and institutional support for participatory action research, community-focused science shops, and collaborations with communities in research ventures. As noted, marketisation has stunted and stifled the opportunities for such ventures in Hungary as well as Europe. An important model of such research and academic innovation has been the Central European University, but as this book recounts, authoritarianism pressured this university to relocate much of its academic activity from Budapest to Vienna. More broadly, critical approaches to academia that place great value on empowering subaltern communities and voices remain at the periphery of many universities and are not given the recognition or status they deserve.

Making the academy a more inclusive place should also involve making universities less sexist, and as revealed in the book institutional sexism remains a serious point of concern. In Hungary what has been described as a 'macho cult' has assiduously attacked feminism and Gender Studies (Ziegler, 2021a). However, such forms of patriarchy predate the premiership of Orbán, being as with many European societies deeply ingrained in the cultural practices and institutions of society. Orbán and his authoritarian style of politics have been able to manipulate such sentiments, and this has been a central feature of his regime particularly in its combative rhetoric and strident search for enemies and battles to be had. The aforementioned traits have come close to destroying democracy in Hungary. It is for this reason that the inclusive academy should deconstruct and challenge patriarchy through Gender Studies degrees and modules and enabling more women to reach senior positions and challenging the dominance of a male elite in academia. The feminisation of the university would also move away from the audit culture of recent years with its masculinised competitivity and individualism and towards solidarity, support, and collective development.

My vision of inclusive education has been influenced by Said's (1996) conception of the public intellectual, which can be defined as having a deep commitment to the greater public. The public intellectual should involve a diverse range of communities in intellectual debate and take a position on controversial issues that threaten justice and freedom. The public intellectual should present challenges to authoritarianism, patriarchy, elitism, and white supremacy (Rangel, 2020). However, the public intellectual is somewhat in retreat in Hungary, as evidenced by the testimony in the book that referred to fear and intimidation within the academy, the same would inevitably happen in other countries experiencing the political forces evident in Hungary and indeed it is a process that is happening elsewhere. Despite these pressures some academics continue to speak truth to power and the courage of those that do so in Hungary and countries like Turkey and India is deeply awe-inspiring. Such is the scale of the challenge in Hungary academics should be raising the alarm about the dangers posed to inclusivity and academic freedom by the Hungarian government's deeply radical but also dangerous higher education reforms and the other raft of reforms introduced over the last decade that have seriously undermined democracy. It is through such action that academics can help justify their value in society, and in the process, do much to dismantle elite 'ivory tower' practices and conventions that at times has left those engaged in the battle for academic freedom feeling they have little support or understanding from the wider public. Of course, ultimately the inclusive university is contingent upon making an inclusive society.

Transforming Society

As noted at the start of this book Fukuyama's (1992) boast of an 'end of history' and triumph of liberalism now seems misplaced, especially in light of the boldness and some would say supreme sense of self-belief of populist leaders like Trump, Orbán, Erdoğan, Modi, and Putin who have with stealth and confidence challenged or swept away numerous liberal conventions. The drift towards illiberalism coupled with the economic uncertainty evident since the financial crisis of 2008 and the huge shock of the Covid 19 pandemic has contributed to a growing sense of vulnerability and anxiety. This growing mood of uncertainty though might prompt a greater sense of reflection of what happened and what might or should happen. This mood of reflection might be conducive to transformative change. Of course, there is a chance that the voices of reaction might be strengthened and emboldened by such a mood, and the drift into authoritarianism might continue unabated. Equally, though there is a chance that change can be guided by the principles of social justice and freedoms of an open society. In such a world the university will be an important instrument and agent of equality, by creating, as outlined above, an inclusive higher education system and by speaking truth to power.

The foundation of transformative change premised on the principles of social justice would warrant a change of the economic system. In chapter one, I outlined how the 'Les Trente Glorieuses', a thirty-year period of post-war economic expansion and rising living standards guided by Keynesian economics had been interrupted by a crisis of confidence that nurtured neoliberalism. Neoliberalism has now been in the ascendancy for longer than the welfarist and interventionist system that preceded it, but as with its forebear is now facing a serious crisis of confidence. The 2008 financial crisis may be just the tremor before the earthquake. Perhaps such a disaster can be averted by global and systemic change and a new economic order.

The model of 'Les Trentes Glorieuses,' an age of unprecedented welfarism and consumerism, may not be one that can be revived in a mirror image of how it existed before. Such a model may also not be sustainable environmentally because of the huge volume of resources that were and would be consumed. Post-war growth was also fuelled by cheap materials and the exploitation of low-wage labour from regions of the periphery contributing to third world inequality. In addition, technological advancements and the increasing automation of production and services will make full employment an impossible aspiration in terms of how it existed in the past. It should also be noted that statism created overbearing bureaucracies, creating inefficiencies and stifling creativity and agency. Such traits were even more apparent in the highly centralised command economies of soviet central Eastern Europe, which of course Hungary was a part of.

Although we cannot turn the clock back and replicate life precisely as it was during the progressive post-war consensus, new structural reorientation can come about shaped by many of the principles and values of this time of consensus, namely intervention, redistribution, and an active role for the state. Wilkinson and Pickett (2009) in their ground-breaking book the 'Spirit Level' argue that progressive social reform centred on redistribution and social justice can be to the benefit of the whole of society, creating higher levels of well-being and contentment and also having the propensity to stimulate economic growth. Such parameters of debate invoking 'common sense' and efficiency could do much to foster a new radical consensus, continuing the trajectory of that established during the 'glorious thirty' of post-war social democracy and interrupted by the Washington consensus.

In a globalised interconnected economy, change will need to come about through large economic blocs or trading areas moving together simultaneously. Countries that venture on such a path on their own would be subject to the wrath of markets that would retaliate through disinvestment. In other words, the only realistic option for such change in Europe is the realisation of a Social Europe within the EU that countenances intervention and redistribution (Ryder, 2020). However, within the EU ordoliberalism and technocratic approaches to capitalism where the state upholds market freedom has been the mainstay approach. However, the stimulus package, the 'EU Covid Recovery Fund', that will seek to revive the European economy through fiscal stimulus in the aftermath of the pandemic, could be a turning point (Ryder et al, 2021). Growing impatience with Hungary and Poland and their democratic backsliding has seen the EU initiate article 7 proceedings against both countries. This could be another indicator of a sea change in European Union governance and the protection of European values.

188 —— 9 Conclusion: Speaking Truth to Power

What is the role of universities in this process of transformation? Universities should assist in illuminating the difficult and painful debates that would lay ahead of such transformation, challenging the forces of reaction and the irrationality and emotion that change is likely to generate. Fact and reasoned argument through dialogue and deliberation will have an important role in facilitating and enabling transformative change. To perform such a role universities need to be unfettered of political and economic interests that might seek to unfairly steer their contributions to the vital debates that lie ahead. Universities need to liberate themselves from the pettiness and tedium of micro-management and audit culture.

Transforming society will also warrant democratic reform. As noted during the course of the book the Hungarian government under Orbán has been adept at manipulating the political and constitutional framework of the country to slant it in the favour of the ruling Fidesz Party, leading to its capture of the judiciary, the media, and cultural and educational institutions as well as key sections of the economy. In effect, an oligarchy has been created and the Government is mired in cronyism and corruption. Hungary has a short history of practising democratic ideals. Some would venture to say that it only had a democracy in the modern sense between 1990 and 2010 while it has had a long history of authoritarianism, but this does not mean such a political approach is inevitable. The two-decade experience of democracy and Hungary's membership in the EU has created a strong support base for the creation of a robust democracy which is especially evident among young Hungarians.

With some justification, Laclau and Mouffe (1985) contend that liberal democracy and anodyne forms of consensus have created an empty and meaningless form of politics in which politicians in the mainstream sound the same and premise their thoughts and actions on an unquestioning adherence to neoliberalism. In Hungary, the choice is now sharper between an authoritarian government and a centrist liberal coalition. Is there though the danger that if the opposition achieves power, the democracy they establish will resemble that which Laclau and Mouffe warn against? A compromised form of democracy between 1990 and 2010 could be said through its failure to have spawned authoritarianism with its pledge to end a failed status quo. How can future disappointment with democracy be avoided?

As I have argued a new radical economic consensus centred on social justice, a new social contract, and economic intervention will give democracies a better foundation, in the EU this would take the form of a Social Europe. How would nation-state democracies fit into this utopian vision? What would be the role of universities? To return to Laclau and Mouffe, they advocate a renewed liberal democracy (radical pluralism) as a means by which transformative politics can be advanced. It can be described as the politics of choice, contrast, and contestation (agonism), in which an adversarial politics of "us" and "them" comes into play (Mouffe, 1999). It should be noted though that such views were shaped by Schmitt's (1976) adversarial view of politics, where the chances of reaching consensus are minimised through a collective nation-building dynamic at the centre of politics. In contrast, radical pluralists have sought to focus on frames centred on economic and social justice rather than nationalism. The French thinker Fassin has criticised what he perceives as the leftist populism of Laclau and Mouffe, claiming it is fuelled by resentment, which ultimately, as with nationalist populism, cannot be immune to reaction and scapegoating (cited in Hamburger, 2018). Agonism is a phenomenon that is susceptible to binary speech acts and irrationalism, but also manipulation.

In contrast deliberative democracy, a discursive form of politics that encourages informed and collective conversation and decision-making might be a more effective remedy to the current ills of the Hungarian political system, offering the prospect of mediation and reconciliation. Deliberative democracy can be said to promote forms of reciprocity where even those on the losing side of an argument might respect the outcome and decision made on account of the process and reasoning used to reach a decision (Smith, 2000). This is a quality that has left Hungarian politics where division and polarisation have become endemic. Habermas, a key proponent of deliberative democracy, has been derided as a naïve universalist on account of his desire to see a consensus forged by deliberation. However, argumentation and deliberation, although being slower and less decisive than coercion and collective "will," might be a more secure means of developing long-term, stable transformative policy trajectories (Garnham, 2007). Deliberative democracy and reasoning also have something of the quality of Gandhi's notion of satyagraha (see preface), in that it seeks to generate understanding and win over opponents rather than grind them into the ground.

In a deliberative democracy, universities would serve as important centres of intellectual aspiration where knowledge production and debate within the university would muster not only support for democratic reform but criticism and guidance that might improve and strengthen such reform. An argument that resonates with some of the thinking of the philosopher John Stuart Mill (1859). The philosopher Hannah Arendt (2005) had a vision of pluralism that argued the search for truth involved a range of conceptions of the world and truth will always differ because such conceptions are shaped and correspond to the observer's standpoint in the world. As far as Arendt was concerned freedom of speech meant that those different conceptions should be heard, and we can only comprehend the world by understanding it as something that is shared by many people with differing conceptions. Through the freedom of sharing these differing conceptions and entering into dialogue does the visibility of the world become apparent on all sides, according to Arendt. Deliberative reasoning in this sense can help reinterpret and understand tradition, helping to better reflect not only on something that comes closer to a truth relevant for the present day, but helping to win over those who have been seduced by conservative visions of tradition and the past. Transformative change can come about by such reinterpretations of tradition and history as a cultural foundation for change.

Academics also have the skills and experience to make a deliberative democracy reach communities at the grassroots through deliberative polling, participatory research and community profiles, forms of information gathering that are collaborative and that can feed into policy change and help end the disconnection between central government and local communities that in part has fired the appetite for nostalgia and charismatic leadership in Hungary. Perhaps the most important contribution universities can make to the development of deliberative democracy is to demonstrate the power and value of dialogic reasoning and deliberation.

As part of the culture war, universities have been accused of creating a tyranny of political correctness and a cancel culture that seeks to marginalise alternative worldviews. In some respects, the dispute reflects a long-standing point of contention between the radical right and left. The right argues for unlimited freedom of speech, yet often criticise or attempt to silence academics on particular topics related to, for example, social justice, gender or race. The left emphasises that freedom of speech does not include the freedom to harm and cherish the right to 'speak truth to power' without censure or reprimand (Dutt-Ballerstadt and Bhattacharya, 2021). Universities and academics need to walk a fine line between upholding free speech but also not tolerating racist and sexist sentiments.

A response to these challenges could be met through the established convention of academic dissensus. Academic dissensus allows for difference and disagreement to be valued, this tension is recognised as a central engine in knowledge production, allowing established views to be challenged and perhaps strengthened by being exposed to contestation, or for new ideas to become established (paradigm shift). However, effective academic dissensus relies on genuinely seeking to understand an opponent's counterview and shaping argumentation through scientific fact, practices which could prove challenging to authoritarian populism with its reliance on sharp invective and emotion. The convention of civility that is promoted as a central value in the US higher education system emphasises settling disagreements in a manner that does not lead to open conflict and a commitment to participate in respectful reasoning and dialogue. Such an approach might help resolve the schism and increasingly sharp invective between some transexuals and feminists about what constitutes female gender identity that in some cases has led to either side trying to shut down and ostracise its opponents, disputes that have found their way into universities and challenged academic freedom. A consensus may be possible but will require much deliberation over an extended period of time. However, current furores in this area risk creating permanent discord.

Civility is a concept that resonates with and is relevant to an understanding of academic dissensus, but care is needed in how such an approach is managed to ensure academic freedom is not compromised. In the US Civility has been weaponised in academia to silence and suppress critical voices accused of inverse prejudices and intemperate views because of the stand they have taken against patriarchy, racism, or other forms of elitism. Such charges are used to justify and create space for non-egalitarian viewpoints and undermine academic freedom by putting critical voices on their guard. Civility means speaking your mind with an opponent. It enables people to disagree without denying the possibility of their commonality. Conversely, incivility also has the function of demystifying the powers of authority and enabling the critical thinker to conclude that having a 'civil' conversation is not sustainable with people who use it to provide cover for oppression (Williams, 2021).

Of course, not just universities have a role in establishing new conventions and standards in dialogue. These are conventions that should also be upheld in the public sphere and political forums. Universities need to perform their historic function of being catalysts for utopian change and reform, innovators in connecting those at the margins with the centre of power and exemplars of deliberation, academic freedom and autonomy. However, it can also be argued that the marketised and/or authoritarian university is not conducive to nurturing such roles and these are points that have been highlighted during the discussion in this book.

What Next?

Writing this book is in some respects my letter of resignation from the Corvinus University, which I left due to my concerns about the threat to institutional autonomy and perceived poor response to student welfare needs during the pandemic. It has been an interesting but strange experience. Strange in the sense that rather than being the detached observer that in some respects has been a feature of my previous writing, this is a story where I am located directly within the social terrain under investigation. I have written about the challenges and dangers presented by Orbánism to my institutional home, namely academia, but also my adoptive home and country Hungary. The concerns and fears I have for the future of both are intense.

I agree with the views formulated by Karl Polányi and Ralph Dahrendorf that neoliberalism might transform into forms of fascism and authoritarianism (Fekete, 2016). As argued in this book there are signs of such a process happening in Hungary, a chilling realisation that has placed some responsibility on me as an avowed public intellectual. I wonder though what the consequences might be for me. Such concerns have been heightened through my connections with George Soros entities: I sit on the board of the Roma Education Fund. As noted in the book, Orbán has sought to demonise Soros and has made wild claims about an army of Soros agents being in Hungary. Such assertions have added to my personal anxieties about living in Hungary, so why stay here? Why not go somewhere else? The answer to the question posed is that I am worried about what will happen if people like me do not speak out or flee. Also, where should I flee to? My native home of the UK with its post-Brexit politics seems to be on something of the same self-destructive trajectory as Hungary and some of the forces I am seeking to resist such as marketisation are of course now near-universal. On a personal level, and this might be a point of vanity, I worry as to the impact on my self-conception if I do not speak out. I fear being compromised. I fear not being the person I thought I was. I also feel some shame for the years my criticism was muted. I felt shamed and inspired to do something on account of the brave example of the SZFE students and teachers that were detailed in this book, who valiantly occupied their university in defence of academic freedom. I also felt moved to action by the fact that Hungary really is my home. I have lived here on and off for twenty-five years, my child was born here and through my partner I have been welcomed into a Hungarian family. I know and believe Hungary can come through the difficult moment it finds itself in and be so much better than what it is today. I yearn for the Freirian pedagogy of hope, a sense that change can happen.

The role of the university should be, in the tradition of Socrates, to challenge and question hegemony and it is in that spirit that I have laboured upon and present this book. In an age of global crisis and anxiety profound change and transformation seem inevitable., The nature and benevolence of that change will be determined by the contestation and argumentation between social movements, communities, and hegemony both globally and nationally. Universities have an important role in this process or at least can if they are free and autonomous. History reveals that the progress of equality and even transformative change has often been triggered by moments of darkness, as reflected by forms of despotism and authoritarianism., A counter-revolution will come and I believe social justice, deliberative democracy, and public intellectuals should be vital components of that resistance and ultimate change. I give the last word to a valued and esteemed Hungarian associate, Andras Pap who closes the discussion in this book with an afterword.

Andras L. Pap:[1] Afterword
In Search of (Lost) Freedom

It is always intriguing to read biographies and confessions of actors and witnesses – however diverse their activities and roles and historical positions may be. Especially when the testimonies reveal intricacies of esteemed professions. When academics write about academic freedom, it is always a special kind of speech act. There is always a therapeutical trigger and desire. Andrew Ryder's book on academic freedom in an ever-growing and solidifying illiberal regime provides a unique documentary of how illiberalism is implemented in one of the prominent terrains. It also provides a direct and candid chronicle of its personal imprint. By revealing deeply personal details to uncover motivations, the story of an Englishmen in Budapest resigning from an academic position once his employer, headed by a government spin doctor, was privatised to a government-allied foundation becomes social history. Professor Ryder's testimony is a sapid exemplification of how personal is public and how public is personal. Treatises on academic freedom are almost always also intertwined with coping mechanisms and ethical dilemmas. Freedom, and infringements on freedom are also convoluted with responsibilities: even if one is personally exempt from facing censorship or any of the diverse forms of political pressure, in the field of humanities and social sciences there is always the lingering obligation and question of how to respond to social and political realities and developments.

For contextualizing Ryder's book, it is important to emphasise that although the threat to academic freedom is common, and in many parts of the world, such as China, Turkey, or Brazil, infringements are far more extreme, involving physical atrocities, incarceration, deportation, or withdrawal of travel documents,

1 Adjunct (Recurrent Visiting) Professor, Central European University, Vienna; Professor of Law, Eötvös University Institute for Business Economic/Ludovika University of Public Service Faculty of Law Enforcement; Research Professor and Head of the Constitutional and Administrative Law Department, (formerly Hungarian Academy of Sciences) Centre for Social Sciences Institute for Legal Studies, Budapest, Hungary. Some of the ideas expounded in the afterword were published in Andras L. Pap: Academic freedom: A test and a tool for illiberalism, neoliberalism and liberal democracy, The Brown Journal of World Affairs, Spring/Summer 2021 • Volume XXVI, Issue II. and Andras L. Pap: Piecemeal Devourment: Academic Freedom in Hungary, UIC John Marshall Law Review, January 5th, 2021, https://lawreview.jmls.uic.edu/piecemeal-devourment-academic-freedom-in-hungary/.

https://doi.org/10.1515/9783110749816-012

Hungary is perhaps the most serious case in Europe and consequently an important litmus test for the EU and an enlightenment vision of European identity.

The author of this afterword is in a unique position of being affiliated with two institutions (the Central European University and the Centre for Social Sciences formerly operating within the Hungarian Academy of Sciences) targeted by government encroachment, while also teaching at one of the Government's primary academic beneficiaries, the Ludovika University of Public Service – all discussed in the book. Besides deliberating all sorts of ethical conundrums, I am also permanently struggling with how to construct a meaningful and valid conceptualisation for teaching constitutional law in an illiberal hybrid autocracy (for students of social sciences and business).

What follows is an interpretational framework of Ryder's book, I will identify contextual dimensions for academic freedom – a term actually quite underdeveloped in terms of conceptual tools, operationalizing mechanisms, monitoring methods, and benchmarking schemes. As I will show, there are competing notions on how to best conceptualise it: as an individual right, a set of requirements for autonomous institutional design, a field to be regulated for market service providers or public commodities, a tool for international policymaking, or academic ranking – not to mention the challenge of how to incorporate challenges brought by social justice movements.

Academic freedom involves teaching, research, and dissemination, and can be performed at research institutes as well as educational institutions. For example a 2020 Council of Europe Report[2] identifies the following essential elements: academic freedom is a professional freedom granted to individual academics including the freedom to teach and do research (freely determine what shall be taught; how it shall be taught; who shall be allowed to study; who shall teach; how students' learning may be assessed and graded and who shall receive academic awards, the right to determine without duress what shall – or shall not- be researched; how it shall be researched; who shall research, with whom and for what purpose research shall be pursued; the methods by which, and avenues through which, research findings shall be disseminated. The supportive elements are: tenure, shared governance and autonomy (both individual and institutional and the latter including academic staff having an equal right to voice their opinions on their institution's educational policies and priorities without the imposi-

---

2 Council of Europe Parliamentary Assembly Report 15167 (2020), Threats to academic freedom and autonomy of higher education institutions in Europe, Rapporteur: Brenner Koloman, Paras 17–21 and 27.

tion or threat of punitive action), and academic freedom needs to include students' academic freedom as well as scholars'.

A 2020 Council of Europe Resolution points out that *"academic freedom and institutional autonomy of higher education institutions are not only crucial for the quality of education and research; they are essential components of democratic societies."*[3] As far as formal commitments go, the aforementioned report[4] points out that in the majority of (CoE) member states, some form of constitutional or legal protection for academic freedom is provided. 11 constitutions of EU countries provide protection for teaching, 15 for research, and eight set forth protection for institutional autonomy. Among other CoE member States: five provide protection for teaching and for autonomy, and four for academic freedom generically.

This takes us to our first contextual dimension: academic freedom means the prohibition and protection from infringement on various forms of academic activity from the Government – practically illiberal autocracies, which habitually cement and solidify illiberalism once the capture of constitutional institutions has been accomplished (or sometimes simultaneously). As Professor Ryder's book documents, attacks on academic freedom can target teaching, research, and dissemination, and be aimed at research institutes as well as universities. Governments outlawing or refusing to cooperate with or provide information to nongovernmental organisations ("NGOs") and human rights defenders, which are valuable sources for research can also have a chilling effect on academic freedom. The Hungarian case thus provides a vivid example for the multiple ways a government can curtail academic freedom, without jailing or denying exit visas for academics: Limitations on academic freedom in the field of research can take the form of bringing independent public research institutions under more direct government control (also see for example Halmai, 2019a and b; Vass, 2020) reallocating funds to an alternative network of government-dependent and government-friendly research institutes, think-tanks, and GONGO's; or adopting legislation, based on which government agencies can refuse to provide information to NGO's or excessively charge for public data requests.

Intrusions on academic freedom in the field of teaching have even more avenues. University autonomy can be curtailed through legislation reorganizing financial management with government appointed chancellors (Ziegler, 2019); cutting and divesting certain singled-out programmes from state-funded institutions; denying accreditations for certain programmes in public universities (Hun-

---

3 Council of Europe Parliamentary Assembly Res. 2352 (2020), Threats to academic freedom and autonomy of higher education institutions in Europe. Para 3.
4 Paras 55–56.

garian Network of Academics., 2020, 30 – 31); denying and withdrawing accreditation for a certain, singled out institutions; taking-over the national accreditation board; privatising public universities to foundations controlled by government cronies (Szirtes, 2020); nationalizing public education; centralising and taking control over public education-curricula; distorting the academic labour market by diverting funding to directly government-operated or favoured institutions; and of course, firing faculty.

In the field of dissemination and publishing of research findings academic freedom can be curtailed by blatant or very subtle forms of censorship; blocking academic events that would involve blacklisted human rights NGO's or dissident academics; hosting political or propaganda events on university premises (incentivising students to attend); launching media campaigns to intimidate critical academics (Körtvélyesi, 2020, Enyedi, 2018)[5]; or retaliating against institutions where faculty or students protest against the Government.

In sum, infringement of academic freedom has many faces: censorship, defunding or banning academic programmes, harassment, intimidation, tax raids, existential threats (termination or denial of promotion or simply losing access to discretionary travel grants and other subsidies), and closing institutions or units. Self-censorship is a natural consequence: it is prudent and logical for university management to only recruit conformists. Thus, academics can face all sorts of external and internal pressures: psychological, existential, and institutional. The effect of these pressures can be manifold: harassment and intimidation consume an incredible amount of energy and time. Institutional insecurity (concerning university programmes or entire institutions) paralyzes strategic planning, grant applications, and student recruitment. The increased level of stress and fatigue radically diminishes performance, be it research or teaching. Dismantling research centers, academic programmes, or institutions causes irreversible harms: these communities can hardly be rebuilt, even if the political regime would change abruptly. Also, restrictions on academic freedom disproportionally target junior faculty, as senior academics with tenure, established international networks, potential access to grants, and with non-government based resources are less affected.

It needs to be added that as a reaction, recently initiatives surfaced to incorporate academic freedom in academic ranking, thereby forcing stakeholders to take infringements seriously. The 2020 CoE Resolution points out that "*academic freedom and autonomy are not properly taken into account in any university rankings today, making some higher educational institutions of countries with the low-*

---

5 For a Polish case see for example (Gráinne de Búrca et al., 2019).

est scores of AFI appear to excel,"[6] and the Assembly *"calls upon the relevant stakeholders, including international organisations, national authorities, academic professional associations, universities and funders, to integrate the assessment of academic freedom into their review processes, institutional partnerships as well as ranking and financial support mechanisms."*[7]

The report on which the resolution was based specifically mentions[8] a new Academic Freedom Index and global time-series dataset, developed by the Global Public Policy Institute (GPPi), the Friedrich-Alexander-Universität Erlangen-Nürnberg (FAU), the Scholars at Risk Network, and the V-Dem Institute, introduced in March 2020, which is composed of five expert-coded indicators that capture key elements in the *de facto* realisation of academic freedom. (Freedom to research and teach; academic exchange and dissemination; institutional autonomy; campus integrity;[9] and freedom of academic and cultural expression). The index is complemented by additional, factual indicators, assessing States' *de jure* commitments to academic freedom at constitutional and international levels, incorporating events-based data,[10] self-reporting data, survey data, legal analyses, and expert-coded data. The authors point out that a formal legal analysis is likely to miss the point, in 2019, for example, close to one-third of countries with the worst performances on academic freedom had constitutional protections for academic freedom in place.[11]

This brings us to a second dimension of academic freedom: a limit to corporate interests. It is an important feature of academic freedom that it is situated within the Scylla and Charybdis of neoliberalism and illiberalism, as analysts and stakeholders are wary of not only the encroachment of illiberal governments, but also the marketisation of the higher educational and research sector. As the aforementioned CoE Report holds,[12] in the *"rise of the neo-liberal global*

---

6 Council of Europe Parliamentary Assembly Res. 2352 (2020), Threats to academic freedom and autonomy of higher education institutions in Europe. Para 7.

7 Council of Europe Parliamentary Assembly Res. 2352 (2020), Threats to academic freedom and autonomy of higher education institutions in Europe. Para 11.

8 Para 74.

9 Campus integrity means the preservation of an open learning and research environment marked by an absence of a deliberately, externally induced climate of insecurity or intimidation on campus. Examples of infringements of campus integrity are politically motivated (physical or digital) surveillance, presence of intelligence or security forces or student militias, attacks by third parties to repress academic life. See (Spannagel et al., 2020).

10 Events-based data on attacks against academics and students have been collected by Scholars at Risk's Academic Freedom Monitoring Project since 2013., Id.

11 Id.

12 Paras 42–44.

knowledge economy, ... higher education is ... a monetised private good (where) [...]
the university is more concerned with maximising cash, than delivering learning."
The question (which cannot be answered in general terms) is then: who is in general terms more trustworthy: the state or the corporate sector? The Hungarian
case, as demonstrated in Ryder's book, shows that (neo)liberal and illiberal
threats can even be combined and cumulative.

Academic freedom also has a third, international affairs/security dimension.
Scholars highlight various concerns academic cooperation with non-democratic
regimes can involve. There are two approaches: subscribing to the 'change by exchange-ideal', based on the assumption that 'cooperation contributes to political
and social progress' and bilateral people-to-people exchanges on education, will
assert soft power in autocracies. The other argument calls for disengagement and
divestment, because democratic change through engagement did not work as expected, and cooperation even comes with risks, such as involuntary technology
transfer, theft of intellectual property, espionage, dual-use technology (meaning
research meant for civilian purposes but can also have military applications).
Baykal and Benner (2020)[13] provide a detailed account of the potential risks
that come with non-democracies offering funding opportunities to universities
and think tanks in democracies (such as Confucius Institutes, the China-United
States Exchange Foundation, the pro-Kremlin Dialogue of Civilizations Research
Institute, or the German-Russian Forum) funded chairs or project funding partly
channelled through state-owned or nominally private companies, as well as individual scholars from democracies (such as lucrative visiting scholar positions
at research institutions in non-democracies). Along with university exchange
programmes used for 'educational diplomacy,' these institutions and projects
are thus instrumentalised to popularise or legitimise autocratic narratives. Baykal and Benner[14] highlight that several national university systems (especially in
the UK, Australia and the US) increasingly depend on fees paid by students from
non-democracies. This all creates channels of influence from non-democracies
into open societies, while at home, non-democracies tighten the screws on foreign NGOs, foundations, think tanks, and universities by limiting their ability
to run their own programmes, and even local collaborators of a Western project
may be exposed to danger of government repression. Baykal and Benner argue
that large funding funnelled into think tanks like the Atlantic Council from
China, Turkey, and Russia are aimed at shaping foreign policy debates. Citing
a Freedom House inquiry, they point to leading universities in the West accepting

---

13 Id.
14 Id.

sponsorship worth hundreds of millions from authoritarian regimes to establish research centers and other kinds of partnerships.

Dependence risks are not necessarily limited to funding: Many research institutes resist disengaging from cooperation with partners in non-democracies, because there can be circumstances where research requires specific natural or demographic conditions that are only present in a few countries, making replication outside of these contexts almost impossible.[15] Thus, dependence often brings about self-censorship. This not only affects students coming from non-democracies. Self-censorship is also prevalent for regional scholars who cannot risk declined visa applications to do fieldwork.[16]

As a fourth contextual dimension, academic freedom is also a challenge for identity politics and social justice debates and is in the centre of culture wars beyond illiberal autocracies as well. Here, debates often turn to career-threatening battles between camps labelling dissenters as 'woke social justice warriors for grievance studies engaged in research' on the one side, and privileged paternalistic conservatives who endorse backlashes against identity politics on the other. Where the population of tenured professors is dwindling and even those left are threatened by new forms of self-censorship, avoiding at all costs to be accused of "cultural appropriation." Avoiding classroom friction with unpopular opinions is an existential necessity for adjuncts, instructors, and part-time faculty with renewable contracts who make up a majority of teaching staff (Kipnis, 2015).

The aforementioned 2020 Council of Europe Report[17] states that according to an EU-wide study, 21% of respondents practiced self-censorship and 15.5% reported being bullied by other academic staff. A study based on eight surveys of academic and graduate student opinion in the Anglo-American world showed that in the U.S seven in ten conservative academics in the social sciences or humanities said they engage in self-censorship (Kaufmann, 2021a, 2021b). An August 2020 survey found that four in ten American academics would not hire a known Trump supporter and one in three British academics would discriminate against a known Brexit supporter for a job (where 52 percent of the population voted to leave the European Union).

This brief overview of what academic freedom entails was only intended to provide a contextualizing framework for Professor Ryder's book, which offers delicious food for thought on a wide variety of issues. It is important to highlight

---

15 Id.

16 Id.

17 Council of Europe Parliamentary Assembly Res. 2352 (2020), Threats to academic freedom and autonomy of higher education institutions in Europe. Paras 37 and 41.

that restraints on academic freedom and subsequent hardship disproportionally target academics living in geographic, political, and socioeconomic peripheries, most of which are already burdened by linguistic barriers. This further accelerates the widening gap between the East and West, North and South, along with the central and periphery, and has a devastating effect on national, local, and regional academia and science.

Bibliography

Adam, C., (2018). Hungarian Academy of Sciences rejects conference proposals on political grounds – *Hungarian Free Press*. [Viewed 15th August 2021]. Available from: https://hun garianfreepress.com/2018/10/02/hungarian-academy-of-sciences-rejects-conference-pro posals-on-political-grounds/

Alter, K., and Zürn, M., (2020). Conceptualising backlash politics: Introduction to a special issue on backlash politics in comparison. *The British Journal of Politics and International Relations*. 22(4), 563–584

Agence France-Presse, (2020). Hungary's parliament blocks domestic violence treaty. *Guardian*. [Viewed 15th August 2021]. Available from: https://www.theguardian.com/ world/2020/may/05/hungarys-parliament-blocks-domestic-violence-treaty

Alexander, J., Eyerman, R., Giesen, B., Smelser, N., Sztompka, P., (2004). *Cultural Trauma and Collective Identity*. Berkeley: University of California Press.

Anderson, R., (2004). *Germany and the Humboldtian Model: European Universities from the Enlightenment to 1914*. Oxford: Oxford Scholarship.

Apuzzo, M., and Novak, B., (2019). In Hungary, a Freewheeling Trump Ambassador Undermines U.S. Diplomats. *New York Times*. [Viewed 15th August 2021]. Available from: https://www.nytimes.com/2019/10/22/world/europe/david-cornstein-hungary-trump-orban.html

Apperly, E., (2019). Why Europe's Far Right Is Targeting Gender Studies. *The Atlantic*. [Viewed 15th August 2021]. Available from: https://www.theatlantic.com/international/archive/ 2019/06/europe-far-right-target-gender-studies/591208/

Arendt, H., (2005). The Promise of Politics. In: J. Kohn, ed. New York: Shocken Books.

Ariel/Humphreys, C., (2019). Clare Ariel/Humphreys' recent commencement address at Corvinus University, Budapest. *Hungarian Free Press*. [Viewed 15th August 2021]. Available from: https://hungarianfreepress.com/2019/08/14/clare-humphreys-recent-com mencement-address-at-corvinus-university-budapest/

Baker, J., (1939). Counterblast to Bernalism. *New Statesman and Nation*.

Bal, M., Kordowicz, M., and Brookes, A., (2020). A Workplace Dignity Perspective on Resilience: Moving Beyond Individualized Instrumentalization to Dignified Resilience. *Advances in Developing Human Resources*. 22(4), 453–466

Balla, Z., (2018). Under pressure, university closes its doors to refugee students. *UNHCR*. [Viewed 15th August 2021]. Available from: https://www.unhcr.org/ceu/10284-under-pres sure-university-closes-its-doors-to-refugee-students.html

Ballai, V., (2021). University Pudding: We looked at what experience was the first to change model at Corvinus. *HVG*. [Viewed 15th August 2021]. Available from: https://hvg.hu/it thon/20210402_corvinus_modellvaltas_tapasztalatok?fbclid=IwAR1LiWL6lhC0jmZunM D70EctjeedpKrdPGEA0UUx1enTL_hA5-aBaC0-zco

Baird, M., (2020). The academic as activist: managing tension and creating impact. *Community, Work and Family*. 23(5), 612–621.

Barát, E., (2020). Gender craze Revoking the MA in gender studies in Hungary and right-wing populist rhetoric. *Eurozine*. [Viewed 15th August 2021]. Available from: https://www.euro zine.com/gender-craze/

Barát, E., (2021). Populist Discourse and Desire for Social Justice. In: K. Hall and R. Barret, eds. *The Oxford Handbook of Language and Sexuality*. Oxford: Oxford University.

https://doi.org/10.1515/9783110749816-013

Bárd, P., and Pech, L., (2019). *How to build and consolidate a partly free pseudo democracy by constitutional means in three steps: The Hungarian model*. Working Paper No. 4. Reconnect. [Viewed 15th August 2021]. Available from: https://reconnect-europe.eu/wp-content/uploads/2019/10/RECONNECT-WP4-final.pdf

Barnes, J., (1985). *The Complete Works of Aristotle: The Revised Oxford Translation*. Princeton: Princeton University Press.

Baskerville, S., (2019). Academic Freedom and the Central European University. *Academic Question*. 32(2), 257–262.

Bayer, L., (2020). How Orbán broke the EU – and got away with it – Hungary's prime minister exploited vulnerabilities in the bloc's legal and political systems. *Politico*. [Viewed 15th August 2021]. Available from: https://www.politico.eu/article/how-viktor-orban-broke-the-eu-and-got-away-with-it-hungary-rule-of-law/

Baykal, E. and Benner, T., (2020). Risky Business. Rethinking Research Cooperation and Exchange with Non-Democracies – Strategies for Foundations, Universities, Civil Society Organizations, and Think Tanks. *Global Public Policy Institute*. [Viewed 15th August 2021]. Available from: https://www.gppi.net/media/GPPi_Baykal_Benner_2020_Risky_ Business_final.pdf.

Bayrakali, E. and Hafez, F., (2016) European Islamophobia Report 2015, Ankara: Foundation for Political, Economic and Social Research. [Viewed 15th August 2021]. Available from: https://www.islamophobiaeurope.com/reports/2015/en/EIR_2015.pdf

BBC, (2017). Hungary passes bill targeting Central European University. *BBC*. [Viewed 15th August 2021]. Available from: https://www.bbc.com/news/world-europe-39493758

BBC, (2017). Large protest in support of Hungary's Soros-backed university. *BBC*. [Viewed 15th August 2021]. Available from: https://www.bbc.com/news/world-europe-39549120

BBJ, (2019). Foundation with 10% stakes in MOL, Richter to fund Corvinus University. *Budapest Business Journal*. [Viewed 15th August 2021]. Available from: https://bbj.hu/economy/environment/initiatives/foundation-with-10-stakes-in-mol-richter-to-fund-corvinus-uni

Beddeleem, M., (2017). *Fighting for the mantle of science: the epistemological foundations of neoliberalism, 1931–1951*. Dissertation, Université de Montréal.

Beddeleem, M., (2020). Recoding Liberalism: Philosophy and Sociology of Science Against Planning. In: D. Plehwe, Q. Slobodian and P. Mirowski, eds. *Nine Lives of Neoliberalism*. London and New York: Verso.

Bellamy, A., (2003). *The Formation of Croatian National Identity: A Centuries-Old Dream?* Manchester: Manchester University Press.

Benczes, I., (2016). From goulash communism to goulash populism: the unwanted legacy of Hungarian reform socialism. *Post-Communist Economies*. 28(2), 146–166.

Béni, A., (2018). Corvinus University to have 4 million tuition fee and more foreign students. *Hungary Today*. [Viewed 15th August 2021]. Available from: https://dailynewshungary.com/corvinus-university-to-have-4-million-tuition-fee-and-more-foreign-students/

Benneworth, P. and Fitjar, R., (2019). Contextualizing the role of universities to regional development: introduction to the special issue. *Regional Studies, Regional Science*. 6(1), 331–338.

Berbas, H. and Republikon Institute, (2020). From Public to Private Universities: Model Change in Hungarian Higher Education. *4Liberty.eu*. [Viewed 15th August 2021]. Available from: http://4liberty.eu/from-public-to-private-universities-model-change-in-hungarian-higher-education/

Berdahl, R., (1990). Academic freedom, autonomy and accountability in British universities. *Studies in Higher Education.* 15(2), 169–180.

Bergson, H., (1932). *Les Deux Sources de la morale et de la religion.* Paris: PUF.

Bernal, J., (1975). Science and Industry. In: D. Hall, ed. *The Frustration of Science.* New York: Arno Press. Original edition, 1935

Bernal, J., (1939). *The Social Function of Science.* London: Routledge.

Berács, J., Derényi, A., Kádár-Csoboth, P., Kováts, G., Polónyi, I., Temesi, J., (2017). Hungarian Higher Education 2016 Strategic Progress Report. *Centre for Higher Education Studies.* Budapest: Corvinus University. [Viewed 15th August 2021]. Available from: http://unipub. lib.uni-corvinus.hu/2828/1/Strat_progress_Report_Hungary_2016.pdf

Beveridge, Lord., (1959). A Defence of Free Learning. New York, Toronto: Oxford University Press.

Blokker, P., (2017). Populism as a Constitutional Project. *Public law and New Populism, NYU School of Law.*

Bódis, A., (2021). Hungary's Government in Reality Controls More Than Half of Leading Media. *Balkan Insight.* [Viewed 15th August 2021]. Available from: https://balkaninsight. com/2021/01/14/hungarys-government-in-reality-controls-more-than-half-of-leading-media/

Bodnár, Z., (2021). Felfalhatja az autonómiájuktól megfosztott magyar egyetemeket a Budapestre készülő kínai egyetem, a Fudan. *Qubit.* [Viewed 15th August 2021]. Available from: https://qubit.hu/2021/03/03/felfalhatja-az-autonomiajuktol-megfosztott-magyar-egyetemeket-a-budapestre-keszulo-kinai-egyetem-a-fudan

Bodó, M., (2015). Eastern Feminism? Some Considerations on Women and Religion in a Post-Communist Context (Romania, Hungary). *Feminist Theology.* 24(1), 23–34.

Bodwell, W. and Chermack, T., (2010). Organizational Ambidexterity: Integrating Deliberate and Emergent Strategy with Scenario Planning. *Technological Forecasting and Social Change.* 77(2), 193.

Bőgel, G. and Mátyás, L., (2021). May the power be with you! Thoughts on university model change. *Telex.* [Viewed 15th August 2021]. Available from: https://telex.hu/velemeny/2021/01/31/az-ero-legyen-veletek-gondolatok-az-egyetemi-modellvaltasrol

Bohle, D. and Greskovits, B., (2019). Staring through the mocking glass Three misperceptions of the east-west divide since 1989. *Eurozine.* [Viewed 15th August 2021]. Available from: https://www.eurozine.com/staring-through-the-mocking-glass/

Boldyrev, O. and Benke, E., (2017). Is Hungary copying Russia by targeting Soros-backed university?. *BBC News, Budapest.* [Viewed 15th August 2021]. Available from: https://www.bbc.com/news/world-europe-39640474

Boros, T., (2018). *The Hungarian "STOP Soros" Act: Why does the government fight human rights organisations?* Budapest: Friedrich-Ebert-Stiftung. [Viewed 15th August 2021]. Available from: https://library.fes.de/pdf-files/bueros/budapest/14205.pdf

Bothwell, E., (2021). Free Speech Debate in England: Government proposes system to assure free speech, but faculty and student groups object. *The Times Higher Education.* [Viewed 15th August 2021]. Available from: https://www.insidehighered.com/news/2021/02/18/english-faculty-and-student-groups-object-free-speech-rules

Bourdieu, P., (1983). The Field of Cultural Production, or: The Economic World Reversed. *Poetics.* 12(4–5), 311–356.

Bourdieu, P., (1986). The forms of capital. In J. Richardson, ed. *Handbook of theory and research for sociology of education.* New York, NY: Greenwood Press.

Bourdieu, P., (1988). *Homo Academicus.* Stanford, California: Stanford University Press

Bourdieu, P. and Wacquant, L., (1992). *An Invitation to Reflexive Sociology.* Chicago, IL: University of Chicago Press; Cambridge: Polity Press.

Bourdieu, P., (1993). *The field of cultural production.* Cambridge, UK: Polity Press.

Bowes-Catton, H., Brewis, J., Clarke, C., Drake, D., Gilmour, A. and Penn, A., (2020). Talkin' 'bout a revolution? From quiescence to resistance in the contemporary university. *Management Learning.* 51(4), 378–397.

Braham, R., (2016). *The Politics of Genocide: The Holocaust in Hungary.* New York: Columbia University Press.

Braun, R., (2019). Resignation letter from Corvinus University. *Hungarian Spectrum.* [Viewed 15th August 2021]. Available from: thttp://hungarianspectrum.org/2019/09/05/professor-robert-brauns-resignation-letter-from-corvinus-university/

Brückner, G., (2017). He Plays Cards with Orbán, Is Friends with Csányi, and Storck Cries on his Shoulder. *Index.* [Viewed 15th August 2021]. Available from: https://index.hu/english/2017/11/30/he_plays_cards_with_orban_is_friends_with_csanyi_and_storck_cries_on_his_shoulder/

Brühwiler, C. and Goktepe, K., (2021). Populism with a Ph.D: education levels and populist leaders. *Journal of Political Power.*

Brown, W., (2015). *Undoing the Demos: Neoliberalism's Stealth Revolution.* Massachusetts: MIT Press.

Brown, L. and Strega, S., (2005). *Research As Resistance: Critical, Indigenous, and Anti-Oppressive Approaches.* Toronto: Canadian Scholars' Press/Women's Press.

Brubaker, R., (2017). Why Populism? *Theory and Society: Renewal and Society.* 46(5), 357–385.

Burawoy, M., (2004). American Sociological Association Presidential address: For public sociology. *The British Journal of Sociology.* 56 (2), 259–294.

Byrne, A., (2017). Hungary takes aim at Soros as parliament backs university curbs. *Financial Times.* [Viewed 15th August 2021]. Available from: https://www.ft.com/content/9d03da8e-189f-11e7-9c35-0dd2cb31823a

Caffentzis, G. and Federici, S., (2011). Notes on the Edu-Factory and Cognitive Capitalism. *Dispatches from the Ruins: Documents and Analyses from University Struggles, Experiments in Self-Education.* 26–29. [Viewed 15th August 2021]. Available from: https://libcom.org/files/dispatch_ruins_final3.pdf

Castells, M., (2012). *Networks of Outrage and Hope: Social Movements in the Internet Age.* Cambridge: Polity Press.

Cemlyn, S., and Ryder, A., (2017). Gypsy, Roma and Traveller Communities. In: A. Peterson, R. Hattam, M. Zembylas, J. Arthur, eds. *The Palgrave International Handbook of Education for Citizenship and Social Justice.* Basingstoke: Palgrave.

CEU Press Release, (2017). 20 Nobel Laureates, Other Leading Academics Urge Hungarian Government to Withdraw Tabled Legislation Targeting Central European University. *CEU.* [Viewed 15th August 2021]. Available from: https://www.ceu.edu/article/2017-03-31/20-nobel-laureates-other-leading-academics-urge-hungarian-government-withdraw

CEU Office of the President and Rector., (2017). CEU Refutes Prime Minister Viktor Orban's Statement in the European Parliament. *CEU*. [Viewed 15th August 2021]. Available from: https://www.ceu.edu/article/2017-04-26/ceu-refutes-prime-minister-viktor-orbans-state ment-european-parliament

CEU, (2017). Response To Justice Minister's Statement. *CEU*. [Viewed 15th August 2021]. Available from: https://www.ceu.edu/article/2017-10-13/ceu-response-justice-ministers-statement

CEU Press release, (2019). CEU "says goodbye" to its spiritual home, awards Open Society Prize to Nobel laureate Joseph Stiglitz. *CEU*. [Viewed 15th August 2021]. Available from: https://www.ceu.edu/article/2019-06- 25/ceu-says-goodbye-its-spiritual-home-awards-open-society-prize-nobel-laureate

CEU Office of the President and Rector, (2020). "Landmark Judgment" – Lex CEU Struck Down by European Court of Justice. *CEU*. [Viewed 15th August 2021]. Available from: https://www.ceu.edu/node/25161/

Cheng, M., (2010). Audit cultures and quality assurance mechanisms in England: a study of their perceived impact on the work of academics. *Teaching in Higher Education*, 15(3), 259 – 271.

Choat, S., (2017). Horseshoe theory is nonsense – the far right and far left have little in common. *The Conversation*. [Viewed 15th August 2021]. Available from: https://the conversation.com/horseshoe-theory-is-nonsense-the-far-right-and-far-left-have-little-in-common-77588

Coffe, H., (2018). Gender and the radical right. In J. Rydgren, ed. *The Oxford Handbook of the Radical Right*. 200 – 211. Oxford: Oxford University Press.

Cohen, R., (2010). *The Berkeley Rebellion: Mario Savio's Design for a Free Speech Monument, California*, (Spring), 20 – 21.

Cohen, S., (2016). *Folk Devils and Moral Panics. Notes and References. Appendix. The Creation of Mods and Rockers*. London: MacGibbon and Kee.

Cole, R. and Heinecke, W., (2020). Higher education after neoliberalism: Student activism as a guiding light. *Policy Futures in Education*. 18(1), 90 – 116.

Collyer, F., (2015). Practices of conformity and resistance in the marketisation of the academy: Bourdieu, professionalism and academic capitalism. *Critical Studies in Education*. 56(3), 315 – 331.

Corvinus, (2019). Anthony Radev will be the president of the Corvinus University of Budapest. *CEU*. [Viewed 15th August 2021]. Available from: https://www.uni-corvinus.hu/hir/an thony-radev-will-be-the-president-of-the-corvinus-university-of-budapest/?lang=en

Coté, M., Day, R. and de Peuter, G., (2007). Utopian Pedagogy: Creating Radical Alternatives in the Neoliberal Age. *The Review of Education, Pedagogy, and Cultural Studies*. 29(4), 317 – 336.

Courpasson, D., Younes, D. and Reed, M., (2021). Durkheim in the Neoliberal Organization: Taking Resistance and Solidarity Seriously. *Organization Theory*. 2(1), 1 – 24.

Csernai, M., (2021). letter of resignation – 17th January

Dahlum, S., and Wig, T., (2021). Chaos on Campus: Universities and Mass Political Protest. *Comparative Political Studies*. 54(1), 3 – 32.

Dahl, R., (1998). *On Democracy*. New Haven: Yale University Press

Daily News Hungary, (2014). Corvinus University head dismisses ChristDem call to remove Marx statue. *Daily News Hungary*. [Viewed 15th August 2021]. Available from: https://dai

lynewshungary.com/corvinus-university-head-dismisses-christdem-call-to-remove-marx-statue/

Daum, A., (2009). Varieties of Popular Science and the Transformations of Public Knowledge: Some Historical Reflections. *Isis.* 100(2), 319 – 332. Chicago: The University of Chicago Press on behalf of The History of Science Society Stable

Dawson, G., (2011). Thirty Hours in the Radical Camera. In: D. Hancox, ed. *Fight Back: A Reader on the Winter of Protest.* London: openDemocracy. 109 – 114.

Deák, Z., (2017). Lex CEU: The beginning of the end of Hungary's academic independence – Heinrich Böll Foundation. [Viewed 15ᵗʰ August 2021]. Available from: https://www.boell. de/en/2017/04/07/lex-ceu-beginning-end-hungarys-academic-independence

Deák, D., (2019). Vagyonjuttatás és felelősségelhárítás. *Public Statistis.* LXIII (11). [Viewed 15ᵗʰ August 2021]. Available from: https://www.es.hu/cikk/2019-03-14/deak-daniel/va gyonjuttatas-es-felelossegelharitas.html?fbclid=IwAR1DvqTpMqlL9Tr9kFKlioyBNqzNxwl s40y97MEFUYgsqtTvOV-QKuRnwvM

Deluca, K. M. and Peeples, J., (2002). From public sphere to public screen: Democracy, activism, and the violence of Seattle. *Critical Studies in Media Communication.* 19(2), 125 – 151.

Department of Education, (2021). Landmark proposals to strengthen free speech at universities. *Press Release.* [Viewed 15ᵗʰ August 2021]. Available from: https://www.gov. uk/government/news/landmark-proposals-to-strengthen-free-speech-at-universities

Deutsche Welle, (2018). Hungary: George Soros' Open Society Foundations to move from Hungary to Germany. *Deutsche Welle.* [Viewed 15ᵗʰ August 2021]. Available from: https:// www.dw.com/en/hungary-george-soros-open-society-foundations-to-move-from-hungary-to-germany/a-43787319

Di Napoli, R., (2014). Value gaming and political ontology: between resistance and compliance in academic development. *International Journal for Academic Development.* 19(1), 4 – 11.

Dorahy, J., (2020). Agnes Heller: A Philosopher for Today. *Critical Horizons: A Journal of Philosophy and Social Theory.* 21(4), 303 – 317.

Domány, A., (2021). Bíróság támadta meg a felsőoktatási átalakítást – az Alkotmánybíróságnak 90 napon belül döntenie kell. *Itthon.* [Viewed 15ᵗʰ August 2021]. Available from: https://hvg.hu/itthon/20210226_alkotmanyellenes_a_felsooktatas_atalaki tasa_fovarosi_torvenyszek_alkotmanybirosag

Donovan, J., (2018). After the #Keyword: Eliciting, Sustaining, and Coordinating Participation Across the Occupy Movement. *Social Media and Society.* 1 – 1 – 12

Dunn Cavelty, M., Kaufmann, M., Søby Kristensen, K., (2015). Resilience and (in)security: Practices, subjects, temporalities. *Security Dialogue.* 46(1), 3 – 14.

Durkheim, E., (1972). *Emile Durkheim: Selected writings.* Cambridge: Cambridge University Press.

Dutt-Ballerstadt, R. and Bhattacharya, K., (2021). *Civility, Free Speech, and Academic Freedom in Higher Education: Faculty on the Margins.* London: Routledge.

Eberhardt, D., (2006). Ethical Issues On Campus: Responding to Student Complaints of Liberal Bias in the Classroom. *Journal of College and Character.* 7(1).

Economist, (2016). Post-truth politics: art of the lie. *The Economist.* [Viewed 15ᵗʰ August 2021]. Available from: https://www.economist.com/leaders/2016/09/10/art-of-the-lie

Enyedi, Z., (2018). Democratic Backsliding and Academic Freedom in Hungary. *Perspectives on Politics.* 6(4), 1067–1074.

European Review of History/REH Editorial Committee, (2020). Introduction to the dossier Academic Freedom in Historical Perspective. *European Review of History: Revue européenne d'histoire.* 27(5), 579–581.

Etl, A., (2020). Liminal Populism – The Transformation of the Hungarian Migration Discourse, Journal of Borderlands Studies. *Journal of Borderland Studies.*

European Commission, (2017). *Special Eurobarometer 465 Survey requested by the European Commission, Directorate-General for Justice and Consumers, November 2017.* Brussels: *Eurobarometer.* [Viewed 15th August 2021]. Available from: https://data.europa.eu/data/datasets/s2154_87_4_465_eng?locale=en

European Commission, (2017). Hungary: Commission takes legal action on Higher Education Law and sets record straight on Stop Brussels consultation. *Press Release.* [Viewed 15th August 2021]. Available from: https://ec.europa.eu/commission/presscorner/detail/en/MEX_17_1116

European Commission, (2017). Commission refers Hungary to the European Court of Justice of the EU over the Higher Education Law. *Press release.* [Viewed 15th August 2021]. Available from: https://ec.europa.eu/commission/presscorner/detail/en/IP_17_5004

European Film Academy, (2020). EFA Supports the Students and Senate of the Budapest University of Theatre and Film Arts. [Viewed 15th August 2021]. Available from: https://www.europeanfilmacademy.org/News-detail.155.0.html?&tx_ttnews%5Btt_news%5D=810&cHash=9708c141703b8240bbd1a0fc933636ef

European Parliament, (2018). *Backlash in Gender Equality and Women's and Girls' Rights – Policy Department for Citizens' Rights and Constitutional Affairs Directorate General for Internal Policies of the Union PE 604.955.* Committee on Women's Rights and Gender Equality. . [Viewed 15th August 2021]. Available from: https://www.europarl.europa.eu/RegData/etudes/STUD/2018/604955/IPOL_STU(2018)604955_EN.pdf

European Institute of Gender Equality, (2020). Gender Equality Index 2020: Hungary. *EIGE'S publications.* [Viewed 15th August 2021]. Available from: https://eige.europa.eu/publications/gender-equality-index-2020-hungary

European University Association, (2018). EUA condemns Hungarian government plan to ban gender studies. [Viewed 15th August 2021]. Available from: https://eua.eu/news/130:eua-condemns-hungarian-government-plan-to-ban-gender-studies.html

Ewalt, J., Ohl, J. and Pfister, S., (2013). Activism, Deliberation, and Networked Public Screens: Rhetorical Scenes From the Occupy Moment in Lincoln, Nebraska (Part 1). *Cultural Studies ↔ Critical Methodologies.* 13(3), 173–190.

Fabók, B., (2020). Alighogy bevezették, máris megroppan a kormány új egyetemi modellje. *G7 ÜZLET.* [Viewed 15th August 2021]. Available from: https://g7.hu/kozelet/20200408/alighogy-bevezettek-maris-megroppan-a-kormany-uj-egyetemi-modellje/?fbclid=IwAR2_5bsuf0mN1OYl0RgwiWYlKawf1nwaFZY8Yd4xeXAHQOUpxw1ePkd31yA

Fekete, L., (2016). Flying the flag for neoliberalism. *Race and Class.* 58(3), 3–22.

Felix, A., (2015). Hungary. In: E. Kováts and M. Põim, eds. *Gender as symbolic glue: The Position and Role of Conservative and Far Right Parties in the Anti-Gender Mobilizations in Europe.* Budapest: Friedrich-Ebert-Stiftung. [Viewed 15th August 2021]. Available from: https://library.fes.de/pdf-files/bueros/budapest/11382.pdf

Fleck, Z., Kovács, A., Lázár, D. and Majtényi, L., (2021). Fighting for Autonomies. *Eötvös Károly Institute, March 2021.*

Foa, R., (2018). Modernization and Authoritarianism. *Journal of Democracy.* 29(3), 129–140.

Fodor, E., (2013). The Policy on Gender Equality in Hungary. European Parliament. . [Viewed 15th August 2021]. Available from: https://www.europarl.europa.eu/RegData/etudes/note/join/2013/493017/IPOL-FEMM_NT(2013)493017_EN.pdf

Foer, F., (2019). Viktor Orbán's War on Intellect. *The Atlantic.* [Viewed 15th August 2021]. Available from: https://www.theatlantic.com/magazine/archive/2019/06/george-soros-viktor-orban-ceu/588070/

Foucault, M., (1977). *Discipline and Punish: The Birth of the Prison.* New York: Random House.

Foucault, M., (1988). Technologies of the Self. In: L. Martin, H. Gutman and P. Hutton, eds. *Technologies of the Self: A Seminar with Michel.* London: Tavistock publications. 16–49.

Fourastié, J., (1979). *Les Trente Glorieuses, ou la révolution invisible de 1946 à 1975.* Paris: Fayard.

Fraser, N., (1995). From redistribution to recognition? Dilemmas of justice in a postsocialist age. *New Left Review,* 212 (1), 68–93.

Freire, P., (1972). *Pedagogy of the oppressed.* New York: Herder and Herder.

Freire, P., (1994). *Pedagogy of Hope: Reliving Pedagogy of the Oppressed.* New York: Continuum.

Frei, B., (2020). After 71 Days, Theater Uni Blockade Ends Due to New Coronavirus Restrictions. *Hungary Today.* [Viewed 15th August 2021]. Available from: https://hungarytoday.hu/szfe-barricade-blockade-restrictions/

Fukuyama, F., (1992). *The End of History and the Last Man.* New York: Free Press.

Fuzessi, K., (2013). Hungary in chaos over higher education plans. *University World News.* [Viewed 15th August 2021]. Available from: https://www.universityworldnews.com/post.php?story=20130220151416428

Gall, L., (2019). Hungary Renews its War on Academic Freedom. *Human Rights Watch.* [Viewed 15th August 2021]. Available from: https://www.hrw.org/news/2019/07/02/hungary-renews-its-war-academic-freedom

Galasso, N., (2019). Confronting Far-Right Masculinities: implications for NGOs. *TPQ.* [Viewed 15th August 2021]. Available from: http://turkishpolicy.com/article/985/confronting-far-right-masculinities-implications-for-ngos

Gardner, M., (2019). European rectors fear for academic freedom in Hungary. *University World News.* [Viewed 15th August 2021]. Available from: https://www.universityworldnews.com/post.php?story=20190806103103293

Garnham, N., (2007). Habermas and the public sphere. *Global Media and Communication.* 3(2), 201–214.

Gawkowski, J., (2018). Orbán, keep your hands off our universities!. *PoliticalCritique.org* [Viewed 15th August 2021]. Available from: http://politicalcritique.org/cee/hungary/2018/orban-keep-your-hands-off-our-universities/

Gellner, E., (1983). *Nations and Nationalism.* Oxford: Basil Blackwell

Gessen, M., (2018). How George Soros's University in Budapest Fell Victim to a Nationalist Bureaucracy. *New Yorker.* [Viewed 15th August 2021]. Available from: https://www.newyorker.com/news/our-columnists/how-george-soross-university-in-budapest-fell-victim-to-a-nationalist-bureaucracy

Geva, D., (2021). Orban's Ordonationalism as Post-Neoliberal Hegemony. *Theory, Culture and Society.* (special issue) 1–23.

Gibson, S., (2015). When rights are not enough: What is? Moving towards new pedagogy for inclusive education within UK universities. *International Journal of Inclusive Education.* 19(8), 875–886.

Giddens, A. and Pierson, C., (1998). *Conversations with Anthony Giddens: Making sense of Modernity.* Stanford: Stanford University Press.

Giroux, H., (2014). *Neoliberalism's War on Higher Education.* Chicago, IL: Haymarket Books.

Goffman, E., (1959). *The Presentation of Self In Everyday Life.* New York: Doubleday

González-Calvo, G. and Arias-Carballal, M., (2018). Effects from audit culture and neoliberalism on university teaching: an autoethnographic perspective. *Ethnography and Education.* 13(4), 413–427.

Graham, L., (2004). *Science in Russia and the Soviet Union. A Short History. Series: Cambridge Studies in the History of Science.* Cambridge: Cambridge University Press

Gross, N., (2008). SIX. Pragmatism, Phenomenology, and Twentieth- Century American Sociology. In: C. Calhoun, ed. *Sociology in America: A History.* Chicago: University of Chicago Press, 183–224.

Grzebalska, W., Kováts, E. and Pető, A., (2017). Gender as symbolic glue: How Gender became an umbrella term for the rejection of the (neo)liberal order. *Political Critique.* [Viewed 15th August 2021]. Available from: http://politicalcritique.org/long-read/2017/

Guterl, M., (2016). I'm on the Professor Watchlist – and it's exposed a radical truth about the future of social justice. *Quartz.* [Viewed 15th August 2021]. Available from: https://qz.com/868513/im-on-the-professor-watchlist-and-its-woken-me-up-to-the-radical-truth-about-america-and-social-progress/

Habermas, J., (1989). *The Structural Transformation of the Public Sphere: An Inquiry into a Category of Bourgeois Society.* Cambridge Massachusetts: Thomas Burger.

Habermas, J. and Nida-Rümelin, J., (2011). Protect the Philosophers. *Süddeutsche Zeitung.* [Viewed 15th August 2021]. Available from: http://www.sueddeutsche.de/kultur/aufruf-von-habermas-und-nida-ruemelin-schuetzt-die-philosophen-1.1050449

Habermas, J. and Nida-Rümelin, J., (2011). *Protect the Philosophers.* Translated from German by D. P. O'Connell. [Viewed 15th August 2021]. Available from: https://www.newappsblog.com/2011/01/translation-of-habermas-and-nida-r%C3%BCmelin-on-the-hungarian-situation.html

Hadas, M., (2007). Much Ado About Nothing? *The American Sociologist.* 38, 309–322.

Halász, A., (2015). Merkel clashes with Orban on meaning of democracy. *EU Observer.* [Viewed 15th August 2021]. Available from: https://euobserver.com/beyond-brussels/127468

Halkó, P. and Megadja, G., (2021). Lánczi András: Nincs végtelen fejlődés. *Kontra.* [Viewed 15th August 2021]. Available from: https://kontra.hu/lanczi-andras-nincs-vegtelen-fejlodes?fbclid=IwAR1wYKYSWckT6m41g_oKcYVwWuOEuckgu98aE8a8T_Noh2hmntz12TxgIG4

Hall, R. and Bowles, K., (2016). Re-engineering higher education: The subsumption of academic labour and the exploitation of anxiety. *Workplace: A Journal of Academic Labor* 28, 30–47.

Hall, B., (2019). Gendering Resistance to Right-Wing Populism: Black Protest and a New Wave of Feminist Activism in Poland? *American Behavioral Scientist.* 63(10), 1497–1515.

Hallonsten, O., (2021). Stop evaluating science: A historical-sociological argument. *Social Science Information*. 60(1), 7 – 26.

Halmai, G., (2019a). Populism, authoritarianism and constitutionalism. *German Law Journal* (2019), 20, 296 – 313

Halmai, G ., (2019b) The End of Academic Freedom in Hungary. *Hypotheses: Droit and Société*. [Viewed 15th August 2021]. Available from: https://ds.hypotheses.org/6368

Halffman, W. and Radder, H., (2015). The Academic Manifesto: From an Occupied to a Public University. *Minerva*. 53, 165 – 187.

Hagmann, J. and Dunn Cavelty, M., (2012). National risk registers: Security scientism and the propagation of permanent insecurity. *Security Dialogue*. 43(1), 79 – 96.

Hamburger, J., (2018). Can There Be a Left Populism? *Jacobin*. [Viewed 15th August 2021. Available from: https://www.jacobinmag.com/2018/03/left-populism-mouffe-fassin-france-insoumise

Hann, C., (2020). In search of civil society: From peasant populism to post peasant illiberalism in provincial Hungary. *Social Science Information*. 59(3), 459 – 483.

Haraway, D., (1988). Situated Knowledges: The Science Question in Feminism and the Privilege of Partial Perspective. *Feminist Studies*. 14(3), 575 – 599.

Harding, S., (1991). *Whose Science? Whose Knowledge? Thinking from Women's Lives*. Ithaca, NY: Cornell University.

Hargittai, I., (2006). *The Martians of Science: Five Physicists Who Changed the Twentieth Century*. Oxford, New York: Oxford University Press.

Harsányi, G. and Vincze, S., (2012). Characteristics of Hungarian Higher Education in an International Perspective. *Public Finance Quarterly, State Audit Office of Hungary*. 57(2), 213 – 233.

Hartl, P., (2012). Michael Polányi on freedom of science. *Synthesis Philosphica*. 27(2), 307 – 321.

Health and Safety Executive, (2020). Making your workplace COVID-secure during the coronavirus pandemic. [Viewed 15th August 2021]. Available from: https://www.hse.gov.uk/coronavirus/working-safely/index.htm#risk_assessment

Hensby, A., (2019). Millbank tendency: The strengths and limitations of mediated protest events in UK student activism cycles. *Current Sociology*. 67(7), 960 – 977.

Hirado.hu, (2017). Kósa szerint sokan felültek "Georgie bácsi trükkjének". [According to Kósa, many were scammed by "Uncle Georgie's Tricks"]. *Hirado.hu*. [Viewed 15th August 2021]. Available from: https://www.hirado. hu/2017/04/12/kosa-sokan-felultek-georgie-bacsi-trukkjenek/

Holloway, J., (2005). *Change the World Without Taking the Power: The Meaning of Revolution Today*. London: Pluto Press.

Hooks, B., (2014). *Teaching to transgress: Education as the practice of freedom*. New York, NY: Routledge.

Horn, D. and Keller, T., (2015). Hungary: The Impact of Gender Culture. In: E. Elgar, ed. *Gender, Education and Employment: An International Comparison of School-to-Work Transitions*. 280 – 296.

Horváth, K (2021) Alkotmánybíróság: nem alaptörvény-ellenes az SZFE-s hallgatók félévének felfüggesztése – Merce. [Viewed 15th August 2021]. Available from: https://merce.hu/2021/10/18/alkotmanybirosag-nem-alaptorveny-ellenes-az-szfe-s-hallgatok-felevenek-felfuggesztese/

Huemer, M., (2013). *The Problem of Political Authority.* Basingstoke: Palgrave Macmillan

Hungary Academy Staff Forum, (2019). Chapter 6 on Academic Freedom. In: Amnesty International Hungary, Hungarian Civil Liberties Union, Hungarian Helsinki Committee, Hungarian LGBT Alliance, Mertel Media Monitor, and Transparency International Hungary, prepared. *Stating the obvious.* [Viewed 15th August 2021]. Available from: https://helsin ki.hu/en/stating-the-obvious/

Hungarian Network of Academics., (2020). *Hungary Turns Its Back on Europe: Dismantling Culture, Education, Science and the Media in Hungary 2010–2019.* Budapest: Oktatói Há lózat Hungarian Network of Academics.

Hungarian Academy of Sciences, (2018). ERC grantees joint statement regarding Government plans concerning the budgetary funding and operation of the Hungarian Academy of Sciences. *Hungarian Academy of Sciences.* [Viewed 15th August 2021]. Available from: https://mta.hu/english/joint-statement-of-hungarian-erc-grant-winners-regarding-govern ment-plans-concerning-the-budgetary-funding-and-operation-of-the-hungarian-academy- of-sciences-108866

Hungary. Hungarian Government, (2017). *Prime Minister Viktor Orban on Kussuth Radio's 180 Minutes Programme.* Hungarian Government. [Viewed 15th August 2021]. Available from: http://www.kormany.hu/en/the-prime-minister/ the-prime-minister-s-speeches/prime- minister-viktor-orban-on-kossuth-radio-s-180-minutesprogramme20170602.

Hungary. Hungarian Ministry, (2018). *Gábor Fodor Member of Parliament – Question and Response – Who is harmed by gender?* [Viewed 15th August 2021]. Available from: https://www.parlament.hu/irom40/14056/14056-0001.pdf

Hungary. Hungarian Accreditation Committee, (2018). *Statement by the Board of the HAC concerning the study programme Gender Studies.* [Viewed 15th August 2021]. Available from: http://old.mab.hu/web/index.php?option=com_content&view=category&layout= blog&id=95&Itemid=667&lang=en

Hungarian Spectrum, (2014). Imre Kerényi and Lajos Kósa: Boorishness and prejudice in Orbán's Hungary. *Hungarian Spectrum.* [Viewed 15th August 2021]. Available from: https://hungarianspectrum.org/TAG/IMRE-KERENYI/

Hungarian Spectrum, (2018). Another leap in the dark: Privatization of Hungarian Universities. *Hungarian Spectrum.* [Viewed 15th August 2021]. Available from: https://hun garianspectrum.org/2018/10/07/another-leap-in-the-dark-privatization-of-hungarian-uni versities/

Hungarian Spectrum, (2019). The Agony of the Hungarian Academy of Sciences. *Hungarian Spectrum.* [Viewed 15th August 2021]. Available from: https://hungarianspectrum.org/ 2019/02/06/THE-AGONY-OF-THE-HUNGARIAN-ACADEMY-OF-SCIENCES/

Hungary Today, (2020). SZFE's New Leadership: Classes May Resume as of Feb. 1. *Hungary Today.* [Viewed 15th August 2021]. Available from: https://hungarytoday.hu/theater-uni- szfe-new-leadership-classes-resume-feb-1/

Hungary Today, (2021). Question on Controversial Anti-LGBT+ Law Included in Upcoming National Consultation. *Hungary Today.* [Viewed 15th August 2021]. Available from: https://hungarytoday.hu/question-anti-lgbt-law-upcoming-national-consultation/

Hungary Today, (2021) Croatia Top Court Affirms Prison Sentence for MOL Chief Hernádi. *Hungary Today.* [Viewed 28h October 2021]. Available from: https://hungarytoday.hu/her nadi-croatia-sentence-court-mol-leader/

HVG, (2018). Ötszáz tudós állt ki társuk mellett, akit Orbán fenyegetően a szájára vett. *HVG*. [Viewed 15th August 2021]. Available from: https://hvg.hu/itthon/20180301_otszaz_tudos_orban_viktor_melegh_attila

HVG, (2018). Interview with Ádám Török. *HVG*. [Viewed 15th August 2021]. Available from: https://mta.hu/english/interview-with-adam-torok-in-hvg-on-20-july-2018-a-summary-108994

HVG, (2020). Szolidaritási nyilatkozatban állnak ki a Corvinus polgárai is a Színművészeti mellett. *HVG*. [Viewed 15th August 2021]. Available from: https://m.hvg.hu/itthon/20201028_corvinus_egyetem_polgarai_szolidaritasi_nyilatkozat_szfe_mellett?fbclid=IwAR0PoRmECxQ3U_tX3Pv5kML3Fnb2xm0Hj6Tagi_aHBAZd5ZtJT0rKoE04uU

Index (2019) Hungarian Academy of Sciences turns to Constitutional Court against law taking away research institutes [Viewed 15th August 2021]. Available from: https://index.hu/english/2019/09/04/constitutional_court_hungarian_academy_of_sciences_research_network_miklos_maroth_laszlo_lovasz/

Index, (2020). Megszenvedheti az olajár esését a Corvinus Egyetem. *Index*. [Viewed 15th August 2021]. Available from: https://index.hu/gazdasag/2020/04/08/corvinus_mol_olajar/?fbclid=IwAR1OfvIsmZAVJZAZcsrwtwM7GMKS66jm2EMmWjyBWZk7zORpTwkPqHp8LcI

Inglehart, R.F. and Norris, P., (2016). *Trump, Brexit, and the Rise of Populism: Economic have-nots and cultural backlash*. Harvard: Harvard Kennedy School.

Innes, A., (2015). Hungary's Illiberal Democracy. *Current History*. 114(770), 95–100.

Inotai, E., (2020). Legal Victory for Central European University is Too Little, Too Late. *Balkan Insight*. [Viewed 15th August 2021]. Available from: https://balkaninsight.com/2020/10/06/legal-victory-for-central-european-university-is-too-little-too-late/

Inter-Parliamentary Union, (2021). Global information on national parliaments. [Viewed 15th August 2021]. Available from: https://data.ipu.org/compare?field=chamber%3A%3Acurrent_women_percent&structure=any__lower_chamber#map

Iroux, H., (2014). *Neoliberalism's War on Higher Education*. Chicago, IL: Haymarket Books.

Ivancheva, M., (2011). The Role of Dissident-Intellectuals in the Formation of Civil Society in (Post-) Communist East-Central Europe. In: H.Kouki and E.Romanos, eds. *Re-Visiting Protests: New Approaches to Social Mobilization in Europe since 1945*. Berghahn Press

Ivancheva, M., (2015). The age of precarity and the new challenges to the academic profession. *Studia Universitatis Babes-Bolyai-Studia Europaea*. 60(1), 39–48.

Jenkins, R., (2007). *Bourdieu*. London: Routledge.

Jemielniak, D. and Greenwood, D., (2015). Wake Up or Perish: Neo-Liberalism, the Social Sciences, and Salvaging the Public University. *Cultural Studies Critical Methodologies*. 15(1), 72–82.

Jeszenszky, G., (2005). *The New (Post-Communist) Europe and Its Ethnic Problems*. Budapest: Kairosz Kiadó.

Jones, R., (1986). *Emile Durkheim: An Introduction to Four Major Works*. Beverly Hills, CA: Sage Publications.

Kafkadesk, (2020). SZFE: Art students fight for independence in Hungary's intensifying culture wars. *Kafkadesk*. [Viewed 15th August 2021]. Available from: https://kafkadesk.org/2020/10/13/szfe-art-students-fight-for-independence-in-hungarys-intensifying-culture-wars/

Kalan, D., (2020). Orban's Macbeth: The tragic figure behind the Hungarian populist leader's efforts to remake his country's theater. *Dispatch*. [Viewed 15th August 2021]. Available

from: https://foreignpolicy.com/2020/10/13/orban-hungary-theater-vidnyanszky-popu
lism/

Karran, T., (2009). Academic Freedom in Europe: Reviewing UNESO'S Recommendation. *British Journal of Educational Studies.* 57(2), 191–215.

Karter, J., Robbins, B. and McInerney, R., (2019). Student Activism in the Neoliberal University: A Hermeneutic Phenomenological Analysis. *Journal of Humanistic Psychology.*

Kasnyikm, M., (2017). Rector of Corvinus seizes the moment to warn university citizens about the limitations of expression. *444.* [Viewed 15th August 2021]. Available from: https:// 444.hu/2017/04/04/a-corvinus-rektora-megragadta-a-pillanatot-hogy-figyelmeztesse-az-egyetemi-polgarokat-a-velemenynyilvanitas-korlataira

Kaufmann, E., (2021a). *Academic Freedom in Crisis: Punishment, Political Discrimination, and Self-Censorship* Report No. 2. March 1, 2021. Center for the Study of Partisanship and Ideology

Kaufmann, E., (2021b). We Have the Data to Prove It: Universities Are Hostile to Conservatives. *Newsweek.* [Viewed 15th August 2021]. Available from: https://www.news week.com/we-have-data-prove-it-universities-are-hostile-conservatives-opinion-1573551

Keczer, G., (2009). A magyar felsőoktatás és az egyetemirányítás változásai az Osztrák-Magyar Monarchiában. *Közép-Európai Közlemények.* 2(2–3), 16–21.

Kentish, P., (2020). Viktor Orbán's latest victim: Budapest's University for Theatre and Film. *Emerging Europe.* [Viewed 15th August 2021]. Available from: https://emerging-europe. com/news/viktor-orbans-latest-victim-budapests-university-for-theatre-and-film/

Khan, A., Blanchett, C., Tóibín, C., Brook, P., Rushdie, S and others., (2020). Letter: Artists urge Orban to end Hungary's university culture war. *Financial Times.* [Viewed 15th August 2021]. Available from: https://www-ft-com.btpl.idm.oclc.org/content/662bb7af-116b-4769-9e54-6b4c1c9c8f4b

Kingsley, P., (2019). Orban Encourages Mothers in Hungary to Have 4 or More Babies. *New York Times.* [Viewed 15th August 2021]. Available from: https://www.nytimes.com/2019/ 02/11/world/europe/orban-hungary-babies-mothers-population-immigration.html

Kinzelbach, K., Saliba, I., Spannagel, J. and Quinn, R., (2020). *Free Universities: Putting the Academic Freedom Index Into Action.* Berlin: Global Public Policy Institute.

Kinzelbach, K., Saliba, I., Spannagel, J.and Quinn, R., (2021). *Free Universities Report: Putting the Academic Freedom Index into Action.* Berlin: Global Public Policy Institute.

Kipnis, L., (2015). Sexual Paranoia Strikes Academe. *The Chronicle of Higher Education.* [Viewed 15th August 2021]. Available from: www.chronicle.com/article/sexual-paranoia-strikes-academe/?bc_nonce=r446odyu4ycjo0t4ua1vf&cid=reg_wall_signup

Knight, K. and Gall, L., (2020). Hungary Ends Legal Recognition for Transgender and Intersex People. *Human Rights watch.* [Viewed 15th August 2021]. Available from: https://www. hrw.org/news/2020/05/21/hungary-ends-legal-recognition-transgender-and-intersex-peo ple

Kohtamäki, V. and Balbachevsky, E., (2019). An explorative study of the consequences of university autonomy in Finland and Brazil. *Higher Education Quarterly.* 73, 328–342.

Kolozsi, A., (2019). Who is the new head of Hungarian science? *Index.* [Viewed 15th August 2021]. Available from: https://index.hu/english/2019/08/14/miklos_maroth_eotvos_lor and_research_network_hungarian_academy_of_sciences_takeover/

Komjathy, B., (2020). Free SZFE: the arts university on the frontline of Orbán's culture war. *Calvert Journal.* [Viewed 15th August 2021]. Available from: https://www.calvertjournal.com/features/show/12317/hungary-university-protests-free-szfe-orban-culture-war

Körtvélyesi, Z., (2017). *A Magyar Tudományos Akadémia helyzete és reformlehetőségei / The Situation and Reform Opportunities of the Hungarian Academy of Sciences.* Budapest: Osiris. [Viewed 15th August 2021]. Available from: https://jog.tk.hu/a-magyar-tudoma nyos-akademia-helyzete-es-reformlehetosegei

Körtvélyesi, Z., (2020). Fear and (Self-)Censorship in Academia. *Verfassungsblog.* [Viewed 15th August 2021]. Available from: https://verfassungsblog.de/fear-and-self-censorship-in-aca demia/

Kori, E., (2016). Challenges to academic freedom and institutional autonomy in South African universities. *International Journal of Teaching & Education.* IV(1), 45–53.

Kósa, A., (2019). Egyetem Zrt. -Radikálisan átszabják a Corvinust. *Népszava.* [Viewed 15th August 2021]. Available from: https://nepszava.hu/3058397_egyetem-zrt-radikalisan-atszabjak-a-corvinust

Kovács, M., (2012). *Törvénytől sújtva – a numerus clausus Magyarországon, 1920–1945/ Down by the Law – the Numerus Clausus in Hungary, 1920–1945.* Budapest: Napvilág Kiadó

Kovács, Z., (2019). Hungarian Academy of Sciences turns to Constitutional Court against law taking away research institutes. *Index.* [Viewed 15th August 2021]. Available from: https://index.hu/english/2019/09/04/constitutional_court_hungarian_academy_of_scien ces_research_network_miklos_maroth_laszlo_lovasz/

Kovai, M., (2016). *Lélektan és (köz)politika: Pszicho-tudományok a magyarországi államszocializmusban 1945–1970.* Budapest: L'Harmattan Kiadó. [Viewed 15th August 2021]. Available from: http://real.mtak.hu/73169/1/Kovai_Melinda_Lelektan_es_politika._Pszi.pdf

Kováts, E., (2018). Questioning Consensuses: Right-Wing Populism, Anti-Populism, and the Threat of Gender Ideology. *Sociological Research Online 2018.* 23(2), 528–538.

Kováts, E., (2019). Limits of the Human Rights Vocabulary in Addressing Inequalities – Dilemmas of Justice in the Age of Culture Wars in Hungary. *Intersections: East European Journal of Society and Politics.* 2(5), 60–80.

Kováts, E., (2020). Post-Socialist Conditions and the Orbán Government's Gender Politics between 2010 and 2019 in Hungary. In: G. Dietze and J. Roth, eds. *Right-Wing Populism and Gender.* Bielefeld: transcript Verlag. 75–100.

Kováts, E. and Põim, M., eds., (2015). *Gender as symbolic glue: The Position and Role of Conservative and Far Right Parties in the Anti-Gender Mobilizations in Europe.* Budapest: Friedrich-Ebert-Stiftung. [Viewed 15th August 2021]. Available from: https://library.fes.de/pdf-files/bueros/budapest/11382.pdf

Laclau, E., (1996). *Emancipation(s).* London: Verso

Laclau, E. and Mouffe, C., (1985). *Hegemony and Socialist Strategy: Towards a Radical Democratic Politics.* London: Verso.

Lendvai, P., (2012). *Hungary: Between Democracy and Authoritarianism.* New York: Columbia University Press.

Lendvai, P., (2014). *The Hungarians: A Thousand Years of Victory in Defeat.* Princeton: Princeton University Press.

Lewis, N. and Shore, C., (2019). From unbundling to market making: reimagining, reassembling and reinventing the public university. *Globalisation, Societies and Education.* 17(1), 11–27.

Liviu, M., (2021). The West's Crisis of Academic Freedom. *CEU.* [Viewed 15th August 2021]. Available from: https://www.ceu.edu/article/2021-03-30/ceu-provost-liviu-matei-wests-crisis-academic-freedom

Litván, G., (1996). *The Hungarian Revolution of 1956: Reform, Revolt and Repression 1953–1963.* Edited and translated from Hungarian by János M. Bak and Lyman H. Legters. London: Longman

Lojdová, K., (2016). The End of Academic Freedom in the Era of Neoliberalism? *Pedagogická Orientace.* 26(4), 605–630.

Lorde, A., (2007). The Master's Tools Will Never Dismantle the Master's House. In A. Lorde, ed. *Sister Outsider: Essays and Speeches.* New York: Random House and Crossing Press. 110–114.

Lukacs, J., (1990). *Budapest 1900: A Historical Portrait of a City and Its Culture.* New York: Grove Press.

Lynch, K. and Ivancheva, M., (2015). Academic freedom and the commercialisation of universities: a critical ethical analysis. *Ethics in Science and Environmental Politics.* 15(1), 6.

Mackay, F., (2021). Dilemmas of an Academic Feminist as Manager in the Neoliberal Academy: Negotiating Institutional Authority, Oppositional Knowledge and Change. *Political Studies Review.* 19(1), 75–95.

MacLaughlin, D., (2018). Budapest protesters rally to try and keep Soros-funded college in Hungary. *Irish Times.* [Viewed 15th August 2021]. Available from: https://www.irishtimes.com/news/world/europe/budapest-protesters-rally-to-try-and-keep-soros-funded-college-in-hungary-1.3710010

Macfarlane, B., (2017). *Freedom to Learn: The threat to student academic freedom and why it needs to be reclaimed.* London: Routledge.

Magna Charta Universitatum, (2020). The Magna Charta. *Observatory Magna Charta Universitatum.* [Viewed 15th August 2021]. Available from: www.magna-charta.org/resources/files/the-magna-charta/english

Magyar, B., (2016). *Post-Communist Mafia State: The case of Hungary.* Budapest: Central European University Press.

Maiguashca, B., (2019). Resisting the populist hype: a feminist critique of a globalising concept. *Review of International Studies.* 45(5), 768–785.

Marcuse, H., (1986). *One-Dimensional Man.* London: Ark.

Matras, Y., (2015). Why are they setting up a European Roma Institute. Circulated on the Romani Studies Network. *Romea.* [Viewed 15th August 2021]. Available from: http://www.romea.cz/en/news/world/commentary-why-are-they-setting-up-a-european-roma-institute

Matras, Y., (2017). Letter from the outgoing Editor. *Romani Studies.* 27(2), 113–123.

Matthews, A., McLinden, M. and Greenway, C., (2021). Rising to the pedagogical challenges of the Fourth Industrial Age in the university of the future: an integrated model of scholarship. *Higher Education Pedagogies.* 6(1), 1–21.

Mayer, N., (2015). The Closing of the Radical Right Gender Gap in France? *French Politics.* 13(4), 391–414.

McBride, D. and Mazur, A., (2013). Women's Policy Agencies and State Feminism. In: G. Waylen, K. Celis, J. Kantola and L. Weldon, eds. *The Oxford Handbook of Gender and Politics*. Oxford: Oxford University Press. 654–679

McLaughlin, D., (2006). 150 injured as Hungarians riot over PM's lies. *Guardian*. [Viewed 15th August 2021]. Available from: https://www.theguardian.com/world/2006/sep/19/1

McCann, L., Granter, E., Hyde, P. and Aroles, J., (2020). Upon the gears and upon the wheels: Terror convergence and total administration in the neoliberal university. *Management Learning*. 51(4), 431–451.

Mede, N. and Schafer, M., (2020). Science-related populism: Conceptualizing populist demands toward science. *Public Understanding of Science*. 29(5), 473–491.

Mendonça, S., (2013). Hungary's Viktor Orban condemns anti-Semitism. *BBC*. [Viewed 15th August 2021]. Available from: https://www.bbc.com/news/av/world-europe-22423980

Merton, R., (1970). *Science, Technology and Society in Seventeenth Century England. Atlantic Highlands*. New Jersey: Humanities Press.

Merton, R., (1996). Social Structure and Anomie. In: P. Sztompka, ed. *Social Structure and Social Science*. Chicago: Chicago University Press.

Miles, T., (2015). U.N. office outraged by biased Hungarian survey on migration. *Reuters*. [Viewed 15th August 2021]. Available from: https://www.reuters.com/article/us-europe-migrants-hungary-un-idUSKBN0O71N620150522

Mill, J., (1859). *On Liberty*. London: John W. Parker and Son.

Miller, B., (2010). Skills for Sale: What is being commodified in higher education? *Journal of Further and Higher Education*. 34(2), 199–206.

Mohos, M., (2021). Kúria: jogszerű volt az SZFE tanárainak *sztrájkja*. *24.HU*. [Viewed 15th August 2021]. Available from: https://24.hu/kultura/2021/04/26/szfe-sztrajk-kuria-dontes/?fbclid=IwAR2mutWUHpiuxS-mHaUqgPxXgzIelt6Tlb5TlpNx25YoGhZuyG256B-c89c

Mok, K., (2000). Impact of Globalization: A Study of Quality Assurance Systems of Higher Education in Hong Kong and Singapore. *Comparative Education Review*. 44, 148–174.

Monnet Chairs, (2018). Europe's Shameful Silence – An Open Letter to EU Leaders from Jean Monnet Chairs. *Verfassungsblog*. [Viewed 15th August 2021]. Available from: https://verfassungsblog.de/europes-shameful-silence-an-open-letter-to-eu-leaders-from-jean-monnet-chairs/

Moskal, M., (2016). Spaces of Not Belonging: Inclusive Nationalism and Education in Scotland. *Scottish Geographical Journal*. 132(1), 85–102.

Mouffe, C., (1999). Deliberative democracy or agonistic pluralism? *Social Research*, 66(3), 745–758.

Mouffe, C., (2005). *On the Political*. New York: Routledge.

MTA/HAS, (2016). Megalakult a Nők a Kutatói Életpályán Elnöki Bizottság/Presidential Committee on Academic Career of Women Established. *MTA/HAS*. [Viewed 15th August 2021]. Available from: http://mta.hu/mta_hirei/ megalakult-a-nok-a-kutatoi-eletpalyan-elnoki-bizottsag-107348

MTA/HAS, (2018). The Academy stands by its independence and the freedom of research. *MTA/HAS*. [Viewed 15th August 2021]. Available from: https://mta.hu/english/the-academy-stands-by-its-independence-and-the-freedom-of-research-108816

MTA/HAS, (n.d.) A Magyar Tudományos Akadémia, Magyar Tudományos Akadémia Kommunikációs Főosztálya. *MTA/HAS*. [Viewed 15th August 2021]. Available from: http://mta.hu/data/dokumentumok/egyeb_dokumentumok/MTA_Bemutas.pdf.

Mudde, C., (2007). *Populist Radical Right Parties in Europe*. Cambridge: Cambridge University Press.

Mudde, C. and Kaltwasser, C., (2017). *Populism: A very short Introduction*. Oxford: Oxford University Press.

Mudde, C., (2017a). The EU has tolerated Viktor Orbán for too long. It has to take a stand now. *Guardian*. [Viewed 15th August 2021]. Available from: https://www.theguardian.com/commentisfree/2017/apr/03/eu-tolerated-viktor-orban-hungarian-central-european-university

Mudde, C., (2017b). Populism: An ideational approach. In: C. Rovira Kaltwasser, P. Taggart, P. Ochoa Espejo and P. Ostiguy, eds. *The Oxford Handbook of Populism*. Oxford: Oxford University Press, 27–47.

Neary, M., (2010). Student as Producer: A Pedagogy for the Avant. *Garde*. [Viewed 15th August 2021]. Available from: http://eprints.lincoln.ac.uk/4186/1/15–72-1-pb-1.pdf

Nelson, C., (2010). Defining Academic Freedom. *Inside Higher Education*. [Viewed 15th August 2021]. Available from: https://www.insidehighered.com/views/2010/12/21/defining-academic-freedom

Nepstad, S., (2004). Persistent Resistance: Commitment and Community in the Plowshares Movement. *Social Problems*. 51(1), 43–60.

Nepszava, (2021). Bencsik: az SZFE egy szutykos odú volt, ahol egy büdös, ótvaros szekta lapult. *Nepszava*. [Viewed 15th August 2021]. Available from: https://nepszava.hu/3108311_bencsik-az-szfe-egy-szutykos-odu-volt-ahol-egy-budos-otvaros-szekta-lapult

New York Times, (2013). A scholar is back home and defiant. *NYT*. [Viewed 15th August 2021]. Available from: https://www.nytimes.com/2013/12/09/world/europe/a-scholar-is-back-home-and-defiant-in-hungary.html

Nolan, D., (2018). Hungary's unscientific swivel: First they came for the humanities and now Hungary's government is after the sciences. *Index on Censorship*. 47(3), 46–48.

Norris, P., (2020). *Closed Minds? Is a Cancel Culture Stifling Academic Freedom and Intellectual Debate in Political Science?* HKS Working Paper No. RWP20–025. Harvard Kennedy School.

Novak, B., (2020). Student Blockade Protests Viktor Orban's Reach at a Top Arts University. *New York Times*. [Viewed 15th August 2021]. Available from: https://www.nytimes.com/2020/09/06/world/europe/hungary-students-blockade-orban.html?

Novak, B., (2021). The Hungarian government transfers public assets to foundations – including most of the universities. *The New York Times*. [Viewed 15th August 2021]. Available from: https://www.universityworldnews.com/post.php?story=20210501152426649

Nye, M., (2011). *Michael Polányi and His Generation: Origins of the Social Construction of Science*. Chicago, London: The University of Chicago Press.

O'Grady, S., (2018). Hungary's Stop Soros bill suggests jail time for those who help migrants. *Washington Post*. [Viewed 15th August 2021]. Available from: https://www.washingtonpost.com/news/worldviews/wp/2018/05/30/hungarys-stop-soros-bill-suggests-jail-time-for-those-who-help-migrants/

Olssen, M. and Raaper, R., (2016). On neoliberalisation of higher education and academic lives: An interview. *Policy Futures in Education 2016*. 14(2), 147–163.

Open Society, (2018). The Open Society Foundations to Close International Operations in Budapest. *Open Society*. [Viewed 15th August 2021]. Available from: https://www.open

societyfoundations.org/newsroom/open-society-foundations-close-international-oper
ations-budapest

Oppenheim, M., (2018). Hungarian Prime Minister Viktor Orban bans gender studies
programmes. *Independent.* [Viewed 15th August 2021]. Available from: https://www.in
dependent.co.uk/news/world/europe/hungary-bans-gender-studies-programmes-viktor-
orban-central-european-university-budapest-a8599796.html

Orbán, V., (2017). Will Europe belong to Europeans? 22nd July, 2017, speech during annual
speech at at the Tusványos Summer University and Student Camp (Tusványos Nyári
Szabadegyetem és Diáktábor) in Tusnádfürdő (Băile Tuşnad), Romania. [Viewed 15th
August 2021]. Available from: https://visegradpost.com/en/2017/07/24/full-speech-of-v-
orban-will-europe-belong-to-europeans/

Orbán, V., (2018. speech at the 29th Bálványos Summer Open University and Student Camp,
28 July 2018, Tusnádfürdő (Băile Tuşnad). [Viewed 15th August 2021]. Available from:
https://miniszterelnok.hu/prime-minister-viktor-orbans-speech-at-the-29th-balvanyos-
summer-open-university-and-student-camp/

Orbán, V., (2020). Together we will succeed again. *Fidesz.* [Viewed 15th August 2021].
Available from: https://fidesz.hu/int/news/together-we-will-succeed-again

OSUN, (2020). George Soros's Open Society University Network: The power to transform
global higher education. *CEU.* [Viewed 15th August 2021]. Available from: https://www.
ceu.edu/article/2020-01-24/george-soross-open-society-university-network-power-trans
form-global-higher

Özdemir, S., (2021). Civic death as a mechanism of retributive punishment: Academic purges
in Turkey. *Punishment and Society.* 23(2), 145–163.

Pap, A., (2018). *Democratic Decline in Hungary: Law and Society in an Illiberal Democracy
(Comparative Constitutional Change).* London: Routledge.

Pap, A., (2021). Academic Freedom: A Test and a Tool for Illiberalism, Neoliberalism, and
Liberal Democrac. *The Brown Journal of World Affairs.* Xxvii (i).

Papp, R., (2019). Doomed to Failure: Orban's neoconservative family policies in Hungary.
European Alternatives. [Viewed 15th August 2021]. Available from: http://politicalcritique.
org/archive/2019/doomed-failure-orbans/

Patai, R., (1996). *The Jews of Hungary: History, Culture, Psychology.* Detroit: Wayne State
University Press.

Paxton, R., (2007). *The Anatomy of Fascism.* London: Penguin.

Pető, A., (2018). Attack on Freedom of Education in Hungary. The case of gender studies. *LSE
blogs.* [Viewed 15th August 2021]. Available from: https://blogs.lse.ac.uk/gender/2018/
09/24/attack-on-freedom-of-education-in-hungary-the-case-of-gender-studies/

Pető, A., (2020). After resistance: Lessons learned from banning gender studies in Hungary.
Matter: Journal of New Materialist Research. 1(1), 91–95. [Viewed 15th August 2021].
Available from: https://nbn-resolving.org/urn:nbn:de:0168-ssoar-72985-5

Piketty, T., (2014). *Capital.* Cambridge, MA: Bellnap Press.

Pluckrose, H. and Lindsay, J., (2020). *Cynical Theories: How Activist Scholarship Made
Everything about Race, Gender, and Identity – and Why This Harms Everybody.* Durham,
North Carolina: Pitchstone Publishing.

Polányi, M., (1939). Rights and Duties of Science. *The Manchester School of Economic and
Social Studies.* 10, 175–193.

Polányi, M., (1936). The Struggle between Truth and Propaganda. *The Manchester School of Economic and Social Studies.* 7(2), 105–118.

Polányi, M., (1962). The Republic of Science: Its Political and Economic Theory. *Minerva.* 1(1), 54–74.

Polányi, M., (1998). *The Logic of Liberty: Reflections and Rejoinders.* Abingdon: Routledge.

Political Studies Association, (2018). Statement on Hungarian Proposal to Ban Gender Studies. *PSA.* [Viewed 15th August 2021]. Available from: https://www.psa.ac.uk/psa/news/psa-statement-hungarian-proposal-ban-gender-studies#:~:text=Gender%20Studies%20is%20an%20integral%20part%20of%20understanding,the%20Minister%20of%20Education%20to%20reject%20this%20amendment

Popper, K., (2006). *The Open Society and Its Enemies, Volume One.* Abingdon: Routledge.

Pótó, J. and Fónagy, Z., (2016). A Magyar Tudományos Akadémia Története / History of the Hungarian Academy of Sciences. Hungarian Academy of Sciences. [Viewed 15th August 2021]. Available from: http://mta.hu/data/dokumentumok/egyeb_dokumentumok/MTA_Tortenete_net.pdf. 2–3

Priester, K., (2011). Definitionen und Typologien des Populismus / Definitions and typologies of populism. *Soziale Welt* 62(2), 185–198.

Pronay, N., (2002). The Budapest Connection: Seeing Red-Hungarian Intellectuals in Exile and the Challenge of Communism. *American Communist History.* 1(2), 183–190.

Raaper, R. and Olssen, M., (2016). Mark Olssen on neoliberalisation of higher education and academic lives : an interview. *Policy futures in education.* 14 (2), 147–163.

Radev, A., (2020). President of BCE: We can truly make it real. [Viewed 15th August 2021]. Available from: https://www.uni-corvinus.hu/anthony-radev-president-of-bce-we-can-truly-make-it-real/?lang=en

Rains, S., (2013). The nature of psychological reactance revisited: a meta-analytic review. *Hum. Commun. Res.* 39, 47–73.

Rangel, N., (2020). The Stratification of Freedom: An Intersectional Analysis of Activist-Scholars and Academic Freedom at U.S. Public Universities. *Equity and Excellence in Education.* 53(3), 365–381.

Rankin, J., (2021). Hungary passes law banning LGBT content in schools or kids' TV. *Guardian.* [Viewed 15th August 2021]. Available from: https://www.theguardian.com/world/2021/jun/15/hungary-passes-law-banning-lbgt-content-in-schools

Ramet, S., (2007). *The Liberal Project and the Transformation of Democracy: The Case of East Central Europe.* College Station Texas: A and M University Press.

Redden, E., (2018). Central European University says the Hungarian government has forced it to move its main campus from Budapest to Vienna. *Inside Higher Education.* [Viewed 15th August 2021]. Available from: https://www.insidehighered.com/news/2018/12/04/central-european-university-forced-out-hungary-moving-vienna

Reinisch, J., (2000). *The Society for Freedom in Science, 1940–1963.* M.Sc. Dissertation, Imperial College, London.

Reuters, (2018a). Hungary to stop financing gender studies courses: PM aide. *Reuters.* [Viewed 15th August 2021]. Available from: https://www.reuters.com/article/us-hungary-government-education-idUSKBN1KZ1M0

Reuters, (2018b). Interpol renews arrest warrant for MOL's CEO, Croatia says. *Reuters.* [Viewed 15th August 2021]. Available from: https://www.reuters.com/article/us-croatia-hernadi-idUSKCN1NM0QK

Reuters, (2020). Hungary government proposes constitutional amendment mandating Christian gender roles. *Reuters.* [Viewed 15th August 2021]. Available from: https://www.reuters.com/article/instant-article/idUKKBN27Q34W?edition-redirect=uk

Riess, H., (2021). Institutional Resilience: The Foundation for Individual Resilience, Especially During COVID-19. Global Advances in Health and Medicine.

Rodríguez-Dorans, E., Murray, F., de Andrade, M., Wyatt, J. and Stenhouse, R., (2021). Qualitative Inquiry, Activism, the Academy, and the Infinite Game: An Introduction to the Special Issue. *International Review of Qualitative Research.* 14(1), 3 – 16.

Rogers, C., (1969). *Freedom to Learn: A view of what education might become.* Columbus, OH: Merrill Publishing.

Roma Civil Monitor (2020) Synthesis Report (research and report funded by the European Commission – edited by Andrew Ryder). Budapest: CEU

Rónay, Z., (2018). Centralizations and Autonomies: The Delimitation of Education by the Hungarian Government. In: N. Popov, Ch. Wolhuter, J. M. Smith, G. Hilton, J. Ogunleye, E. Achinewhu-Nworgu and E. Niemczyk, ed. *Education in Modern Society, BCES Conference Books* Volume 16. Sofia: Bulgarian Comparative Education Society. 177 – 182.

Rónay Z., (2019). Consistory – The Obscure Subject of State Control. In: G. Kováts and Z. Rónay, eds. *Search of Excellence in Higher Education.* Budapest, Corvinus University of Budapest Digital Press. 71 – 87.

Russell, C., (1993). *Academic Freedom.* New York: Routledge.

Ryder, A., Nagy, B. and Rostás, I., (2013). A Note on Roma Mental Health and the Statement by Géza Jeszenszky. *Corvinus University Social Policy Journal.* 4(2), 89 – 97.

Ryder, A., Bogdán, M., Dunajeva, K., Junghaus, T., Kóczé, A., Rövid, M., Rostas, I., Szilvási, M. and Taba, M., (2015). Roma rights 2 2015: Nothing about us without us? Roma participation in policy making and knowledge production. *Journal of the European Roma Rights Center.* Budapest: ERRC. [Viewed 15th August 2021]. Available from: http://www.errc.org/roma-rights-journal/roma-rights2 – 2015-nothing-about-us-without-us-roma-participation-in-policy making-and-knowledge-production

Ryder, A., (2017). *Sites of Resistance: Gypsies, Roma and Travellers in the Community, School and Academy.* London: Trentham Press IOE (Institute of Education)

Ryder, A., (2018). Paradigm Shift and Romani Studies: Research On or For and With the Roma. In: S. Beck and A. Ivasiuc, eds. *Roma Activism: Reimagining Power and Knowledge.* New York: Berghahn Books. 91 – 111.

Ryder, A., (2019). A Game of Thrones: Power Struggles and Contestation in Romani Studies. *International Journal of Roma Studies.* 1(2), 120 – 143.

Ryder, A., (2020). *Britain and Europe at a crossroads: The Politics of Anxiety and Transformation.* Bristol: Policy Press.

Ryder, A., Taba, M. and Trehan, N., eds., (2021). *Romani Communities and Transformative Change: A New Social Europe.* Bristol: Bristol University Press.

Ryder, A., (2021). *Roma Challenges to Illiberalism and Marginality: The case for liberating empowerment and participatory monitoring.* Budapest: CEU Policy Studies.

Said, E., (1978). *Orientalism.* New York: Pantheon Books.

Said, E., (1996). *Representations of the intellectual: The 1993 Reith lectures.* New York City: Random House LLC.

Sárosi, P., (2020). David Takes on Goliath: The Struggle for Academic Freedom in Hungary. *Autocracy Analyst*. [Viewed 15th August 2021]. Available from: https://autocracyanalyst. net/david-takes-on-goliath-struggle-for-academic-freedom-in-hungary/

Saurette, P. and Gunster, S., (2011). Ears wide shut: Epistemological populism, argutainment and Canadian conservative talk radio. *Canadian Journal of Political Science*. 44(1), 195–218.

Sayan-Cengiz, F. and Tekin, C., (2019). The gender turn of the populist radical right. *Open Democracy*. [Viewed 15th August 2021]. Available from: https://www.opendemocracy.net/ en/rethinking-populism/the-gender-turn-of-the-populist-radical-right/

Scheiring, G., (2020). *The Retreat of Liberal Democracy. Authoritarian Capitalism and the Accumulative State in Hungary*. London: Palgrave Macmillan.

Schmitt, C., (1976). *The Concept of the Political*. New Brunswick: Rutgers University Press.

Scheppele, K., Kochenov, D. and Grabowska-Moroz, B., (2021). EU Values Are Law, after All: Enforcing EU Values through Systemic Infringement Actions by the European Commission and the Member States of the European Union. *Yearbook of European Law*. 39(1), 1–121.

Scheppele, K., (2016). Enforcing the Basic Principles of EU Law through Systemic Infringement Actions. In C. Closa and D. Kochenov, eds. *Reinforcing Rule of Law Oversight in the European Union*. Cambridge: Cambridge University Press.

Scholars at Risk Network (2021) Submission to the Third Cycle of the Universal Periodic Review of Hungary 39th Session of the United Nations Human Rights Council [Viewed 5th November 2021]. Available from: https://www.scholarsatrisk.org/wp-content/uploads/ 2021/04/Hungary-UPR-Submission.pdf

Seidler, V., (2018). *Making Sense of Brexit: Democracy, Europe and Uncertain Futures*. Bristol: Policy Press.

Serughetti, G., (2019). Why Orban's Hungary is afraid of Feminism and Academic Freedom (and George Soros, of course). *ResetDialogues*. [Viewed 15th August 2021]. Available from: https://www.resetdoc.org/story/orbans-hungary-afraid-feminism-academic-freedom-george-soros-course/

Shanes, J., (2019). Netanyahu, Orbán, and the Resurgence of Antisemitism: Lessons of the Last Century. *Shofar: An Interdisciplinary Journal of Jewish Studies*. 37(1), 108–120. Project MUSE

Sherman, S. and Gorkin, L., (1980). Attitude bolstering when behavior is inconsistent with central attitudes. *J. Exp. Soc. Psychol*. 16 (4), 388–403.

Smeltzer, S. and A. Hearn., (2015). Student Rights in an Age of Austerity? Security, Freedom of Expression and the Neoliberal University. *Social Movement Studies*. 14(3), 352–258.

Smith, D., (1991). *National Identity*. London: Penguin.

Smith, A., (2003). *Routledge Philosophy Guidebook to Husserl and the Cartesian Meditations*. London: Routledge.

Smith, G., (2000). Citizens' Juries and Deliberative Democracy. *Political Studies*. 48(1), 51–65.

Somfai, P., (2020). Company or university? – The reasons for the privatization of Corvinus University are still obscure. *168*. [Viewed 15th August 2021]. Available from: https://168. hu/itthon/budapesti-corvinus-egyetem-alapitvany-maganositas-palkovics-laszlo-188186? fbclid=IwAR1c_T5gbQA1TGZTAv3Z9blkbUll7hQx6x8-iImGsrxrV_9zoUfi5rxnj2Q

Soros, G., (2020). The Costs of Merkel's Surrender to Hungarian and Polish Extortion. *Project syndicate*. [Viewed 15th August 2021]. Available from: https://www.project-syndicate.org/ commentary/merkel-surrenders-europe-to-hungary-poland-extortion-by-george-soros-

2020-12?utm_source=twitter&utm_medium=organic-social&utm_campaign=page-posts-december20&utm_post-type=link&utm_format=16%3A9&utm_creative=link-image&utm_post-date=2020-12-14

Sparkes, A., (2000). Autoethnography and narratives of self: Reflections on criteria in action. *Sociology of Sport Journal.* 17(1), 21–43.

Sparkes, A., (2007). Embodiment, academics, and the audit culture: a story seeking consideration. *Qualitative Research.* 7(4), 521–550.

Sparkes, A., (2013). Qualitative Research in Sport, Exercise and Health in the era of Neoliberalism, Audit and New Public Manageent: Understanding the Conditions for the (Im)Possibilities of a New Paradigm Dialogue. *Qualitative Research in Sport, Exercise and Health.* 5(3), 440–459.

Spike, J., (2020). Students occupy top arts university after leadership resigns over autonomy fears. *Insight Hungary.* [Viewed 15th August 2021]. Available from: https://insighthungary.444.hu/2020/09/03/students-occupy-top-arts-university-after-leadership-resigns-over-autonomy-fears

Spirk, J., (2020). Még a Kádár-rendszerben sem történt ilyen: Palkovicsék belenyúltak az OTKA pénzosztásába. *24.HU.* [Viewed 15th August 2021]. Available from: https://24.hu/belfold/2020/08/31/kadar-rendszer-palkovics-belenyultak-otka-penzosztas/

Spooner, M., (2018). Qualitative research and global audit culture: The politics of productivity, accountability, and possibility. In N. Denzin and Y. Lincoln, eds. *The Sage handbook of qualitative research* (5th ed., 894–914). Sage

Statewatch, (2020). Hungary's restrictions on civil society groups are discriminatory and unjustified, Court of Justice rules. *Statewatch.* [Viewed 15th August 2021]. Available from: https://www.statewatch.org/news/2020/july/hungary-s-restrictions-on-civil-society-groups-are-discriminatory-and-unjustified-court-of-justice-rules/

Stehr, N. and Meja, V., (2005). *Society and Knowledge Contemporary Perspectives in the Sociology of Knowledge and Science.* Abingdon: Routledge.

Stepan, A., (2009). The Early Years of Central European University as a Network: A Memoir. *Social Research.* 76(2), 687–71.

Stewart, M., (2017). Nothing about us without us, or the dangers of a closed society research paradigm. *Romani Studies.* 27(2),125–146.

Stiglitz, J., (2009). Moving beyond Market Fundamentalism to a More Balanced Economy. *Annals of Public and Cooperative Economics.* 80(3), 345–360.

Stockdill, B. and Yu Danico, M., (2012). The Ivory Tower paradox: Higher education as a site of oppression and resistance. *Transforming the Ivory Tower.* Honolulu: University of Hawaii Press. 1–30.

Saunders, F., (2000). *Who paid the piper: the CIA and the cultural cold war.* London: Granta.

Suissa, J. and Sullivan, A., (2021). The Gender Wars, Academic Freedom and Education. *Journal of Philosophy of Education.* 55(1), 55–82.

Szegedy-Maszák, M., (1994). Conservatism, Modernity, and Populism in Hungarian Culture. *Hungarian Studies.* 9(1–2), 15–40.

Szigeti, T., (2018). Fidesz-Linked Magazine Publishes List Attacking Supposedly Liberal Academy Researchers. *Hungary Today.* [Viewed 15th August 2021]. Available from: https://hungarytoday.hu/fidesz-linked-magazine-publishes-list-attacking-supposedly-liberal-academy-researchers/

Szirtes, G., (2020). Hungary's students are making a last stand against Viktor Orbán's power grab. *Guardian.* [Viewed 15th August 2021]. Available from: https://www.theguardian.com/commentisfree/2020/sep/15/hungary-students-viktor-orban-university-theatre-budapest

Szögi, L., (2015). *Az Eötvös Loránd Tudományegyetem története képekben / The Illustrated History of the Eötvös Loránd University.* Budapest: ELTE. [Viewed 15th August 2021]. Available from: https://www.elte.hu/file/ELTE_tortenete_SzogiL.pdf

Szokolszky, A., (2016). Hungarian Psychology in Context: Reclaiming the Past. *Hungarian Studies.* 30(1), 17–55.

Sztompka, P., (2000). *The ambivalence of social change: Triumph or trauma?* WZB Discussion Paper No. P 00–001. Berlin: Wissenschaftszentrum Berlin für Sozialforschung.

Szűcs, Z., (2019). The Battle of the Academy: The war on academic freedom in Hungary enters its next phase. *Heinrich-Böll-Stiftung.* [Viewed 15th August 2021]. Available from: https://www.boell.de/en/2019/03/12/battle-academy-war-academic-freedom-hungary-enters-its-next-phase

Takács, K., (2019). Justification letter (principal investigator Evil Tongue). *Linkoping University.* [Viewed 15th August 2021]. Available from: https://liu.se/en/news-item/regimens-kontroll-tvingar-forskare-fran-ungern-flytta-till-liu

Takács, J. and Szalma, I., (2020). Democracy deficit and homophobic divergence in 21st century Europe. *Gender, Place and Culture.* 27(4), 459–478.

Tang, S., (2019). Some Reflections on Science Popularization and Science Culture in China. *Cultures of Science.* 2(3), 227–234.

Tarrósy, I., (2002). *Higher Education in Hungary Heading for the Third Millennium.* Budapest: Ministry of Education.

Teczár, S., (2019). A kormány odaültet öt embert a Corvinus fölé, akiket senki nem tud majd leváltani. *Magyar Naranc.* [Viewed 15th August 2021]. Available from: https://magyarnarancs.hu/belpol/a-kormany-odaultet-ot-embert-a-corvinus-fole-akiket-aztan-senki-nem-tud-majd-levaltani-117706

Teczár, S., (2020). A demokrácia maradékát is felszámolná a kormány az alapítványosított egyetemeken. *Magyar Naranc.* [Viewed 15th August 2021]. Available from: https://magyarnarancs.hu/BELPOL/A-DEMOKRACIA-MARADEKAT-IS-FELSZAMOLNA-A-KORMANY-AZ-ALAPITVANYOSITOTT-EGYETEMEKEN-128464?FBCLID=IWAR0GLPB_FNXWV9C5DFZRBRTQZX887FPHXK9LOFZXNXCKSEMACFNDBHBGGLW

Teczár, S., (2020). Igazságtalan és káros módszerrel sorolják új fizetési kategóriákba a Corvinus oktatóit. *Magyar Narance.* [Viewed 15th August 2021]. Available from: https://magyarnarancs.hu/belpol/igazsagtalan-es-karos-modszerrel-soroljak-uj-fizetesi-kategoriakba-a-corvinus-oktatoit-126618

Teczár, S., (2021). Feszültségek az alapítványi fenntartásba adott Corvinuson. *Magyar Narance.* [Viewed 15th August 2021]. Available from: https://magyarnarancs.hu/belpol/rontas-alatt-236030

Tedlock, B., (2013). Introduction: Braiding Evocative and Analytic Autoethnography. In Handbook of Autoethnography, edited by S. Holman Jones, T. Adams, and C. Ellis, Walnut Creek, CA: Left Coast Press. 358–362

Temkina, A. and Zdravomyslova, E., (2014). Gender's crooked path: Feminism confronts Russian patriarchy. *Current Sociology.* 62(2), 253–270.

Than, K., (2013). Hungary's Orban accuses Europe of Soviet-style meddling. *Reuters*. [Viewed 15th August 2021]. Available from: https://www.reuters.com/article/us-hungary-eu-orban-idUSBRE9640BR20130705

Toarniczky, A. Klér, A. Kun, Z. Vajda, E. Harmat, V and Komáromi, B (2019). Coping with Paradoxes or How to Construct a Sustainable Career in Academia? In the 2nd Danube Conference for Higher Education Management: In Search of Excellence in Higher Education

Trencsényi, B., Rieber, A., Iordachi, C. and Hîncu, A., (2017). Academic Freedom in Danger. Fact Files on the CEU Affair. *Comparative Southest European Studies*. De Gruyter. 65(2), 412–436.

Trehan, N. and Matache, M., (2021). Transatlantic dialogues and the solidarity of the oppressed: Critical race activism in the US and Canada. In A. Ryder, M. Taba and N. Trehan, eds. *Romani Communities and Transformative Change: A New Social Europe*. 145–178.

Tóth, C., (2014). University rector to keep Karl Marx statue on campus. *Budapest Beacon*. [Viewed 15th August 2021]. Available from: https://budapestbeacon.com/university-rector-keep-karl-marx-statue-campus/

Tressler, R., (2020). After all they've been through, it's time to take students' mental health seriously. *Independent*. [Viewed 15th August 2021]. Available from: https://www.in dependent.co.uk/voices/students-university-lockdown-coronavirus-mental-health-b938847.html?fbclid=IwAR2LUwAevrg_NrwP1XlCOZwFIZd-DO3 L4o6pk8Y9TJ2LoKMO5yjtMRSv8ng

TRTWorld, (2021). Students at Soros-funded university endure nightmare Vienna move. *TRTWorld*. [Viewed 15th August 2021]. Available from: https://www.trtworld.com/magazine/students-at-soros-funded-university-endure-nightmare-vienna-move-43717

Tsatsou, P., (2018). Social Media and Informal Organisation of Citizen Activism: Lessons From the Use of Facebook in the Sunflower Movement. *Social Media + Society*.

Tufts, S. and Thomas, M., (2017). The university in the populist age. *Academic Matters*. [Viewed 15th August 2021]. Available from: https://academicmatters.ca/the-university-in-the-populist-age/

UNESCO, (1997). Recommendation concerning the Status of Higher-Education Teaching Personnel. [Viewed 15th August 2021]. Available from: http://portal.unesco.org/en/ev. php-URL_ID=1&3144URL_DO=DO_TOPIC&URL_SECTION=201.html

Vaski, T., (2021). Hungary's Planned Fudan University Budapest Location Faces Backlash. *Hungary Today*. [Viewed 15th August 2021]. Available from: https://hungarytoday.hu/hun garys-planned-fudan-university-budapest-location-faces-backlash/

Vaski, T., (2021). SZFE's New Administration: Necessary Model Change or Autocratic Coup? *Hungary Today*. [Viewed 15th August 2021]. Available from: https://hungarytoday.hu/free szfe-model-change/

Vass, Á., (2020). Science Academy President Shocked After Ministry Unilaterally Modifies Basic Research Scholarship Results. *Hungary Today*. [Viewed 15th August 2021]. Available from: hungarytoday.hu/mta-science-academy-shock-ministry-palkovics-freund-basic-research/

Vass, A., (2021). Opposition Turns to Constitutional Court over Ruling Parties Outsourcing Public Assets and Unis. *Hungary Today*. [Viewed 15th August 2021]. Available from: https://hungarytoday.hu/opposition-court-fidesz-orban-government-outsourcing-public-as sets-universities/

Verseck, K., (2012). Hungary's thinkers protest cultural suppression. *Deutsche Welle*. [Viewed 15th August 2021]. Available from: https://www.dw.com/en/hungarys-thinkers-protest-cultural-suppression/a-15842557

Vida, B., (2019). New waves of anti-sexual and reproductive health and rights strategies in the European Union: the anti-gender discourse in Hungary. *Sexual and Reproductive Health Matters*. 27(2), 13–16.

Vidal, F., (2018). Introduction: From The Popularization of Science through Film to The Public Understanding of Science. *Science in Context*. 31(1), 1–14.

Vrielink, J., Lemmens, P. and Parmentier, S., (2011). Academic Freedom as a Fundamental Right. *Procedia – Social and Behavioral Sciences*. 13, 117–141.

Walker, J. and Cooper, M., (2011). Genealogies of resilience: From systems ecology to the political economy of crisis adaptation. *Security Dialogue*. 42(2), 143–160.

Walker, S., (2018). Hungarian leader says Europe is now under invasion by migrants. *Guardian*. [Viewed 15th August 2021]. Available from: https://www.theguardian.com/world/2018/mar/15/hungarian-leader-says-europe-is-now-under-invasion-by-migrants

Walker, S., (2019a). Classes move to Vienna as Hungary makes rare decision to oust university. *Guardian*. [Viewed 15th August 2021]. Available from: https://www.theguardian.com/world/2019/nov/16/ceu-classes-move-to-vienna-orban-hungary-ousts-university

Walker, S., (2019b). Hungary eyes science research as latest target for state control: Academy will be managed by nationalist government in unprecedented move. *The Guardian*. [Viewed 15th August 2021]. Available from: https://www.theguardian.com/world/2019/jun/13/hungary-eyes-science-research-as-latest-target-for-state-control

Walker, S., (2020). George Soros: Orbán turns to familiar scapegoat as Hungary rows with EU. *The Guardian*. [Viewed 15th August 2021]. Available from: https://www.theguardian.com/world/2020/dec/05/george-soros-orban-turns-to-familiar-scapegoat-as-hungary-rows-with-eu

Wall, S., (2006). An Autoethnography on Learning About Autoethnography. *International Journal of Qualitative Methods*. 5(2), 146–160.

Webb, D., (2018). Bolt-holes and breathing spaces in the system: On forms of academic resistance (or, can the university be a site of utopian possibility?). *Review of Education, Pedagogy, and Cultural Studies*. 40(2), 96–118.

Weldon, S., (2008). Intersectionality. In: G. Goertz and A. Mazur, eds. *Politics, Gender, and Concepts: Theory and Methodology*. Cambridge: Cambridge University Press. 193–218.

Weiler, H., (2009). Whose Knowledge Matters? Development and the Politics of Knowledge. In: T. Hanf, H. Weiler and H, Dickow, eds. *Entwicklung als Beruf*. Baden-Baden: Nomos. 485–496.

Weis, L. and Fine, M., (2012). Critical Bifocality and Circuits of Privilege: Expanding Critical Ethnographic Theory and Design. *Harvard Educational Review*. 82(2), 173–201.

Wilkin, P., (2020). The Rise of Illiberal Democracy: The Orbánization of Hungarian Political Culture. *Journal of World-Systems Research*. 24(1), 5–42.

Wilkinson, R. and Pickett, K., (2009). *The Spirit Level: Why More Equal Societies Almost Always Do Better*. London: Allen Lane.

Williams, E., (2021). Afterword. In: R. Dutt-Ballerstadt and K. Bhattacharya, eds. *Civility, Free Speech, and Academic Freedom in Higher Education: Faculty on the Margins*. Abingdon: Routledge.

Wilson, L., (1995). *The Academic Man: A Study in the Sociology of a Profession*. Abingdon: Routledge.

Windisch, J. and Nagy, I., (2020). Ilyen mélyen még soha nem láttunk bele, miért várat magára a kiállás az SZFE mellett. *HVG*. [Viewed 15th August 2021]. Available from: https://hvg.hu/itthon/20201026_szfe_corvinus_lanczi

Witte, G., (2018). The Trump administration tried to save a U.S. university by playing nice with an autocrat. It failed. *Washington Post*. [Viewed 15th August 2021]. Available from: https://www.washingtonpost.com/world/europe/the-trump-administration-tried-to-save-a-us-university-by-playing-nice-with-an-autocrat-it-failed/2018/11/30/f028718a-e831-11e8-8449-1ff263609a31_story.html

Wodak, R., (2015). *The Politics of Fear What Right-Wing Populist Discourses Mean*. Thousand Oaks: Sage

Wolin, R., (2011). Ghosts of a tortured past: Europe's right turn. *Dissent*. 58(1), 58 – 65.

Wood, F., (2010). Occult innovations in higher education: corporate magic and the mysteries of managerialism. *Prometheus*. 28(3), 227 – 244.

Wray-Bliss, E., (2005). Abstract Ethics, Embodied Ethics: The Strange Marriage of Marx and Foucault and Positivism in Labour Process Theory. In: H. Willmott and C. Grey, eds. *Critical Management Studies: A Reader*. Oxford: Oxford University Press. 383 – 414.

Záborszky, E., (2019). How will Corvinus University be transformed? *Hungarian Spectrum*. [Viewed 15th August 2021]. Available from: https://hungarianspectrum.org/2018/10/07/another-leap-in-the-dark-privatization-of-hungarian-universities/

Zalan, E., (2020). MEPs hear clash over occupied Hungarian drama school. *EU Observer*. [Viewed 15th August 2021]. Available from: https://euobserver.com/political/149891

Zarycki, T., Smoczyński, R. and Warczok, T., (2017). The Roots of Polish Culture-Centered Politics: Toward a Non–Purely Cultural Model of Cultural Domination in Central and Eastern Europe. *East European Politics and Societies*. 31(2), 360 – 381.

Zeigler, T., (2019). *Academic Freedom in the European Union – Why the Single European Market is a Bad Reference Point*. Max Planck Institute for Comparative Public Law and International Law (MPIL) Research Paper No. 2019 – 03. 4 – 33.

Ziegler, T., (2021a). The Anti-Enlightenment Tradition as a Common Framework of Fascism and the Contemporary Far-Right. *Fascism: Journal of Comparative Fascist Studies*. 10, (1), 16 – 51.

Ziegler, T., (2021b). Using EU Citizenship to Protect Academic Freedom: An Alternative Method. In: D. Kostakopoulou and D. Thym, eds. *Research Handbook on EU Citizenship*. Cheltenham, Egyesült Királyság / Anglia: Edward Elgar.

Zimmermann, S., (2005). L'Homme: Europäische Zeitschrift für feministische Geschichtswissenschaft. 16 (2005), 63 – 88.

Zontea, A., (2015). The Hungarian Student Network: A Counterculture in the Making. In P. Krasztev and J. Van Til, eds. *The Hungarian Patient: Social Opposition to an Illiberal Democracy*. Budapest: Central European University Press. 263 – 290.

Zubascu, F., (2018). Hungary's plan to ban gender studies sparks international backlash. *Science-Business*. [Viewed 15th August 2021]. Available from: https://sciencebusiness.net/news/hungarys-plan-ban-gender-studies-sparks-international-backlash

Zubașcu, F., (2019). Parliament votes to give Hungarian government control over Academy of Sciences – Science Business. [Viewed 15th August 2021]. Available from: https://science

business.net/news/parliament-votes-give-hungarian-government-control-over-academy-sciences

Index

https://doi.org/10.1515/9783110749816-014